THE
WRITER
AS
CELEBRITY

THE
WRITER
AS
CELEBRITY

INTIMATE INTERVIEWS

Maralyn Lois Polak

M. Evans and Company, Inc. New York

These interviews originally appeared in The Philadelphia Inquirer Sunday Magazine.

Library of Congress Cataloging-in-Publication Data
Polak, Maralyn Lois.
    The writer as celebrity.

    "These interviews originally appeared in the Philadelphia Inquirer Sunday magazine"—
    1. Authors, American—20th century—Interviews.
    2. Authors, English—20th century—Interviews.
    3. Authorship.   I. Philadelphia inquirer (Philadelphia, Pa. : 1969) II. Title.
    PS129.P64   1986   810'.9'0054   86-2066
    ISBN 0-87131-477-0

M. Evans and Company, Inc.
216 East 49 Street
New York, New York 10017

Design by Lauren Dong

Manufactured in the United States of America

9 8 7 6 5 4 3 2 1

For Gene Roberts

My deepest gratitude to Sharon Crippen, Bill Eddins, David Boldt, Bev Mowbray, the late Annson Kenney, Boo Reinecke, Ann Shine, Michael Sokolove, Jane Biberman, Sally Jo Sorensen, Rod Nordland, Peggy Morgan, Joan Auritt, Pete Dexter, Joe Carter, and Joseph Franklin. They know what they did.

THE INTERVIEWS
(In Alphabetical Order)

INTRODUCTION

My new dictionary defines *celebrity* as a famous or well-known person, while my old dictionary has a different way of putting it: the condition of being celebrated; fame, renown (the *celebrity* of the Duke of Wellington, of Homer, or of *The Iliad*); a person of distinction. Somewhere between those two dictionaries lies my personal definition of the Writer as Celebrity; not really someone we know from appearances on "The Tonight Show," but someone who has distinguished himself through important work, whose name excites us.

In my eleven years interviewing celebrities for my weekly column in the *Philadelphia Inquirer Sunday Magazine*, those who stand out most in my mind are the writers. Few among us are not curious about the lives of writers. Writers are their own heroes, and sometimes ours: alone in their room, they reinvent worlds, create people, design adventures, fulfill fantasies; there is almost no limit to what a writer can achieve through, or in, the imagination.

What interests me is not *how* they do it; that's like asking a lovely milkmaid who whistles beautifully how she purses her lips. What interests me is the human being between the lines, behind the words: real people who have become known through their writing. The writers I've talked to range from Pulitzer winner to pulp, poet to playwright, sacred to profane. What interests me is the notion of writers talking, the writer as character, who writers are as a basis for why they write.

I hope this book will be a companion to literature, for lovers of the word—readers and students alike. Unlike many other famous individuals in our society, writers can't really fake it; they can't really be permanently levitated by hype; their product, the book, poem, play, or article, speaks for itself; a bad writer ultimately unmasks himself on the page. All this intrigues me—the writer's mind, personality, self, soul—and I sought to capture it.

Maralyn Lois Polak
Philadelphia
October 1985

GERMAINE GREER
A Satisfied Woman

Germaine Greer is a fascinating/appalling amalgam of the sacred and the profane—the Shakespearean scholar who talks like a slut, the Melbourne convent child who became one of the world's most articulate advocates of sexual freedom, the serious thinker whose deeper discoveries about the accomplishments of women in history are often obscured by her own lurid public persona, the Cambridge Ph.D. feminist who debated macho Norman Mailer in a media zoo, the victim of a loveless girlhood (domineering mother, disabled father) who now finds herself an international celebrity dividing her time between a London flat and a Tuscany farmhouse, the "middle-aged gardener" who is godmother to eight and mother to none.

She is sitting on a couch at the Barclay, sipping a glass of white wine left over from a dinner of oysters Rockefeller. She is a statuesque, large-hipped woman in a loose teal-blue dress, matching stockings, red shoes, and red earrings. Her graying hair is rakish and unstyled. Her eyes are deeply circled. She has frown lines. She is frightfully clever and frightfully funny.

In her 1971 best-seller, *The Female Eunuch*, Germaine Greer declared, "It's not wrong or promiscuous to have several lovers," and in her latest book, *Sex and Destiny: The Politics of Human Fertility*, she has decided that "it's not wrong to have several babies." She has none of the latter, and some of the former.

So now she's forty-five. "I don't mind. I quite like it," she says. Is she with younger men or older men or no men at all? "Oh, the bliss of being with no men at all," she says, laughing. "But, oh no, they're always around. The less you want them, the more tenacious they are. Haven't you noticed that? You can't get rid of them. No matter how I insult them, drive them away with blows and curses, tell them please be gone by morning and all that, they're still there!"

She sounds rather delighted with herself, no? "No!" She laughs. "I sometimes get desperate. I think, oh God, if I don't wake up in this bed by myself just once!" Where does she find these men? "I don't find them at all." Then where do they find her? "I just can't lose them. I don't try very hard to lose them. I don't try very hard to keep them. . . . I just don't worry about it anymore. One thing there'll never be any shortage of is men. . . .

"Well, let me say, in terms of complete practicalities, that I consider myself to be"—she pauses dramatically, and then guffaws—"one of the [most sexually satisfied] women I know." I caution her that this is a family magazine. "I am terribly, terribly spoiled. And one of my hopes is that I have a very slow terminal disease for which they give me lots of super drugs. I want lots of . . . atropine, morphia, heroin, the works, ah, so that my memories just come floating up without me editorializing them at all. Because I want to have time to write a very long thank-you letter to all the people who made a fuss of me.

"And they're all men. Well, no, they're not all men; there's a couple of women. But the women I didn't really enjoy or understand. I just—it didn't threaten me; I mean, I did it," she says. Oh, women lovers. "But it didn't turn me on. . . . I have nothing to complain of, really nothing. But I've never let them know that I appreciated it, really. Because I've usually been busy and done something else and moved on. I've been a little bit boorish, I think. And preoccupied. I've put other things first. I found other things more interesting. I catch my plane. I don't care who's tearing his hair out in handfuls at the airport; I'm on my plane. And maybe when I come back, he's still there, and maybe he isn't. But I do appreciate it, really. Sort of," she amends.

". . . I have never had a man in my life I didn't learn something from. It's just that I think I'm intelligent enough to know the sorts of things I can be taught by a man who has a different background from mine. I mean, believe me, I would never, ever have looked for love from my academic colleagues. Never. They were too insecure and pathetic. They were terrified that I was going to be better than they were"—she giggles—"and they were quite correct in this terror."

Better sexually or intellectually? "Oh, intellectually. . . . No, they were afraid of everything about me. . . . I never wanted anything to do with those people. I never thought that what I should be doing is, you know, trying to mate with, oh, [a cerebral writer such as] Anthony Burgess. . . . Um, no, no.

"At present I have, there are at least, well, I don't know how many men there are in my life, but when I last checked, there were two in particular. One of them is"—she hesitates—"well, how would I explain? One of them drives a bulldozer for a living. He doesn't actually drive a bulldozer, he owns a whole lot of earth-moving equipment. And he makes swimming pools and roads and things like that. And I always consult him about all of that. He's in Italy.

"And the other man's a mechanic. He's wonderful. I never knew anything about such things, I wouldn't have known what a ball bearing was five years ago, but this man in my life is a mechanical genius." She grins. "He can't talk, he can't communicate verbally at all. He gets terribly flustered and the words come out wrong and he doesn't say what he wants to say. But I can put any piece of metal in his hand, and he can tell me, from the way the metal has been milled and worked, what job it's supposed to do. And I'm left-handed, so it's hard for me to learn how to use tools because I can't transpose their function.

"And he taught me, in two minutes, he taught me how to use a scythe because he made me understand the principle of the shape of the scythe's blade. And so now I love scything. It's one of the best jobs there is to do in the garden. It's very hard and you sweat a lot, but it's great fun and the smell of the grass is wonderful and everything looks terrific when you've done it. . . .

"And the thing about this man is, he really, I think he's a

genius. He actually dreams in sound and speed and weight! He doesn't dream about literary things, he doesn't dream about incidents, people, statement, places. He dreams about speed! He dreams about spheres crashing through barriers and things like that!"

How positively *male*. "Oh, but I love it. And he fascinates me, and I'll learn anything from him. I mean . . . he can't *tell* me, he doesn't blind me with science; he just shows me. And I learn. I've learned a thousand things. He'll take a tool out of my hand and show me that I'm holding it the wrong way, that I've got it balanced the wrong way, and I instantly understand. I know the importance of having the right tools. I know that I can't do a job if the screwdriver is the wrong size. I'll just wear myself out trying to do it if my tools are too small or too large. I know the difference between a wood chisel and a stone chisel. And I now do a hundred things I didn't do before, because he taught me how to do them. And he does it in the simplest possible way."

Isn't it important to have someone intelligent she can have discussions with? "No. I can't discuss things with him." But isn't that important? "No. There's nothing to discuss." She laughs. "He *understands*. . . . And in fact the mechanic has had to help the earth-mover, which was a very tricky situation. I mean, he mended his excavator and showed him why the excavator was breaking all the time, what was wrong. . . . [But] the mechanic really wanted to break the earth-mover, crush him and humiliate him—but he crushed him and humiliated him by helping him! You know what men are like!

"My men don't seem to mind whether I'm fat or thin or anything. . . . I'm always expecting at least one or another to be gone. And they never are." She laughs. "I *am* very spoiled. I mean, the older of these relationships has been going on for ten years. I don't lose very many. At this point I'm starting to speak like a brain surgeon."

Some wags have suggested she's bored with sex. "I'm not. I just think we make a tremendous fuss about it: 'You've got to keep a man's sexual interest. And you don't do that by what you do when you're with him. You do that by keeping other men interested in you,'" she says, mimicking advice in women's magazines. "Actually, in Italy, of course, it's perfectly permissible for a woman to put on weight. And that's one reason why I like Italy, because they don't want women to look as if they're sixteen. . . ."

But she's not suffering from sexual excess? "Ah, no, I don't think that's it. I mean, it depends on how you assess these things. Seeing as I think I've had a lot of high-grade sex, and what I've never had is sort of daily sex or weekly, you know, marital-type sex, where because you're sleeping in the same bed, you're gonna do it." (Her only marriage lasted three weeks.)

"When we get to that stage, I behave disgracefully. I mean, my relationships do get to that stage, and then I behave disgracefully. I'm apt to do things like just not come to bed. And so at bedtime I'm just gone. And I've done all kinds of things. I've slept in the fields, and I've slept in trees. I'm really a very difficult woman," Germaine Greer says sagely. "You can never take me for granted."

DECEMBER 16, 1984

BOB GREENE
America Is His Beat

What initially intrigued me about Bob Greene was that he was just twenty-three when he began writing a daily column for a major metropolitan newspaper, that he had published five books before he was thirty, that he had done headline-making interviews with mass murderer Richard Speck in prison and Richard Nixon right after he resigned the presidency, and that, while researching a story on sex symbols, he had posed in tight jeans and unbuttoned shirt, as a joke, for a poster that briefly made him "the first journalistic sex symbol."

I thought he'd be a terrific story about relentless ambition, early success, and perhaps subsequent disillusionment, because though he was still doing his column, syndicated three days a week in hundreds of cities, plus his monthly "American Beat" pieces for *Esquire* and frequent appearances on ABC-TV's "Nightline" and a new book about being a new father after thirteen years of marriage called *Good Morning, Merry Sunshine*, he had yet to achieve that holy grail of his profession, the Pulitzer Prize, and he was pushing forty.

Naturally I had speculated on his beginnings, and was totally wrong. I was surprised to discover that he was not born poor or pushed and pressured to excel. Bob Greene was, *is*, so thoroughly midwestern that he once wanted to be a forest ranger or a tennis pro, his nominally Jewish parents named him Junior, and he still speaks with a twang, and the business his father presided over was actually bronzing baby shoes. A classic firstborn, he grew up in suburban Columbus, Ohio, was a copyboy for his hometown paper at sixteen, and studied journalism at Northwestern, where he wrote a column for the school paper while stringing for the *Chicago Tribune*, "bashful" all the way.

Yet here he is at thirty-seven, no angst, no therapy, no heavy introspection or deep-seated guilt, no escape through watching films or reading fiction, not even coffee or cigarettes—a well-balanced guy in a shot-and-beer town, Chicago, possibly the last city of real men. Is he bored? Is he jaded? Has he peaked? Is he arrogant? Is he street-tough? Is he burned out? Noooooo.

He is, he says, just a storyteller, a guy who likes to wander around and see things and then tell people about it. He sponsors an all-female bowling team called the Greenettes, has appeared on "Late Night with David Letterman" three times in the last six months, and his curiosity—be it about a Trojan condom factory in Trenton, or the lost legend of the Alamo, or the death of this country's last great general, or teenage girls in San Antonio whose lust for rock stars takes weird forms—will absolutely not quit.

Bob Greene has curly dark hair and a chubby, friendly face. He's wearing a star sapphire pinkie ring, blue shirt, and tan cords. He generally lets his wife, Susan, a former paralegal he met in college, handle the checkbook and household finances. He doesn't write letters. He's impatient. He hates flying, waiting in lines, being put on hold, and anything in general that stands in his way, because he moves so fast. He lives in a condo in Chicago. The last time he cried was when the coach cut him from his junior high basketball team. He was twelve.

Has he ever tried to write fiction? "Well, back in the *Sun-Times* [he's now with the *Tribune*] a friend and I . . . wrote a fictional serial called 'Bagtime.' What are you laughing at?" he wonders. It's a funny title. "We wrote it under the name of its fictitious hero, which is Mike Holliday. He's a bag boy at the Treasure Island Supermarket in Chicago, which is a real supermarket. And it ran all summer, five times a week. You talk about ambition. That summer I was writing five Bob Greene columns a week, and I also wrote six 'Bagtimes' a week. So I was writing eleven columns a week. So anyway, that was Mike Holliday, and it ran all summer under his name, Mike Holliday. Then people found out it was myself and [his friend]. And then the next summer it came out as a paperback book, *Bagtime*, by Mike Holliday. And then the summer after that, or two summers after that, I guess, it came out as a musical comedy in Chicago that did quite well."

Where can one get a copy? "If I can find one, I'll send it to you." I tell him I was a supermarket cashier for six years. "See, Mike Holliday is my alter ego. I mean, Mike Holliday is me if I didn't have this ambition. Now I use him all the time, not all the time," he amends, "but once every six weeks. . . . So now about every six weeks in my column, it will start off by saying, 'An envelope has been delivered to this office, and inside the envelope was a long note from Mike Holliday, a bag boy at the Treasure Island Supermarket on Wells Street and author of the best-selling novel *Bagtime*. Here is the contents of Mike Holliday's message.' And then I'll just run in his voice. So Mike Holliday appears in my column writing these fictional letters to me.

"But he really is, I mean, it's like being a different person. I guess the thing I like best about myself, I mean, the most midwestern things are part of Mike. Mike's a guy who went to college and just decided, well, he wasn't cut out for the business world and he wasn't cut out for the world of ambition and achievement, and he's just happy being a bag boy. And I love writing in Mike Holliday's voice. And people love him. I mean . . . a lot of people still don't realize he's fictional—like this stewardess on the plane, this flight attendant, knelt down next to me and asked, 'Is Mike Holliday really thinking about becoming a lifeguard?'

"Because I'd run a column saying that he was thinking about getting out of the bagging business and becoming a lifeguard, because he always idolized lifeguards. And I said, 'Well, yeah.' And she says, 'Well, would he give up the bagging job?' And I realized she didn't know! And I said, 'You do know about Mike Holliday, don't you?' And she goes, 'Yes, he's that bag boy who writes you letters all the time.' And I said, 'Well, you do know that Mike Holliday is me, don't you?' And she had no idea. And at the end of the flight I said, 'Are you disappointed?' And she said, 'Well, I can take it. But I don't know how my kids are going to handle it.'"

What kind of adventures, or nonadventures, does Mike have? "Well, originally I made it sort of racy, for the original serial which ran every day. He found out his ex-wife was involved in a bisexual thrill cult with the Chicago White Sox, the Chicago Bears, and the waitresses from . . . one of those hip seventies restaurants in Chicago. And we built this whole adventure around him trying to find his wife and find out how this had happened. You know, it was one of these planned outrage-type series. But now Mike's sort of more reflective. I mean, he'll just talk about things in his life."

Like what? "Well, this last time, summer was coming and he realized, is it really right for him to keep being a bag boy at his age? Once, before it's too late, he'd like to become a lifeguard and rub the white cream on his nose and sit on the beach. What's wrong?" he asks me. Oh, that's hilarious—my first love was a bag boy. "Yeah," he says sympathetically.

Has he written more fiction? "No. I mean, that was fine for me. I have no real desire to. What I figured out, and I don't think I've ever said it out loud, is that I reach more people every day than a best-selling novelist does. I mean, the idea of becoming a novelist, I guess, is to reach large groups of people with your wonderful novel, which is great. But I have that lucky situation where I sit down every day and reach all those people. And I think I'd reach so many fewer people with a novel. I mean, maybe someday I'll change my mind and maybe someday it will be sort of nice to sit at home and write novels. But now I just want to get on the airplane and go. . . . I mean, I want to go out and see these things. I don't want to sit in my room."

What motivates him, then—the numbers? "No. What I'm saying is reaching people. No, not just the raw numbers. I mean, I assume what drives the novelist is the idea of having his vision reach all those people that a best-selling novel reaches. I mean, maybe, you know, maybe there's some part of art to it." Art? "Maybe writing great fiction is an art that journalism isn't. But I guess that's something I'm willing to give up. . . . I met Irving Wallace once and he just had a best-seller. And it didn't occur to me until about two days later, well, I probably get more mail than he does. I mean, journalism makes it possible for you to do that."

Does he have any thoughts about the journalist as outsider, as ultimate voyeur? "Oh, I've written about it. I mean, I'm aware of the fact that it's a very strange way to make a living, to go into other people's lives and scrape those lives for what you can use for your stories and then go out and display those scrapings in front of others. And most people wouldn't choose to live that way, and I do. And I don't know what you can say beyond that. I'm aware of the fact that most people wouldn't live that way, and, even if they could, wouldn't do it."

Maybe that explains why he wrote *Bagtime:* "To live another life? Maybe." To *live* another life. "Yes, maybe. Although *Bagtime* ain't that good." He laughs. "Really, being Mike Holliday really appeals to me. I mean, I sort of like this line in *Bagtime*. And *Bagtime*, what it means, the reason we used it," he interrupts himself, "was that it was a takeoff on [E. L.] Doctorow, because that same summer his book *Ragtime* was a big hit. Um, Mike Holliday says, you know, 'When I'm off on my own, my time is *my* time, and when I'm in the grocery store, it's bagtime, I bag the groceries, and when I punch out, that's it, the day's over.'

"Well," Bob Greene says, "I sort of like the idea of that."

AUGUST 5, 1984

ISAAC ASIMOV
Revenge of the Nerd

They have called Isaac Asimov many grand and glorious things—Most Intelligent Man in the World, Father of Modern Science Fiction, World's Most Famous Popularizer of Difficult Subjects, Renaissance Man, Writing Machine—but they have forgotten something, something very important.

Isaac Asimov was also the First Nerd.

Sure, you see him now with his string tie and his bushy sideburns, his polyester and his dandruff, a lovable gargoyle exuding avuncular charm and spectacular success (his 262nd book, *Foundation's Edge*, is his first best-seller ever), and nerd-wise, he could fool you.

You know nerds, those clumsy kids with Coke-bottle glasses who can explain the universe to their parents with astounding lucidity, the kids who grow up to be est trainers and chipheads and California millionaires. Well, Isaac Asimov is sixty-three now, short and round, but picture him, precocious and gawky and green, hanging out in his poor Russian immigrant father's Brooklyn candy store, daydreaming of galaxies in collision and robot sweethearts to take to the prom.

Picture him, always the brightest one in class, but tasting deep disappointment early. Missing the word "weigh" to lose a spelling bee. So ugly, his high school yearbook jeered, "When he looks at the clock not only does it stop, it goes backward!" So overeager to tell a story, his essay about larks and daisies in spring was so mawkish the creative writing teacher dismissed it with a harsh but accurate "this is s———."

Nerd's Revenge. Incredibly prolific author, witty raconteur, erstwhile biochemist and college professor: Isaac Asimov's entire career, barely contained by his 640,000-word, 1,500-page autobiography, has been a gigantic "So there," thumbing his nose at those distant, dead detractors.

Nerd's Revenge. He holds a Ph.D. in chemistry from Columbia, but wanted to be a doctor. "I suppose my closest approach to a big disappointment was not getting into medical school. But that was extremely lucky for me, because I would have made a rotten doctor. . . . I quickly recovered, because I think deep in my heart I didn't particularly want to be a doctor. . . . As it turned out, the only thing I really wanted to do was to write or to speak. I wouldn't have been a particularly good anything else."

Briefly, as a young man, he worked as a cancer researcher, but he glosses over that now; writing proved more seductive. He even wrote a textbook for medical students, *Biochemistry and Human Metabolism.* He tends to eat "everything," and it shows. Though he has written about nutrition, he "doesn't particularly practice it," he says, grinning. "I'm all for people *not* eating red meat, because that drives the price down so I can afford it."

He doesn't smoke or drink or gamble or swear or hang out with the boys. Seven days a week he sits down at his typewriter. The words pour onto paper as fast as he can think, 2,000 to 4,000 words a day. He's actually sorry when he finishes a book, and every six weeks for the past thirty years he has finished one. If his doctor told him he had just six months to live, he would type faster. He doesn't have a photographic memory, nor is he a speed reader. His IQ has been measured a number of times, most recently twenty years ago: "When they tested me for Mensa, it turned out to be somewhere over 160. . . . While I'm extremely good in taking tests of that sort, in other respects I'm very stupid.

"I have no sense of direction. I get lost in my bedroom. Ah, I need someone around all the time to keep me from being helpless. I'm not the kind of bright person who knows exactly what to do when things go wrong. At home, my wife, Janet, does most of the repairing and most of the practical everyday decisions. My part is to sort of look around at a loss. I can do that very well."

Does he consider himself a genius? ". . . If by genius you mean someone who does some specific thing very well, and as very few people can do, well, then I guess I am. But being a genius doesn't preclude you from being a dumb jerk nine-tenths of all the ways in which you interact." Hmmm, he's always described as egocentric, but I don't get that sense.

"Well, I'll tell you, that's my persona. I get my humor by flirting with every girl I see, and I'm very self-assured about my own talents. So that I *seem* to be a dirty old man and to have a tremendous ego. But that's not *me*, that's my persona. That's the way I present myself, because I consider it humorous.

"I know what I'm good at. But I don't kid myself into think-ing that's all there is to life. I have probably written more and better on more different subjects than anyone since Aristotle. But once you've said that, that doesn't mean I'm particularly wise or particularly courageous or particularly *anything*. I just can write better on more different subjects than anyone. And faster."

Does the quest for a masterpiece concern him? "No, it never did, largely because I assumed I was never going to write one. I figure it's important in your life's work to know what your limitations are. And from the very start I knew that a Tolstoy or a Shakespeare I was not, and I wasn't aiming to be. I was going to write as best I can, but I wasn't going to tell myself any fairy stories about what the best I can might be."

Now we get to his secret inadequacies. Unlike so many first-borns, he's not adventurous. He came to America from Russia when he was three, but he hates to travel, dislikes vacations, and refuses to fly, though he's written extensively about space travel. "I think probably there's a connection—I've traveled so much in my mind that the thrill is gone. I mean, I don't feel the urge to go places and see things, because I have gone places and seen things, things that no one else has. Ah, I've got a very lively imagination, a very vivid one. I don't therefore feel com-pelled to travel to see the sights. . . ."

Did he ever fly? "Yes, when I was in the Army, a sergeant said to me, 'Private, get on that plane.' And I didn't see my way clear to disappoint him. So I got on the plane, and it took me from Honolulu to San Francisco. That was sometime in the spring of 1945. And I haven't flown since, and I don't intend to.

"If I have to pin it down to anything, it's my acrophobia. I'm not comfortable at heights. That is, I don't mind being high up—I live on the thirty-third floor—as long as I don't look out the window, down. I always use artificial light. My blinds are always down, and I get tired of explaining why. It gives me a sense of being enclosed. I would like to live two hundred feet underground. I wouldn't let anyone come there. I'm a claustrophile. . . . Just the thought of going up in the air is not a comfortable one for me."

Someone else can have his space shuttle ticket. But isn't he curious, having envisioned it? "No, no. I've seen it. I honestly have."

What outsiders label vanity and arrogance, he considers "cheerful self-appreciation." He and his second wife, a psychiatrist, never entertain at home. "Frankly, I'm against it," he reveals. He prefers to take friends to restaurants—his treat. "It saves me, it saves us, a lot of time and effort. I must admit I do it for myself."

He sees himself as "an all-around nice guy with a great many peculiarities—my fear of airplanes, my tendency to be very suave with the young women and the old women too, my well-known egocentricity, and the limitless extent to which I'm anxiously interested in the whole world."

Talking to ordinary people doesn't bore him, and he's *never* bored if he's left to himself. "If I'm trapped with a person who doesn't let a word in edgewise, I can always stop listening, and think. If my thought fails me, I can estimate how many curves there are in the wallpaper. . . . I'm egocentric in the sense that I live inside my own head most of the time, and I'm fascinated by my own thoughts. And I generally have little time to spare to think about other people, not out of viciousness, just out of lack of time, I suppose. . . ."

His regrets are few, and easily overcome. He wishes he could speak Russian, which he has forgotten, and that he played a musical instrument, which he never attempted. When he takes trains, he does an acrostic, or looks out the window and thinks. He's visited England and France on the QE2; doesn't mind ships. He's crazy about cats, but he won't have one because he lives too high up, and cats have a habit of climbing out the window. When he lived in Boston, with his first wife, he always wore bow ties, the clip-on kind, and when he moved to New York and remarried, this new wife said switch to string ties, because they're easier and better; he hates to tie a tie.

"I have a good memory for numbers, dates, whatever things other people tend to forget, but if I were to see you on the street, I couldn't remember that we met. I tend to forget people," he confides, and proceeds to compose a limerick using my last name. "I'm death grip on abstractions, but I forget living people. But if you had come to my apartment to talk, think of the fun we could have had," he twinkles.

For all his compulsive word-making, there is a quiet core to him, humble and precise. "Nothing has ever happened to me in any real sense. I haven't met famous people. I haven't been involved in world-shaking events. I haven't done unusual things like climb Mount Everest. I've led a very quiet life. And yet here I am. It's not as though I was anything else. I'm a science fiction writer, and a professor, and here I am, well-to-do and famous. Twice I read my autobiography to see if I could find out how it happened, and I swear I can't. How the devil did it happen?"

MARCH 27, 1983

BOBBIE ANN MASON
Kentucky on Her Mind

There was this won-der-ful guy who wrote her a fan letter, then showed up at a bookstore with a dozen roses. She was signing autographs. This was the same bookstore that had given a cocktail party for writers last winter, and she was supposed to go, but for some reason she didn't, though the guy went, thinking he'd meet her, and he brought an orchid corsage for her. She doesn't know what he ever did with that corsage, but this time he brought her roses.

The roses came with rose food, a little packet she would add to the water soon, before they began to wilt. Well, *he* didn't actually bring the rose food, the florist put it in. This was the second time in a week she'd had to deal with roses. She just was in Atlanta for a booksellers' convention, and it was very interesting, and she had a great time. And then her publisher sent roses to her room, and there she was with these beautiful roses, but she was only staying overnight, and so she had to take the roses back home on the plane, which wasn't easy.

Bobbie Ann Mason talks, and writes, like that—with a sigh and a drawl and a flutter—about the brief ordinary moments of the small person. Literature's latest darling is a "shy, awkward, retiring, pigeon-toed country girl" from Mayfield, Kentucky, population 10,000; a Pennsylvania housewife of forty-two "haunted" by her rural roots, her relatives, her region; an ex–college professor whose prize-winning short stories about hairdressers and bus drivers and drugstore clerks appear in *The New Yorker*, *The Atlantic*, *Redbook*, *Vanity Fair*—the "best" magazines. Her desperate, dreary characters are blitzed by progress. They face their bleak dreams alone, shop at K mart, live and die daily for Phil Donahue, and talk about TV as if it were real, as if it were happening to them.

More interesting than her fiction, she is a plain woman with pale skin and a plaintive voice. Oldest of four, she grew up on an isolated dairy farm. Her early ambition was to be a secretary. Once she had a "pseudo-glamorous job" with a Manhattan movie magazine. She "loves animals, has a garden, lives in the woods" some place outside Allentown. Where, she will not say. She's jittery about her privacy.

She will say she eats cracked wheat bread with raspberry jam for breakfast, has eight cats and two dogs, stops writing at 5 P.M. because there's "so much to do" around the house. She's been married fourteen years, does not like mentioning her husband's name or discussing why they didn't have children or where he works or what her siblings think of her or which famous writers snubbed her before she became famous overnight (remarkably, she sold her first short story without an agent to *The New Yorker* in 1980, just mailed it in and they bought it). She doesn't need to wear a watch, because she can tell time in her head.

Most of her friends are academics. For eight years she taught journalism part-time at Mansfield State College in upstate Pennsylvania, until she was laid off. She never worked on a newspaper except in college, where she wrote a satirical column. "I know a lot more about [the people I write about] than I knew what went on in academics' heads. That was just a foreign world to me," she tells me after her book-signing and rose-receiving at Encore Books. "I never could quite join the sophisticated world of the Northeast, where I've lived for twenty years. I still have my head in Kentucky. And I'm always deeply aware, when I'm in a lot of sophisticated situations, of who I am and where I come from and what my mother might say. . . . I'm very aware of how far I'd come. . . .

"I never had much confidence until recently. . . . Starting to get published helped," she says. "I was unable to connect with the way the world works, the business of the world. When I was teaching, there were these inevitable committee meetings. And I would never speak up, I would never say a word, not only because I was quiet and shy, but I never understood what they were talking about. I couldn't relate to it. And I think it was because I just didn't care, I didn't want to know. . . . I'm sure they were important issues, but I couldn't relate to the kind of tensions that developed among people in that kind of situation. There's a formal way of going about these kinds of things, you know, with meetings. Ah, they just drove me up the wall.

"I couldn't understand why people weren't laughing and getting down to something at the heart of it, instead of arguing all around it. And I could just not play the game. Well, I guess mainly I see myself, perhaps I see myself, and my lack of confidence, has to do with feeling intellectually inferior," she reveals. "When I left home, I went through a long, long period of very painful and confusing culture shock, because I wasn't prepared. I think I was very poorly educated and I didn't know how to go out into the world. . . .

"I had no imagination when I was a child," she says with a laugh. "That was part of what I mean by poor education. The method of learning was all memorization. In college I started to run into a little trouble, but in graduate school I ran into a *lot* of trouble. Because I didn't know how to think, I didn't know how to analyze, I didn't know how to be in a discussion group. . . . Graduate school [she has a Ph.D. from the University of Connecticut] was the big shift in culture for me. Suddenly I encountered all these very heavy professors in school, very demanding and very very large men, for one thing, just intimidating enough," says the 5-foot-3½-inch author wryly.

"They were on an intellectual level that I felt I couldn't achieve, and I couldn't talk to them. And so I just felt very intimidated, and therefore I felt that I wasn't very smart. And that's a very self-perpetuating kind of thing. If you're so afraid you're not very smart, then obviously you're gonna block your mind so you won't have any ideas to prove that you're smart with, because you're too busy thinking about how inferior you are. So there was a long period where I just was really scared and had no thoughts in my head. And I got through graduate school just by sheer plugging along and working very hard."

But she did her doctoral dissertation on Vladimir Nabokov, a very difficult writer. "Yeah, but he hated ideas. He was somebody I could relate to. Oh well, just his feeling about nature and about memory and about childhood. He was an exile from Russia and an exile from his childhood and he had two opposing cultures in his head." Does she see herself as an exile? "Yeah. I think that's what makes me a little peculiar, I mean, in that I don't fit in either place. . . .

"I didn't enjoy teaching at all," she admits. "I didn't feel I was very good, and my lack of confidence and my feeling of intellectual inferiority really entered into it." Despite all her academic training? "Well, I'll tell you, it's easy. My sense of inferiority has to do with public performance, not with brains, not with my mind. So teaching is being a public performer. And if you get up there and your mind goes blank because you're scared, then you don't have any access to what you know. And my experience was that I was so shy, that what happened to me when I came North was that in effect my mind went blank, and I had an awfully hard time just gaining access to what my mind could do. It certainly wouldn't work when I was up in front of a class. When I talk about it, it sounds extreme. But people do suffer teaching. . . .

"What scares me is related to that intellectual timidity. Now I think I probably should have something articulate to say about writing, but I don't. And I give readings of my work, I answer questions, but I'm very uncomfortable with the idea of giving a lecture or Saying Something." Wisdom. "Yes. I don't have a lot to say about writing or about the state of literature. I know a lot about cats, and I know a few things about gardening and maybe a few things about people. But I can't talk, I don't remember anything I read, I'll put it that way. And so I can't talk about it." Does she remember what she writes? "Yeah, but I don't have anything to say about it. And so I read it."

Has it been difficult adjusting to the overwhelming success of her first book, *Shiloh and Other Stories?* "Well, it's very hard to separate the kind of exaggeration from reality. So I just live my ordinary life. I'm shocked anybody's read my book. People come up to me and say, 'I read your book'—I want to ask, 'Well, really? Where did you find it? You mean you bought it?'" She laughs. "'Why'd you do a fool thing like that?' I mean, it just surprises me.

"Well, it's like at certain periods of your life, or if you're feeling very insecure, you look at your face in the mirror and you don't recognize it. They say that about people who have serious mental illness, that's a stage, a deteriorating stage, when you don't recognize your face in the mirror. Anyway, that's an analogy. It's like you can't quite relate to being known by people who you don't know. And you cannot sit at home and think about that. There's just no way to comprehend it, there's no way to relate to that. It's out there," Bobbie Ann Mason says, "and you're just at home with the cats."

DECEMBER 25, 1983

ANDY WARHOL
The Pope of Pop Art

"I can't dance. I wanted to, but I couldn't learn. I can't drive a car either because my mind wanders and so do my eyes. The dentist told me not to talk about eating candy, and I guess my guiltiest pleasure is another thing my dentist hates—rinsing my mouth out with Lavoris!"

More mythology surrounds Andy Warhol—his techniques, his tactics, his projects, and especially his persona—than possibly any other living artist. "How would I describe myself? That's too hard. I'm forty-seven. I'm wearing a Brooks Brothers shirt, a Liberty tie, an Yves Saint Laurent sweater, blue jeans, boots. Supp-hose socks, and Jockey underwear. I love to shop for underwear. The press always started up saying I was unusual, but they really didn't know me."

He is the Pope of Pop Art who brought us realer-than-real-life Brillo boxes and Campbell soup cans, Marilyn Monroe and Liz Taylor. He is the Sultan of Non Sequiturs: "Someday everybody will be famous for fifteen minutes" and "Someday you'll be able to go to a party and be the only one there." And he is holding court under a moose head, next to a well-stocked marble bar, in the converted Broadway furniture company showroom that houses his creative conglomerate.

In one room is the sober, serious, suit-clad staff of *Interview Magazine*, his 80,000-circulation monthly gazette of glamour and glitter. In another room a henna-frizzed, olive-drab-clad British lass is stitching together huge circles of cherry licorice to make a "candy dress" that Warhol and his crew will actually consume—while it's being worn—at a gallery opening.

Minutes ago he was shooting Polaroids of a fortyish matron in a Mylar dress. She preened, postured, primped, and pouted in a squalid cemetery of poses, for a series of portraits that would become his famous Day-Glo Popsicle-hued 40″ × 40″ silkscreens. They sell for $25,000 for the first one, $15,000 for each additional, and a very rich Texas lady reportedly bought twenty-four at these very prices.

Andy Warhol, so the story goes, didn't see *Snow White* till he was thirty-five because he spent most of his sickly childhood in bed with his Charlie McCarthy doll. Like all heroes and gods and creatures of myth, details of his birth and early life are shrouded in mystery if not confusion. Was his father a construction worker or a coal miner? Andy denies nothing.

Andy Warhol catapulted from the lowly echelons of commercial art—fashion layouts, women's shoes—and even illustrated *Amy Vanderbilt's Complete Cookbook*, highlighted by sprightly yet sparse renderings for a chapter on "Cupcakes, Cookies, and Frostings." *The Philosophy of Andy Warhol* is, by some accounts, his sixteenth book. Others, in limited editions, have sold for as high as $2,000. He has produced more than a dozen films, ranging from the monotonous and interminable to the campy and chic. *Sleep* shows a man in deep repose, slow motion, static camera. *Empire* is twenty hours' worth of the Empire State Building. And then there are, lately, *Frankenstein* and *Dracula*, gaudy, gory, slickly conventional box-office bonanzas, hardly "underground."

Andy Warhol's publisher warns—candidly—that he is fearsome to interview. Will he show up? Will he stalk off in midquestion? Will he bother to speak at all? He does, but it is a conversation of shadow, not substance. His voice is so faint it barely records. He is like Spray Net, a gentle misty haze filling the room. His white-blond hair hangs in spikes across his forehead, and he fixes you with an almost lidless reptilian gaze. If he doesn't have a ready, prefabricated rejoinder, he rolls his eyes, stutters, "I don't know," and waits.

How much time do we have, I ask, slightly apprehensive. "We'll see. When it gets boring, we'll take you on tour." Every museum catalog gives him a different birthplace—McKeesport, Pittsburgh, or Philadelphia, where he supposedly attended Philadelphia College of Art. "I guess I grew up in all those places. But I liked Philadelphia the best because I like painted American furniture and they have lots of that."

What's his earliest memory? "I can't remember. I can't remember from yesterday." He shrugs. I'm trying to picture him as a child. "Oh, I used to skate. Pick wildflowers. Play with baby dolls. That's a good one," he congratulates himself. What kind of kid was he? "Girly. Yeah. And nervous, too. I was nervous then and I'm nervous now."

What, I wonder, is his biggest talent? "Not giving interviews." He grins. Is he shy? "Sort of. Yeah. No. Well, it's just too much work, making up all those answers."

Did he have any artistic impulses when he was young? "I traced. I still do. That's what I do," he says proudly. "Just trace." What kind of ambitions did he have? "I didn't have any. It's all been so . . . accidental.

"When I was eighteen," he backtracks, "a friend stuffed me into a shopping bag and brought me to New York. One of my first jobs was in window dressing. Yeah, I was a staple-gun queen. I loved stooping in windows. When we went around recently promoting my new book, I sat in store windows like a mannequin and people came up to me to sign their books. It was fun. I signed twelve thousand copies by hand. Now my signature's not worth anything," says the man who once used a rubber-stamp autograph as his signature.

I ask him about his ideal feminine beauty. "Tatum O'Neal. We've been dating. Actually," he amends, referring to Ryan O'Neal's prepubescent daughter, "I just saw her a couple of times. I have a new girlfriend every month," says the lifelong bachelor. "Sex is okay. But it's, oh, just too much work. I'd rather sweep up."

These days Andy Warhol parties with the likes of Caroline Kennedy and Princess Lee Bouvier Radziwill and Paulette Goddard. His charm, I suppose, is similar to that of the Pet Rock. And many of the sycophants and show-offs and psychedelic parasites who hung around his human zoo, the Factory, have moved on to careers of their own. "I love gossip," Andy

Warhol says. He tells me Ingrid Superstar, who coined the surname emblematic of her ephemerally blazing status, is running a sewing machine in New Jersey. Viva is writing books and raising a baby. Joe Dallesandro's getting $75,000 a film. Eric Emerson was run over by a truck. Andrea Feldman committed suicide. Candy Darling died of cancer. Holly Woodlawn's nightclub act is packing 'em in. "And you should meet my friend Brigid Polk," he falters, "because she takes a tape recorder when she goes to confession."

Did he grow up Catholic? "Yeah. I still go to church every Sunday," he claims. "I just like the church. It's very pretty." Has being Catholic helped him to be a better artist? "Yeah," he says. "How? Well, I didn't have to go to a psychiatrist, I could go to a priest."

How does he feel about being a celebrity? "Well, I don't think I am," he says, "because I can walk around New York and nobody even notices me." How would he like to be remembered? "I'd rather be forgotten," he deadpans. But what about his prospective posthumous place in art history? "Oh gee." He shakes his head. "Usually I paint with paint that flakes off. It's flaking off now and we're getting calls from people complaining. They'll just have to send their paintings to a restorer. After all," he says grandly, "if you want to own anything, you should be able to afford to keep it."

Is he afraid of anything? "Oh, the dark," he smirks. Does he sleep with the lights on? "No, the television," he explains.

"I never dream. So since I've learned to fall asleep to television, when I wake up I just think I'm dreaming of Barbara Walters."

But that could be a nightmare. "Oh no," he protests. "I like television. I love 'Rhoda.'"

If somebody handed him an hour of network TV, what would he do? "I'd call it 'Nothing Special.' I saw a copy version that someone else did and it was called 'Ordinary'—it was mentioned in somebody's column a couple of weeks ago—a lady would iron and wash dishes. Well, we'd do the same. Just do two things at once, you know, like eat and talk. Nothing special."

If he could furnish one room to represent him, what would he include? "Nothing. I'd just leave it empty. I like a really big room. I just think a lot of space is really exciting. Not too many things—just what you have to use—one spoon, one fork, one plate, one dog. How have I furnished my own living space? Just shopping bags."

And who does he most admire? "God," he chuckles. But when I ask Andy Warhol if he expects to go to heaven, the tape recorder runs out and automatically clicks off. "There's your answer," he says, surrendering to his own technology. It's a classic case of deus ex machina if I ever saw one.

JANUARY 11, 1976

WILLIAM LEAST HEAT MOON
The Irish Osage

In the beginning, there is the name, and it is confusing.

"When I check into a hotel, if somebody else has registered me, I have to look under 'H' for Heat, 'L' for Least, 'M' for Moon, 'T' for Trogdon. I don't know whether there are any other permutations you can work on that name or not," laughs William Least Heat Moon, a/k/a Bill Trogdon, part Anglo, part Osage Indian, part writer, part professor, part photographer, part wanderer, suspended between two cultures, quoting Walt Whitman one minute and Black Elk the next.

"Listen, I was always the writer without the pen I needed to take down the good thing I heard, because I don't like to carry things in my pockets. I think that's part of the Osage coming out; I don't want anything on me. But I *will* carry a knife," he says, showing me a Japanese contraption that is both knife and pen. "It's a pen-knife, that's what they call it. Pen-hyphen-knife. Anyway, I'm no longer caught without a pen. You can always find something to write on, but you can't always get to your quill."

Call him Least Heat Moon. His father is Heat Moon, his older brother Little Heat Moon. Coming last, he is therefore least; it was, he says, a long lesson of a name to learn. "Ah, the name. . . . My father, my brother, and I used it only for, if this doesn't sound too inflated, ah, only for spiritual matters. In other words, in certain ceremonies, we would use it. To each other we would use it. Even some of our closest friends don't know about it," says the slight, soft-spoken bearded man of forty-four in tweed jacket, jeans, gingham shirt, and cowboy boots after a visit to Channel 6's "AM/Philadelphia." "We had never written it down."

Bill Trogdon, laid-off college professor and cuckold, did not really "become" William Least Heat Moon until the eighth—and final—draft of his book *Blue Highways*, which would go on to sell more than a quarter-million copies, phenomenal for an unknown writer's first effort. Six years ago he had lost his teaching job and his wife had left; his life had turned on him, so he just threw it over and took off.

He packed his pain and a few provisions in a used van he named Ghost Dancing, put $450 and a gas credit card in his pocket, carried a tin of chopped liver so he would never go hungry, and began a three-month, 13,000-mile journey along America's back roads, its remote, rural blue highways, blue because on the old maps the main routes were red, blue because there a man can lose—and find—himself, blue because he was.

This was less a travelogue and more a mystical quest, says the Kansas City lawyer's son who had never really been more than mediocre, doing a little teaching here, a little manual labor there. "I'm terrified of this word 'spiritual.' It sounds as bad as the word 'cultural,'" he says, sipping a beer in his hotel. "Somebody says the word 'culture' and I run for a gun. But anyway, all my spiritual values had always been connected with the Osage line—not with Christianity, not with anything else. Even though my parents both attend Presbyterian church, that never spoke to me, it was never part of me."

He realized that "the man who was trying to write this book was not Bill Trogdon, nor was it just Least Heat Moon. The man is William Least Heat Moon. He's a man with one foot in Anglo culture, in which he has grown up and been educated and has blood in. But it's also from the Osage line, which he knows about and has blood in. I've never lived on a reservation, so I can't say I grew up in it, other than what my father would teach us."

What his father taught him was reverent irreverence for his roots. "Some of it was just plain whoppers and tall tales. I remember once when I was very young and I was looking at his navel and asked him what that was. And he said, 'That's where Custer shot me.' Because I knew who Custer was. And I believed that for years—until the point I realized that I had one too, and I didn't get shot. . . .

"When we played cowboys and Indians as kids, I was the one who always wanted to be the Indian, because my father had told me that's a fine thing in itself to be. So I was popular in a way with playmates, because they knew they always had one Indian that they could shoot."

Did he encounter prejudice as a child? "It didn't last very long, because I learned my lesson quickly. But there was a while where I would boast about my Osage interest. I was interested in being the Indian, and I was happy to wear a feather. I would be the one who would take lipstick and put three stripes across my cheeks. They knew that I played it up from time to time. And they began calling me, mocking me, not only because of the Osage business, but because I was small, they began calling me Buck.

"'Buck' is a pejorative term, as you know, for an Indian male. But it had a double edge, since I was also small, too. They were hitting me from both sides. And it disturbed me at first, but then I realized that one of the best ways to get rid of a nickname is to accept it. And even though you might not get rid of the nickname, you can get rid of its negative connotations. . . . And to this day there are a number of people who still know me as Buck."

He is not sure if he has Indian blood on both sides. "Not on my mother's side, as far as I know. However, we've found out about a few ancestors we didn't know about since the book came out. And we're getting some notions now that my mother may have a touch of the blood, which she's not too happy about. She thinks it's fine for her husband and her sons to be Heat Moons, but she doesn't want to be a Heat Moon. I think she's uncomfortable with it. She's Irish. And she loves the notion of being Irish. And certainly she inculcated that in my brother and me. Down-home-dancing-singing-telling-jokes-language Irish. My sense of language comes through my mother."

As a boy he spent most of his time in the woods, building huts and making fires. "I was always the fire-builder. I loved to build fires," he recalls. His earliest ambition? "Probably the usual things, a fireman." Really? "Quite likely." Setting fires and wanting to be a fireman? "I hadn't thought about that." He laughs. "I do find various conflicts. . . . But you've got to realize that human beings are not logic machines. You can talk about Emerson's 'foolish consistency is the hobgoblin of little minds,' but make sure you put 'foolish' in there."

When you consider that his doctoral dissertation was on classical mythology in the poetry of Robert Herrick, that he spent five years getting his Ph.D. and now calls it "wasting my time," that he learned it was of no real value once he was on the road dealing with real people—you get a sense of the heavily credentialed academic trying to unlearn himself.

"Well yes, I think that's symptomatic of what happened to me. I went to the University of Missouri in '57 as a freshman, eighteen years old, to study photojournalism," a degree he completed when he was thirty-six. "I went from being aware of Osage Indian rites, of making complete Indian costumes, headdress . . . loincloth . . . everything, in high school; it was very important to me. And when I got to college, perhaps because of the extreme rigidity of that period, that all just disappeared from me. Within a semester I had lost interest in becoming a photojournalist and wanted to become an English teacher.

"I was infatuated with the tweediness of academic life. The most superficial of values attracted me. And I didn't escape that for another twenty years, until I became aware of what I was doing. And there were conflicts during those twenty years where one aspect of me just could not stand that other side. I don't want to say I was a schizophrenic, but"—he laughs ironically—"close."

Schizophrenic? "I was being pulled two ways. One side would say you behave this way, you write about these things, you read these books, you talk this way to your students. The other side said, oh, that is useless, pointless, empty, and what you need to do, you must have your feet on the ground, you must be talking to the people who do things in this life and who don't make a living *talking* about doing things. I'm speaking now of the professorial life. . . . When one side dominates, when the Western side, the Anglo side, the side believing in progress and technology grows too strong, then I find personally I'm out of balance. I'm a leaning man, and things begin to go wrong.

"And if you're walking entirely in the ways of your grandfathers, then you're going to be blind to what is going on about you in your own life. . . . I would assume that a human being, to be civilized, has to find that concordance, that harmony between what has gone before and what is about to come. . . . When I feel there's a balance, then I think I'm probably most content and I feel most sane and rational."

I was curious to meet Bill Trogdon, to see for myself if he would be a broken man lamenting a lost marriage. He isn't. His first wife, whom he had called "the Cherokee," who had once been his student, has been supplanted by his second wife, a non-Indian who once was his college Spanish teacher. He lives at the edge of the woods in Columbia, Missouri, and wants to find a piece of land *in* the woods. He likes milk shakes and bourbon and books and basketball. But like his Indian grandfather, he makes walking sticks, a symbol of the source of life.

"It's not as easy as it looks to find a straight one, or to straighten them, to finish them, to cut them. You have to deal with shrinkage, and warpage, and all that. I guess the highest gift that I can give to my friends," says William Least Heat Moon/Bill Trogdon, "is a walking stick. I give them away."

JUNE 3, 1984

MARILYN FRENCH
Not Much Use for Men

She tames her rage on the page. When she writes, she uses every part of herself, everything she is—"the vicious, the angry, the loving, the desirous, the yearning, the tender"—and she is fulfilled. She writes best-selling novels that map the chasm between the sexes, and penetrating scholarly studies of Shakespeare and Joyce that have become classics in literary criticism. She sips scotch and smokes cheroots and ignores rude jackhammers that rattle and clatter the macadam as she speaks. She is funny and smart and Phi Beta Kappa and a Harvard Ph.D. and divorced and controversial and fifty-five. She is Marilyn Edwards and Mara Solwoska and Mira Ward and Marilyn French.

Best known to the public for *The Women's Room* and to academia for *The Book As World: James Joyce's Ulysses*, she has now tackled the whole of human history in *Beyond Power: On Women, Men, and Morals*, a massive feminist revision of social philosophy for which her publisher invoked comparisons with Freud, Rousseau, Hegel, and St. Augustine. That's heavy company, even for the oldest of two daughters of a Queens engineer who grew up thinking "women could do anything."

Tell us about the names—are those different selves, in a sense? "No, those are accidents. I feel nameless. I was born Marilyn Soliwoski; my parents changed their name to Edwards. At the time I was very busy wanting to be accepted—I was about eleven—and that suited me fine," she says. "But when I grew older, I came to hate that name. It has no character, I felt. Then I got married, and I became Marilyn French. And I was writing and I wasn't having much success, and someone told me as long as my name was Marilyn French, I would never have success as a writer."

Why not? "That was just a thing she said. You know how people read your tarot cards or they throw the I Ching? It was like that. So I sent out a story under the name Mara Solwoska, and it was immediately published." She laughs. "So it became kind of a thing. Anyway, then I wrote *The Women's Room*, and I wanted to publish it under the name of Mara Solwoska, and my publisher, who is normally a very calm, tranquil man, blew a gasket. He said, 'People will not be able to remember that name.' I said, 'They remember the name of Solzhenitsyn.' He said, 'He's Russian; you're American.'

"Anyway, he really got upset about it, and also my children got very upset about it. I said, 'Well, you know, you have your father's name, but why should I have it? I don't like him, and besides, why should I immortalize his name?' They said, 'He'll die,' which he did, 'and we want you to have the same name we have.' So I kept it."

She kept it, but grudgingly. This name business has her flummoxed. ". . . I couldn't find a name. Because I tried to go to my mother's mother's name, but of course that's her father's name. And besides . . . you can imagine how they would have shortened it," she says of a name she can't even spell for me. "But the name I wanted to take was Mara Solwoska. I don't like Marilyn especially. Never have. Sorry," she says, laughing, "I was forgetting that's your name also." No, I share her sentiments exactly. Please go on. "And Solwoska wasn't as bad as Soliwoski, and it was feminine, Solwos*ka*, you know, so that's the name I chose for myself—with my mother's help. My mother said, 'I can understand why you want a different name.' And so then we came up with this together, and I felt that I had been renamed. But then I couldn't use it.

"You know what 'Mara' means? I started a novel like that many years ago: 'My mother's name was Marah, and I was nursed on her bitter waters.' It means *bitter,* and it's the root from which the name Mary in the Bible comes. And it was named after a well that had bitter water," she says. That's interesting, because some of her most unfriendly reviews inevitably mention that word—they say, oh, she's so bitter. "*Bitter* is a word you use for women who refuse to say that, really, even though they had to give up practicing law and they had to stay home and take care of these three children, they really are happy. That's what's bitter."

Did she really ever say, "People think I cause divorces because women are reading my books. A lot of men like to think it's all me, that it's all my doing. They don't understand where women are coming from, because they don't listen to women, ever"? Does that sound familiar? "Oh, I might have said that. I think I would probably say it in a little bit pithier way. What I say is, I've gone to innumerable parties where innumerable men have come up to me and said, 'Oh, Marilyn French, you've caused my divorce.' And my response is, 'I feel sure you had something to do with it.'"

For years she wanted to end her own marriage, to a lawyer, "but I knew he wouldn't let me go. . . . He was quite smart, but he only had one obsessive passion, and that was me. . . . There are people who can feel great obsessive passion, but they don't understand how to love, because maybe they had trauma in their own lives," she explains.

Some critics—and readers—have noticed more than bitterness; they've been astonished at the amount of anger in her novels. "Well, I think women are very, very angry—quite rightly. I don't know if there's a lot of anger in my novels or not. It's not something I can really judge," she murmurs. ". . . I don't think people probably have any idea how angry women are, because women are trained to be nice. . . . Women are extremely angry. And if my books have anger in them, it's because that anger is out there in the world."

Does she live alone? Yes. Is she heterosexual? "I always have been," she declares. Is she interested in men anymore? "I like some men. I think that it's hard for me to get to know men now. When I taught [in college], when I was just one of the people there and I saw them every day, I had a lot of male friends. But I lead such an isolated life now, and the men I meet go, you know, 'the killer.' I find most of my friends now are women. I have enormously good, loving friendships with women, and that's what really sustains me. And my children. They are very important to me. They're thirty and thirty-one."

But is she interested in men anymore? "I think I've given up on men. I mean, you know, seven years goes by, and that's a long time. Since the last time I met a man, ah, when I was involved with a man that I got anything from. Look, for a lot of years, the way I kept myself going was to get involved with very young men," she says. "But at some point, I mean, these sweet boys, I love them, they're nice, you know, but enough already. I'm tired. I'm a mother. You know. I want to go home and take an aspirin," she intones.

". . . Betty Friedan, the great feminist, came up to me at the cocktail party for *Women's Room* and said, 'Oh, Marilyn, I loved the book, but it was such a sad ending, did [the heroine] have to be alone?' And I said, 'Betty, how nice to see you. Let me introduce you to my friends.' I had this big circle of brilliant, beautiful, all younger-than-I women. Betty's older than I. And I said, 'We're all single. . . . There are no men for these women.' Oh, there are men—there are always men who want you to bandage them.

"Well, who wants to bandage them? The older you get—" She shakes her head. "First of all, look, the men drop dead. They die a lot earlier than we do. I'm fifty-five. The men that would normally be involved with me—men from forty to sixty—half of them are already dead. And the ones who are really wonderful, decent good human beings have wonderful marriages, and they don't want to ruin their lives. So what's left?"

What's left has never been scared away by her brilliance. "And I've never had a problem with men, except they tend not to give anything," she contends. "And that's a huge problem when you get older. Because time is very precious. And from other people, what you need is nourishment. You need to be engrossed in some way that you know you can be yourself fully. You don't have to be there just to bandage their egos or to bolster them. You need someone who you can be a baby or a screaming witch with."

And mostly, she complains, you can't do that with most men. "They need you too badly, because they're too damaged by what they do in the world. They're horribly damaged, I know they are, and I feel sorry for them. But when are they going to rebel? I don't feel like going out with a man and sitting there building up his ego all night. I'm tired and I have a lot of work to do. Besides, I think I can have a lot more fun with my women friends, I really can. They care for me, and they take care of me in ways that men . . . don't."

Aren't younger men less damaged? "Yes, but also less sure, and they need just as much bolstering. And they can't help you at all. I had a long-term relationship with a very young man for many years. He was a sweet guy, really sweet—lovely, smart, beautiful. But when terrible things happened in my life, he was speechless . . . he told a lot of jokes. He didn't know how to help me at all. He didn't know! There wasn't anything bad about him; he was a sweet boy," she repeats. "He just wasn't good enough for what I needed. It was easier to be alone with my sorrow and stress and worry at the time. And that thing has since passed, and everything is fine."

So can a woman have it all? "My normal answer to this question is yes, but not all at one time. But now that I'm in my dotage, um, I think, yes, you can have it all. *If* your children are grown, and *if* you will go to a woman as a lover, and *if* you have good women friends, you can have it all," Marilyn French says knowingly. "But you have to be able to do that."

SEPTEMBER 8, 1985

JERZY KOSINSKI
"Not Everyone Is Tolstoy"

"There are people . . . who won't talk to me. They don't like me. Some won't even sit next to me. They heard I'm peculiar," says novelist Jerzy Kosinski, who is far more "complex, driven, obsessed" than any character of his own invention.

When tall, gaunt Jerzy Kosinski, member of the international jet set, is not playing polo in Latin America or skiing in Switzerland or hobnobbing with Zbigniew Brzezinski or making movies in Italy with Jack Nicholson, he resides in an almost austere two-room Manhattan flat with a copy machine near his bed and a hospital close by. Some nights he reads to dying patients. Some days he takes mundane part-time jobs. He will don gray wig and fake mustache so he can watch others live, so he can live without being watched, so he can pretend he did not publish *Steps*, *Being There*, *The Painted Bird*, so he can pretend he is ordinary, anonymous.

The once mute child who survived Nazi terrors to become a babbling witness to war and depravity now spills forth his tales in a high fast tenor, so fluent in English despite his accent that he has taught it at Princeton and Yale after learning it from TV news and telephone operators. He is the picaresque hero, the former Soviet bureaucrat and social scientist and professional photographer who escaped from behind the Iron Curtain by forging letters of recommendation from men who did not exist. At twenty-four he arrived in America with $2.80 in his pocket and a lust for the unpredictable.

"Regardless of what my readers might think, I always saw my life as being rather typical," he told me on a recent visit to Penn. "Typical. Typical of a great number of people, in fact for most people whether they know that or not. . . . What is controversial? I live a perfectly normal life. I pay religiously my taxes. I vote in every election, even when I'm abroad, which is more than most Americans do. I think my life has been relatively predictable in terms of what I do, looking back, not looking forward. Forward, nobody knows. Look, I was married for ten years, I mean, my God, I'm forty-seven, what is the secret? The characters I write about? They should not threaten anybody, that's not my fault, I am not controversial," he protests. "My readers are controversial to themselves. That's what bothers them. Not my life. *Theirs.*"

But he's a writer, that's not typical. "I don't really see myself as a novelist. I don't have the life of a professional man. I really live the life of an amateur. If you tell me right now, if you convince me there's something in Philadelphia that would be of interest, I would move here. I can be here tomorrow morning, I have nothing to prevent me from doing it. My whole life is structured around being mobile. I know Philadelphia quite well. My wife was dying here."

His wife was wealthy steel heiress Mary Weir, who was being treated for brain cancer at the Institute of Pennsylvania Hospital. "So I was coming here, believe me, more than I wanted to. There's hardly anything in Philadelphia of the mid-sixties that I didn't know, because when she was unconscious or semiconscious I would just ride around. So I know this city very well, very well.

"She was dying for a long time. For three years. For three years I was flying to Philadelphia, landing on the river in a plane, picking up a helicopter, driving a car, coming on a train, every conceivable way, back and forth," he recalls. "It was a very comfortable city, and her specialist was here, so whenever she had to be hospitalized quickly, we drove to Philadelphia."

They had a thirty-eight-room duplex in New York, a yacht in Greece, a villa in Italy, an estate in Florida, a mansion in California. "Look, my marriage to Mary didn't change anything in my life, other than emotions. I didn't acquire anything that I wanted during the marriage, I didn't need anything. I always lived in one room. In every house we had, I moved everything to my one room, which drove the servants crazy, because they were not supposed to clean it. I would always clean my own room. And most of the food prepared by our cooks neither Mary nor I could eat, because it was too heavy, and I am a simple eater. So we both dumped the food in the bathroom so the cook wouldn't be upset, but from time to time the cook would discover what was happening—our refusal to eat in front of the cook—and he or she would leave for a 'better' household.

"And most friends I made outside of Mary were rich Americans who did not go through the Second World War and they had households and this [wealth] was not something I wanted to have. I have just as much from a household I visit—if I visit your household I'll probably get as much from it as I would from a household I'd live for a while in. And I always traveled on my own, I would have traveled just as much on my own with Mary as I would without Mary. Ironically, when she was alive I still traveled on my own also.

"What I'm saying is, the marriage contributed emotions, but it did not contribute anything beyond what any other marriage would contribute," since he did not inherit his late wife's estate, "of course not," he declares. "Actually I was ruined financially by the marriage. Because I paid the tips. I took upon myself to pay the tips and it was an obligation I shouldn't have assumed. I did it because I felt I should contribute *something*, and I felt ridiculous that here I was married and I couldn't do anything.

"So I paid for my clothes, that was easy because I don't change clothes very often. I don't change fashion. But in any case, I didn't realize how much it would take to tip. It took everything I had. It took the royalties" from his first three books. "When Mary died [in 1968] I had to apply for a Guggenheim."

Destitution is behind him. *Being There* was made into a movie starring Shirley MacLaine and the late Peter Sellers. Why does Kosinski appear on TV when that book was such a

savage critique of "vidiots," mindless viewers? "I went on television, on Johnny Carson, with whom I shared some life situations, mutual friends, summer houses, and all that, I was on
it because it was no different than any other aspect of life.
Then other television shows began contacting me, they began
saying, 'Well, listen, there's this guy Kosinski, he writes some
strange books but he's perfectly all right on TV shows, he's a
Polish name, there's obviously a Polish audience out there, he
cannot harm anyone,' so I became a guest, though for ambig-
uous reasons. Most of the television audiences do not know
my books.

"People say, 'Well, you went on television, it enlarged your
readership.' It did not at all," he claims, "not at all. I might as
well tell you, I *lost* some readership, because the profound
audience felt somehow bothered by my too easy manner. They
kept saying, 'I thought you were a profound man, I read your
books, you are a metaphysical being, you have letters, and
suddenly I saw you making fun on Johnny Carson, now why
would you go on [the] Johnny Carson show?' And then I would
say, 'What right do I have *not* to? Will I not go on something
which every single American watches for seven and a half
hours each day? Do I have a right not to . . . ?'

"I have always been a very marginal novelist. A lesser talent.
Yes, there's nothing wrong with that. Ninety-nine percent of
mankind is, even in this I'm typical. Would I like more talent?
Yes. But you cannot get more talent. But I'm no different than
most lesser talents. We're all lesser talents. I think the difference is I'm trying to make up for it. Maybe I'm more mobile,
more persistent. At the age of twenty I already knew what I
had. There's nothing wrong with being a lesser talent. Mankind needs them just as much." He laughs.

Lesser talent? He has won the National Book Award and his
work is translated into thirty-eight languages. "A lesser talent is
not mediocre," he stresses. "I remember my father once told
me when I began to write, 'You will be punished one day,
there's no greater punishment than an insufficient talent.'
Look, I have sold 2½ million copies [in paperback]. You can

make some money on Kosinski, you are not going to starve," he jests darkly, "even if you are an agent.

"There is a place for a lesser novelist. Not everyone is Tolstoy. And not everyone is Dickens. There should be a place . . . for even a lesser novelist who writes about minor subjects, like Kosinski," he declares. "And when I say I'm a minor novelist, I say it complainingly. I'm complaining to the world. I'm saying, 'Come on. Reward me.' But I also know how to survive without it."

JANUARY 4, 1981

GRACE PALEY
A Gray-haired Little Girl's Short Story

The woman walks over to the window, in a stranger's office, in a strange city, and examines the familiar leaves of plants. "This is like my grandmother's plant. She died a long time ago. I've given away pieces of her plant to so many people, my friends, my children, and so have they."

She is barely five feet tall, and when she speaks, it is a wondering, wistful voice, childlike through chewing gum and a Bronx accent and crowded cadences. But her hair is wavy silver; absently, she unpins it, rakes her fingers through, then fastens it up again in a coil. How easily she forgets herself, her pleasant face plain of makeup, her shapeless blue cotton housedress covered with little pink and green flowers, her stockings over unshaven legs, her red shoes with small heels.

Author Grace Paley seems like a gray-haired little girl, unconcerned with glamour and glory, standing in for a grown-up. But she is a grandmother herself, born in 1922, a staunch peace activist, a feminist. She writes short stories, great short stories. She has built an extraordinary literary reputation on her "two little books"; *The Little Disturbances of Man* (1959) and *Enormous Changes at the Last Minute* (1975) are classics. With her second husband, poet and landscape architect Bob Nichols, she lives in a Greenwich Village walk-up. Her two children are grown, and twice a week she teaches writing at Sarah Lawrence. Lately her stories have appeared in *Ms.* magazine and *The New Yorker*.

"We're all storytellers. That's something everybody does. You do. You probably told two or three stories today already. No? How come?" she says, laughing, before giving a guest lecture at Temple University Center City. "I think very serious literary people feel that only very serious literary people should write, but the English language is there for everybody—anybody can probably take a pen and start putting words down. We're not the bosses of beauty or truth. It's the people's language. And they should do any damn thing they want with it, you know? It's a sin on God not to write if you want to. I mean, there's so much censorship in the world, who needs *your* censorship? If you want to write, do it!

"Muriel Rukeyser said all writers were once little children who sat under the piano listening to the grown-ups," she relates. And Grace Paley grew up listening to her father, a neighborhood doctor, and her mother, who ran the house and the office. Grace, youngest of three children, answered the door and the phone. "His practice was as much part of my life as going to school." She recalls writing "little rhyming things, the sort of things parents or aunts liked. I never would have written them when I was four or five if I hadn't been encouraged. Not only did my family like it, but the entire middle class of which I was a four-year-old member liked it"—she laughs—"so it was just a natural thing to do."

She views her own parents as heroic. "They came to this country when they were about twenty, and they didn't know any English. They had been socialists in Russia, in prison. My father had been in Siberia when he was eighteen, nineteen, my mother had been exiled," she says. "My father was a big storyteller, he was very good at it. He talked a lot about their lives. When he was old, he wrote a lot of stories about the people on the block. I tried to publish them and I never could, but they were really good."

As a child, she read "everything," both "junk and wonderful things." Poems by Robert Louis Stevenson, horse books, dog books, and "I always liked *Little Women*. I liked what's her name, Josie? She was so tough, the others seemed awfully sissyish. But then I liked a lot of things. I liked war books, soldier books. I'm a pacifist now, but I was really very into heroics. . . .

"I used to feel that I failed at everything until I began writing stories," she admits. "I didn't do well in school. But I had a lot of gratification; I mean, I really had nice things happen. I wanted children and I had children. I've been married to two people I like very much." She smiles, and I ask for specifics. "I didn't do well at school, at college [a year at Hunter, a year at N.Y.U.]. I can't say I flunked out. I just stopped going to classes.

"Oh, I was very young. I just couldn't. I was just tired of school. . . . Actually, after the sixth grade my interest in the academic routine was over. . . . The minute I sat down in class I felt a steel wall coming down in front of my face. I just wrote poetry. I'd hang out in the halls and write poetry. Also I was in love a lot. All that took up time. It took up your mind's time. You didn't do anything with it, but there it was in your mind, all the time."

At nineteen she married her high school sweetheart, film cameraman Jess Paley. During World War II she lived in Army camps; then, when he went overseas, she worked. "I worked in tenant organizations. It was quite an accident that I got those jobs. I was an office worker. That was my only trade—typing. Oh no, I was never bored. I can't stand that word. Kids use it all the time. I mean, you have your head, your head's attached to your shoulders, how can you be bored?"

But still, her family felt she was a failure. "I had not really finished school, I had no chosen profession. I mean, my family was not the kind who thought just because I was married and had kids that I was so great. They really felt that I should have gotten a couple of degrees and done something with myself. Obviously, even at thirty-one or thirty-two, I had done nothing with myself. Then when my book came out, everybody, my family was in heaven."

Eventually she began, in her mid-thirties, to write short stories as exquisitely crafted as her poems. "I sent them out, but no one published them. . . . I could have very easily been discouraged, I'm not that brave." Then, somehow—and here memory and history blur—maybe it was because her kids played with his kids, or maybe her husband showed a friendly

Doubleday editor a manuscript, but somehow "this guy saw my first three stories and said they were fine and he'd like to put out a book, so I should write seven more stories, which I did over the next two years. But I had only written three stories and that's how I got my book. I was very lucky."

Lucky, yes; rich, no. "I never used to see royalties, never. Only in the last few years. Oh, I got paid for my books, I got my advances, which were just comical, I mean, when I first wrote," she says. "When I hear the kind of money people make at writing now, that has nothing to do with me. Those million-dollar advances are not right. I don't think so. They're not right for the same reasons that it's unjust for anybody to sit on the board of U.S. Steel and make a million dollars when somebody else is making nothing. I don't think it's right."

However, "if anybody offered me a lot of money I might accept it, so I could *do something* with it. But I might not accept it, I mean, I might be suspicious of it. I don't really know. See, I think they get a million dollars, but then I think they have big taxes." She laughs. "That sounds funny when you say that, it sounds really stupid. But see, I guess they don't have big taxes 'cause then they could get it over a period of years. It's not my world," she murmurs, "I don't understand it."

Does she socialize with other writers? "I never used to, but in the last few years I have. I was sort of afraid of that life, it just worried me. Besides, I don't enjoy it," she contends. "What I really liked were my friends and their children. I have a lot of good women friends, and we've been together and through a lot since the kids were small. I like the park. I love to go to Washington Square Park, and I used to go. And I liked it when the kids were in school and I liked to go to the PTA, I liked all that stuff." She always hung out on "the block," never in chic saloons like Elaine's. "I just didn't want to, I didn't want to be taken away from ordinary life, from people's lives. I just didn't want to. And at that time, writers were mostly men, anyway," she trails off.

She has lived in the same neighborhood for thirty years. "It's a community of people who are pretty much, I call them radical pacifists, most of them. But a lot of them are not. I've always lived there, even when my kids were small. And being in the same neighborhood is important. . . . Maybe if I moved to another block," she teases, "like three blocks away, I'd be the real typical literary outsider. But living on the same block all these years has really given me a strong sense of being part of a place. I still have the same grocery store. There's a lot of things that are really stable in my life."

Only when she describes her serious causes does she lose her air of bewildered innocence. Two years ago she was arrested, tried, fined, and placed on probation for her part in unfurling an anti-nuclear power banner on the White House lawn. "I'd like to harass people into saving the world, because I don't think it can be saved that easily. If people don't get off their tails, the world will blow up. There's really a very short time for us. If we don't backtrack pretty quick and stop building those things, it can't go on like this. I mean, you'll never be my age, you realize that?"

We discuss her experience of getting older. "Sure, you really feel a sadness about moving toward the exit gate, you really feel sadness about that," she says. "But you'll see this yourself. As you get older, you really don't give a s—— what people think about you." She laughs. "You really don't. So they hate you. Or they think I look like a jerk. I look like a jerk anyway. No, no, I'm just saying you don't think to yourself anymore, 'Oh God, what do they think of me?' You don't care about it so much, you care about it less and less," Grace Paley says. "It's a nice little trade-off. Wait, you'll get freer. You'll love it."

NOVEMBER 23, 1980

JAMES DICKEY
"Have a Beer with Your Soul"

It is 9 A.M. and the Poet is unprepared to meet the Press. Stinking of booze, he is bleary-eyed, and his bare chest barrels over baggy blue boxer shorts. His rapidly reddening body blocks the hotel room door. "We can't talk here," James Dickey drawls, stretching the words out like taffy. "It's a mess."

Dickey has made a career out of "bein' big, tough, masculine, tricky"—and terribly talented. He is a former athlete, night fighter, and adman who wrote jingles for Coca-Cola, Lay's Potato Chips, and Delta Airlines. With a rare combination of humility and perspective, he calls himself "America's greatest living poet," and his "close friend" and fellow Georgian Jimmy Carter warmly concurs.

"God, I hate the city," he moans some ten minutes later when he whisks into the Ben Franklin coffee shop wearing a silver Aquarius medallion over a white Mexican voile shirt, gray suit, impish smile and five (!) wristwatches ("I'm a consultant for a celestial navigation equipment manufacturer"). After ordering "the high-calorie, low-protein breakfast," he relents and requests tomato juice, ham, sunny-side-up eggs, and home fries.

Very shortly we are headed for Camden via the high-speed line. James Dickey, fifty-two, is on his way to Rutgers to read his poetry. Though he once advised an audience rather prosaically to "have a beer with your soul," the democratic idea of getting somewhere under his own steam does not seem to give him pleasure. Looking about as uncomfortable as a Roman senator plopped from a helicopter onto a crowded sidewalk, he lurches along next to his long-haired, short-skirted bride of four months, Deborah, twenty-nine years his junior.

Where, the former Library of Congress Poet must have been wondering, was, if not a proper welcoming committee, at least a cab or one of those nifty horse-drawn carriages? After all, hadn't he swapped tall tales and slurps of beer with Billy Carter on "The Mike Douglas Show"? Didn't he create the President's Official Inaugural Poem ("in plain English even dogs and cats can read")? And hadn't he penned and performed in *Deliverance*, his own movie-from-a-novel that had been burned in North Dakota and incinerated in California high schools? Hadn't he won a National Book Award? And walked under Spanish moss down South with Barbara Walters for the "Today" show? And appeared on the cover of *Esquire* clad in an aluminum life mask that had almost blinded him? Don't these folks here know how to act?

For James Dickey, the descent into the train concourse is a crash course in urban decay. The turnstile sticks, so he must hoist his six-foot-three, 190-pound bulk over it. The magazine stand contains four full feet of nasty magazines, and he turns away genuinely angered and appalled and embarrassed. Strange stuff for a man who once wrote that he "secretly thinks of [myself] as mild-mannered, agreeable, colorless and uninteresting." Well? "I do, I do," he shrugs, boarding the train. "Except the public won't have it. So I have to get drunk all the time to make myself colorful," he chortles. "Just like Dylan Thomas. And believe me, I'm not averse to it."

Why the literary fascination with alcohol? "It's an entirely artificial environment for anybody to be on public show all the time, to be interviewed all the time, to travel all the time," he says. "I used to drink an awful lot, but now I don't need it anymore. It's much better that way. And put that in," he instructs me.

"Yes," Mrs. Dickey injects, "just sit down and have one good resourceful drink together."

"Yeah," he adds, "I don't really need it."

"We both enjoy a beer or a glass of wine," she says very carefully.

"Yeah," he goes on, "that's about it. I'm not one of those

obsessive drinkers like Dylan Thomas, Hart Crane, John Berryman, Hemingway, or Faulkner. I really never was," he contends. "I don't have it in me. I'm not anything like them."

"Maybe they weren't totally happy," his wife suggests.

"Well, I think they probably were," he says.

"I'm getting upset lately," his wife whispers to me, "that more and more Jim's identifying himself as the author of *Deliverance* rather than the poet. He's so worried about making money I'm afraid he might not concentrate on writing anything else important."

James Dickey sold his first poem for $28.50. His first book received $114 in royalties. But selling *Deliverance* to Warner Bros. was another story. "Quite a different story," he offers. Say $200,000? "I don't talk figures," he demurs. "That was only the beginning. Look, don't make a big thing about my earnings. Because, listen, there's only one person, and he's recently dead, who has a more complicated tax situation than I do." He glares. "Even Nixon's tax situation is not that complicated. The only person who would be comparable in complexity to mine is a gentleman named Howard Hughes." Poor James Dickey. He has to juggle income from so many different sources—"book royalties in many languages, reprint rights, film, reruns, residuals. From television shows, readings, reviews." Poor, poor James Dickey. "I'm going to have to what-do-you-call-it," he says, fishing for the right word, "incorporate?

"I have to do something, I'm losing so much damn money. No, I'm not in need, but my income fluctuates like the sine curve in trig. Some days I got a lot, some days I don't have a thing. I've always disagreed with the premise that poets aren't supposed to have anything," he says vigorously. "We've always had a tradition in America of hounding our artists to death. Look at the list of our great artists, you see a continual history of defeat, frustration, poverty, alcoholism, drug addiction. The best poets of my generation are all suicides."

James Dickey's opinions are brutally clever. Of Farrah Fawcett-Majors, he says, "I wish I knew who you were talking about. Oh, that conventional beauty made of plastics and light metal." And poet Erica Jong's success as a novelist? "I don't think anything of it. She's another no-talent . . ." he snorts. "Usually pornography is written by men. . . . Well, she looks sort of like a man, in drag." He giggles. "But don't say that, 'cause she's a nice enough person."

To which his wife counters, "You say the most God-awful things about people and then you don't want to be quoted. Then why don't you learn to keep your thoughts to yourself?"

He grumbles like a little kid reprimanded for putting his fingers into a bowlful of chocolate icing, and I suggest his wife seems to be a moderating influence. "The best." He beams. "She was a student of mine. Let her tell you about it."

"I'm tired of talking about it, I talked about it all last night, you talk about it," says his child bride.

So he explains. "We fight, invariably, but creatively. The situation is this. Deborah just looked to me like a decorative little bric-a-brac in the classroom, a rather spectacular piece of student bric-a-brac. Pretty distinctive-looking, very smart, a good student. I had no further interest than just lookin', which was quite a privilege.

"And then my wife of thirty years died. It wiped me out. Because everything had centered around her. . . . I was pretty close to being totally demoralized by it. It was cataclys-mic. . . . Then this marvelous girl just got me to understand she was there with me. That I was not going to be alone if I didn't want to be. She saved me, and I can never give her enough credit."

According to a *New Republic* writer, Dickey was "famous for his virility." "I don't know what he'd mean"—he grins wickedly—"and besides, he don't know anything about that." He pauses. "A writer is essentially . . . a writer. And for him to be someone who capitalizes on a public image, so much less the writer. I'm essentially a writer, I'm a solitary person. I want that white sheet of paper, and silence, and whatever is coming up in the head at that time."

Is there anything he dislikes about interviews? "Sometimes

it gets a little bit irritating when you see it in print; it's irritating to me at least temporarily, when they describe you physically. If they don't say I'm the best-looking man in the world, very imposing and all that—when they say that I'm a middle-aged, balding, toothless, southern put-on type. You know, I just don't like to be described. It's like the old ladies say when they're raising their daughters—if you can't say something nice, don't say anything a-tall."

Does he envy anyone? "I envy the best of myself, when I'm doing less than I know I can do in writing. I've always found art relatively easy. It's life I find hard." He rises, and leaves the train. "I abhor backsliding. But I have backslid sadly. I can't run as fast as I used to. Or lift as much weight. Or shoot an arrow as well. . . . You don't like doin' these things for any reason except that you just like doing them. That's what you like about the things that fascinate you.

"I have," says James Dickey, "a generic horror of the aging process because the only thing I've ever been is young."

JUNE 19, 1977

GÜNTER GRASS
Between God and Hitler

Trying to interview the great Günter Grass, Germany's most celebrated living author, in the distracting presence of his very tall blond Valkyrie second wife, her teenage son with pierced earring and punk hairdo, an elaborately analytical art critic, a nervously attentive gallery owner, and assorted interruptive hangers-on and hoagie eaters is, to say the least, trying.

But the fifty-six-year-old novelist, humanist, poet, playwright, printmaker, sculptor, jazz drummer, and occasional politician—creator of fiendishly funny Oskar, dwarf percussionist and shatterer of glass, egos, and illusions in *The Tin Drum*, his most famous book—is unperturbed. He puffs on his pipe and peers over his wire-rimmed specs and appears casually dignified in corduroy and tweed and speaks in slightly accented English—part doleful dachshund, part Westphalian ham—before a recent exhibition of his graphics at Philadelphia's Suzanne Gross Gallery.

Dark-eyed, dark-haired, with a huge dark mustache, Günter Grass is a man divided and sometimes tortured by his complicated heritage. His birthplace was Danzig, the free city-state seaport once annexed by the Nazis and now Poland's Gdansk. On his mother's side he is Kashubian, of an old Slavic tribe in Poland. Son of a German grocer and minor official, he was brought up Roman Catholic "between the Holy Ghost and pictures of Hitler."

His commitment to his country has been a sometimes painful choice. At ten he became active in the Hitler Youth movement. (That didn't stop him from writing, at age thirteen, his first novel about his mother's people, "the same thing I do today, I didn't change," he quips.) At sixteen or seventeen he was drafted, served as an aide in the Luftwaffe, was wounded and captured by the Allies during battle shortly before Germany surrendered in 1945. Confined to a hospital bed in Marienbad until he recuperated, he was later shifted to an American POW camp in Bavaria and forced to view the liberated Dachau concentration camp as part of his successful rehabilitation.

His subsequent career has taken the quixotic twists and turns typical of many writers and artists. He has been a black-marketeer, drum and washboard player, farm laborer, potash miner, speech writer for Willy Brandt. He even designs his own book jackets. Trained as an apprentice stonecutter, he went from tombstone carver to student of painting and sculpture to author. There seems to be a continuity between cutting stone, engraving tombstones, etching, drawing, sculpting—making images—and writing. "I like to work with material," he says. "To form, to transform."

Hailed as masterpieces internationally, his books are contraband east of the Berlin Wall. But, he says, "books are stronger than frontiers." In his own country, he has been given prizes, then denied them, denounced as a national disgrace yet praised as a voice of conscience. Because of his irreverent treatment of religion, politics, and romantic love, dozens of attempts have been made in Germany to ban his books as pornographic and blasphemous. Concerned with myth, history, food, and sex, his works are often mordant, perhaps morbid, even grotesque.

He grew up in a two-room apartment, always reading, reading, in his own world. His sister and parents and he would all sleep in the same bedroom; it was very noisy. "If you grow up in a two-room apartment, you have to create larger rooms in your imagination," he says. World War II came to his home town when he was twelve. "And so it became normal to me." At first the Hitler Youth "was all right. We went to the forests, like boy scouts, in tents. But later on, sometimes it got boring, every day, every week, going to meetings. I preferred to sit by myself and read. I didn't like to sing—Boy Scout songs changed to Nazi words," he recalls.

"We believed in it. We thought we were right. In '45, even when the war was over and everything was destroyed and I got the news about the burning of six million Jewish people and other, other terrible crimes, then I saw the background, what had happened, really," he says. ". . . It was all too early for me, yes? I was," he gropes, "I was in uniform when I was fifteen, yes? And the same time I was looking for a girl, but I had no possibilities. I was always in the barracks. This was my problem. I didn't think about war, and you could see that we were losing the war, but that was not my problem. My problem in those years . . . was how to meet a girl."

He was in the prison camp for a year, he says without bitterness, and being shown Dachau "was an education program. They took the young ones, the sixteen and seventeen-year-old boys, like me, and they brought us to Dachau and they showed us. But first we didn't believe it. No, because we said it's not possible the Germans are able to do this. We thought it was propaganda and a bloody lie. But then in prison camp we heard on the radio the beginning of the Nuremberg trials, and then our own people started to speak out and say that it's true."

He speculates that if he had been a few years older, since "I grew up in a *petite bourgeoisie* family, that I think I would have been a Nazi. But nobody can be sure." What about his father? "He entered the party in '36, because the owner of the other grocery on the next corner did, and then he had to do it. It was opportunism. And he liked the uniform. After the war he didn't understand, I tried to teach him the reasons why he lost everything."

Is it disturbing to discuss those days? "To talk, yes. I like to write about it, and I did. Everything we are speaking about, you can find in my books, and better than I can tell you. In these things I am better on paper. . . ."

These days, Günter Grass and his wife wear matching wedding bands from a trip to China. They live in the northern part of Germany, in Schleswig-Holstein, near Hamburg, no longer, as once reported, doing without a car, TV, or telephone. "We have two chickens," his wife volunteers. Always the same two chickens? "We change them," he says, grinning.

"Two died. Yeah, we eat them." Does *he* kill the chickens? "No, a neighbor does it for me. Well, I could do it, but I'd have to learn how. That's not so easy, yes? You have to do it in a good way."

Someone points out a lithograph he has done of a cockfight. It was in the middle of a village in Indonesia, he relates, on a flat roof made of palm leaves, while a crowd of men watched. What interested him, he says, was the atmosphere, and "the movings," the movements of the birds. "I am always drawing," he has said, "even when I'm not drawing, when I'm writing, cooking, making love, or deliberately doing nothing. Long before I wrote the fairy tale of *The Flounder*, I had drawn a big flat fish with a brush, with an etching tool, with charcoal, and with soft pencil. Only then did it take shape in words. . . ." And he cooks a mean flounder, top of the stove, sautéed with butter and capers and white wine and fennel.

I ask him the best thing he's done. "I'm afraid that I am remembered by the interviews I have given." He chuckles. And that distresses him, no? "That distresses me, yes," he says, laughing. "I think that it's a very simple discipline, to make words and print words." A simple discipline? "Yes, because I see how you work. You did read a lot about me. But you read more *about* me, more written about me, than my own writing." Well, I say, I *have* read many of his books, too. "But most of your questions are coming from other interviews, what somebody told, what somebody said. I am feeling I'm answering your questions, but I forgot the reason. But the reason is the exhibition of my etchings," he declares. Certainly we would never forget that.

"But I know it's very difficult to speak about drawings and pictures. Because you have to see it. And you, you hurried up," he accuses me. "You come in the gallery and you can see the pictures." Well, I've been here before to see his work. "The best thing to speak with me about is how to do it, yeah, how to do it." All right. Tell us. "Now? No, no time."

One of Günter Grass's most compelling prints is of a praying mantis. Never kill them, my father told me as a child in New

Jersey, they're good, they eat the bad bugs. And so I grew up thinking the praying mantis was like an insect god. "This is one of the first lithographs I did," he says. "I got her when I was in Italy, yes? And I have a marvelous method to kill them"—trapping the creature in a glass and pouring in "grappa," grape wine. "Very high alcoholic content. They are dead very soon, and a nice death, huh?

"Years ago, I had one in a glass, yes? And I fed her with flies. It was marvelous to see how calm she was." Calm? "Calm, yes. She waited just till the second when the fly was near her, then, whoosh, like this." So why would he kill praying mantises? "No, no, I don't kill them. I killed *one* of them," he stresses, "to make drawings. Because I used it," Günter Grass says with a laugh, "to make a gravestone of her."

JUNE 12, 1983

ERMA BOMBECK
"I Never Asked for Anything"

My father's heroine, Erma Bombeck, heralded as the funniest woman in the country, 31 million readers, syndicated in 900 newspapers, voted one of the most influential women in the United States, regular on "Good Morning America," recipient of ten honorary doctorates, iron-clad contract preventing her copy from being edited, income in excess of half a million dollars a year, feminist who stumped for the ERA, and what does her official bio say her hobby is? Dust!

Dust? "It's really true," she admits with a laugh. "Everyone has to have a hobby, and I just picked something that I seem to have a great collection of. You know, everybody's got a hobby in the whole world today. If you don't have one, you're just un-American. So I thought I gotta have something. I don't collect anything. I don't *do* anything. I am the soul of mediocrity. The soul of mediocrity," she repeats, "in tennis, in needlepoint, in everything. I do a whole lot of stuff, and I don't particularly excel in any of it, but I do have a good time doing it. For someone who started out at thirty-seven, when I got syndicated"—she laughs again—"I mean, it's gonna be a big finish."

Erma Bombeck would rather write than speak but prefers being interviewed to having her picture taken. She portrays herself as Everywoman, Mrs. Mom-God-Country-Flag-and-Apple Pie, three children, married for thirty-four years, daughter of a Dayton crane operator who died when she was nine, just a housewife working at home in Paradise Valley, Arizona. "I'm not a real complicated person. I don't write complicated," she contends. "I'm not that way at all." She feels, she insists, "rotten" about being fifty-six, wants to write plays and perhaps a successful sitcom to erase the sting of "Maggie," an earlier TV flop, she tells me one Saturday morning in Manhattan, on tour to promote her seventh book, *Motherhood: The Second Oldest Profession.*

Yes, terrible things do happen even to Erma. This year her house was struck by lightning and then vandalized. Her sister died. Her son's car was stolen. None of her three kids—ages twenty-five, twenty-eight, and thirty—have made her a grandmother yet, let alone married. Don't be misled by her routine that she's just "real folks, I have a lot of normalcy in my life, this is a ten-year-old gray skirt I'm wearing, we live in a ranch house on the mountainside and drive a six-year-old car, and I get up at 6 A.M., walk a mile, write, take a nap, write some more, go to aerobics class, come home, get dinner, fall into bed, get up and do it again, no big social life, friends for dinner on weekends."

The "very nice" house is custom-built in a posh community, the car is a Mercedes, and her financial affairs grew so complicated that her Ph.D. husband left his job as high school principal to manage "the money . . . we have a couple of little companies . . . we support tons of charities. We made some investments for my old age, which is coming the day after tomorrow." She and hubby are "flaming liberals." Her friends have names like Phyllis Diller, Art Buchwald, Abigail Van Buren, Ann Landers, Liz Carpenter, Dinah Shore. And despite her wealth, success, celebrity, she is, she claims, a stranger to self-confidence. "I am," she declares, "127 pounds of insecurity."

Huh? "I probably have more insecurities than any one person you can imagine," she confides. "And I think it works very well for me. I hope I never lose them." What are they? "Um, I never take anything for granted. I never have. It's not that I'm looking over my shoulder, expecting some housewife in Iowa to be warming up. . . . But I feel if I don't put out . . . the best I've got every week, it could go away, the columns, 'Good Morning America.' I'm very insecure about anything. I can't let up a minute. It's always seemed like a luxury, where you're so good that you don't have to worry about it anymore. I've never been that good and never will be. It's something that I work on all the time, constantly."

She says she's living proof that a former lousy reporter can become a famous, funny columnist—as a reporter, she says, she didn't stick to facts, she'd get so intrigued with her subject she'd forget to take notes, she made the people she wrote about sound like her, and she didn't ask the right questions. Then she discovered the lighter side of car pool–playpen–kitchen–bedroom life, though she never envisioned becoming a star. "I thought my life was going to be married to Bill Bombeck, living in the suburbs, writing a column for a weekly suburban paper. I thought that was the best of all worlds. I could work at home and I could send in the thing once a week, maybe to be read by a couple thousand people, that would be great. . . .

"I've never asked for anything. . . . The television, they came to me. I mean, if you're looking for a real hard success story of someone who clawed their way to the top—I mean, scratch that and substitute a wimp who's just sitting there over her IBM Selectric and just watching all these things happen to her, because that's exactly the way it was. I have never been real aggressive or real ambitious. Never for me. So when I started the column, I thought, 'This is terrific, thirty-eight papers is great, I'll retire with that!'"

Was her transition from behind typewriter to before cameras difficult? "I always tell myself I'm a writer, that's what I am, so I don't worry about what's gonna happen to me out there. I'm not slick. I'm not glib. I don't know television that well. I never pretended to. I'm a writer who's gone on television. And if I can't be myself and screw up"—she laughs—"and make dumb remarks, then they better replace me. Because that's as good as I get. Or as bad as I get. I'm never going to become very polished. . . ." Did TV make her over? "No, not at all," she maintains. She looks good. "No face-lifts, no tucks. None of those things. My own teeth. Oh, I had them bonded because I had a space in between. It's great. . . .

"You know what I have a fear of? That one of these days my

typewriter will break down. I'm serious about this, it's maybe thirteen years old, and I will not be able to buy another typewriter. It is a very, very genuine fear, because there are no typewriters being sold and everything is going to word processors. And I cannot even put my ironing board up and down, that's the truth. I am no mechanic whatsoever. Today my television was humming in my hotel room, and I made fifteen calls down to the desk saying, 'This is going crazy up here and giving me a lot of headaches, can you possibly turn it off?' What happened was someone had set an alarm clock"—she giggles—"and it was the buzzer going off for the alarm. I would have sat in this hotel room for three solid days with my head splitting, do you understand that? I would not know how to turn it off. Can you imagine that?

"I'm serious. I can't pump my own gas. I swear I cannot do that. I tried it once. I use unleaded. And I got the wrong nozzle, and I got thirty-two cents' worth of gas all over my feet. And for thirty-two cents I have nothing in the tank at all. He said, 'Lady, you got the wrong nozzle,' they looked at me like I was crazy. And I said, 'I'm not going to do this anymore, my foot could catch fire at any given moment. I have no gas in my car, I'm not having a good time. I'm going home.'"

Was this—or will it be—a column? "No. Who'd believe it? They wouldn't believe anyone would be that stupid. I just simply do not know how to do that." So she's resisted the technological age? "Oh yes. I have no computers around the house. I only go to the bank when the teller's there, because I don't know how to get money by pushing all those buttons. I don't know how to do any of those things. Nothing. I can't do that. You know what it is? I think it's a lack of patience."

Watch out—she's reinforcing some stereotypes. "Oh, I know, I know, I know, I know. And I'm not saying I'm dumb. I'm saying I have no patience with it. Or something like that. No, I'm not going to take the rap for not being bright enough to figure it out. I just don't want to." She laughs. I didn't say she wasn't bright enough, I point out. "No, I did. No, no, I did. I don't want to do that. I hate being stereotyped that way."

As a little girl, she wanted to be a ballerina "until my can started to grow to epic proportions," she recalls ruefully. Her childhood was complicated. Her father had been previously married, and when he died, Erma's half sister went to live with her own mother, and Erma was raised primarily as an only child. Often lonesome and solitary, she wrote little dramas for paper dolls, had an imaginary playmate, made up her own games, read like crazy, and sat under the eaves at her grandmother's house, having tea parties for invisible guests.

"You have enough for a book," she says. How do real folks react to her? "I think they're just real disappointed, which is maybe why I keep a low profile in a crowded room. I think they expect that I'm going to have a lot of one-liners and be very funny and do a stand-up number on them or something. I think they're real disappointed, because when I talk with people, I usually like to pick their brain on what they do and how they feel about things, I really like to get into some issues. I don't want to sit around and say, 'You think your kids are bad, ha, ha, ha,' and then go on to the next one. See, I do that all day. . . .

"I've always been too short for the public, um, such a disappointment, they always think I'm taller. . . ." Anything else she'd like to say about herself? "I think they know enough already. . . . Gee, this quiz is hard. . . . There's just not a lot to say. I'm really shallow," she teases. Has anyone ever dared to say anything bad about her? "Sure. Oh yeah. Absolutely." Erma Bombeck smiles prettily. "What do you think I am, Doris Day?"

NOVEMBER 20, 1983

BUCKMINSTER FULLER
From Crackpot to Genius

"When I tell you I'm the average man, I assure you I'm utterly convinced of what I say," insists inventor-engineer-architect-philosopher-poet-mathematician-writer-manufacturer-builder-industrialist-teacher Buckminster Fuller. "Anything I've been able to do, just about anyone can."

Average? Growing up in a house designed by the son of Longfellow the poet and learning to ski at seventy-two? Indeed! For years he was dismissed as a "charming crackpot." But lately Buckminster Fuller, who will soon be eighty, is being hailed as "one of the creative giants of the century." Clearly his ideas have come into their own time, even if his self-image hasn't.

Almost fifty years ago, he designed rear-steered cars that could seat ten and go 120 mph, mass-producible dwelling machines, floating cities. He resurrected the ancient Greek word "ecology" and gave us "more for less" and "Spaceship Earth." Fifty thousand of his geodesic domes dot the globe even on the North and South poles and the top of Mount Fuji. Though he holds two thousand patents, he never intended a career as an inventor—his ideas came while exploring experimental math.

These days he's World Fellow in Residence at Philly's University City Science Center, where we're talking over late afternoon tea. Built like a short fence post—sturdy, ruddy, and close to the ground—he has bristly white hair and thick trifocals and is quite hard of hearing. His thick New England–accented voice tends toward a monotone, and our brief chat is a mere clearing of the throat for someone whose lectures have lasted four hours.

"I was born cross-eyed and farsighted," he recalls from behind his desk surrounded by photos of boats, "and I never saw a human hair or a teardrop until I got my glasses at four and a half. I'd see color, but no details. The interesting thing is, all I have to do is take off my glasses and I'll see exactly what I saw from childhood—the lens correction I got was so good and so accurate it hasn't been changed ever since.

"I assumed everyone else saw what I saw. People were colored blobs. I didn't use the word 'blue,' because that's the way things were. The fact that I could feel hair with my fingers yet not see it did not seem any more illogical than the fact that I could smell certain things yet not hear them." When he was a toddler, his eye defect was so bad he thought his older sister was telling tall tales when they compared notes about their visual world. "I assumed she made up stories because I couldn't see what she was seeing. Then I'd tell her about all the things I could see. But what I imagined, *nobody* could see"—he laughs—"so they thought I was just the greatest storyteller.

"When I finally got my glasses and suddenly saw human eyes, I was astounded. Once you have eyes, you latch onto eyes. I saw the eyes of dogs, cats, snakes, toads, and was terribly excited looking at them. I'd made friends with these animals very readily. It was like a new birth," he marvels. "But it had two very important effects on my entire life. One, I had to get along by recognizing big patterns, not details. Two, it also taught me that if I don't see what's going on, if I don't understand things satisfactorily, I am likely to see things clearly considerably later, so it tends to make me quite patient. That's why I've been able to endure some very tiresome long negative experiences on the way to hoping to accomplish something. I don't tend to get discouraged easily."

As a child he was undersized, sensitive, but strong. He played football without his glasses.

It was a family tradition to attend Harvard. "Though I was the fifth generation to attend, what really shocked me were the distasteful social games. None of the parents wanted their kids to room with me. They thought I was a nobody. Though my family was old and respectable, we weren't well-to-do. My father, a Boston merchant, had died when I was twelve.

"I think to assuage my pride I figured out a great trick. I borrowed my sister's dog, a spectacular Russian wolfhound, and stood outside the stage door of a popular musical comedy. After the show all the beautiful girls would come out and stop to pet this lovely dog. This was how I could meet any girl I wanted." He laughs. "I picked out the most attractive girl and took her out to dinner in the most prominent restaurant in Boston so all my classmates could see. I'm sure they were envious.

"My mother was afraid I'd literally end up in the penitentiary. Why? Primarily my utter irresponsibility about money. I never had an allowance until I went to college and suddenly was given a sum to last six months. Naturally I spent it immediately. Once, instead of taking my exams, I went down to New York and took out the entire chorus line at the Winter Garden Theater to dinner. Possibly twelve or eighteen little dancing girls. And I charged it to my family."

Harvard expelled him twice in his first year and finally dropped him for "continued irresponsibility and lack of interest." He tried working in a Canadian cotton mill and a meat packing plant. "The respectable middle-class world, the things they talked about, bored me," he reflects. "There was a time in the twenties when the only honest people I could find to talk with were in brothels. When I talk about finding girls in brothels, certainly they knew about sex, but I really wanted to learn about life. So I went to more than a thousand brothels in eastern America."

Five years of turmoil and crisis began for him in 1922. At four, his first daughter died. "It was a time of incredible unhappiness," he recalls. "She had spinal meningitis and infantile paralysis. I'd drink very hard at night and work fantastically hard during the day. Though I had five factories producing strong, lightweight building materials and had completed 240 buildings, I didn't make any money, even though I did prove the logic and efficiency of my construction system. By all standards I was considered a failure. I was absolutely penniless and lost the support of all my backers. So I contemplated suicide."

In a dramatic dialogue with himself on the shores of Lake Michigan, Fuller decided suicide was selfish—he was too valuable to humanity. "I had enormous expertise in fundamental things—how to feed people, build machinery, run ships. This experience really belongs to other people. One reason I was in such a mess financially was that I had been taught a game—earning a living. But I had a desire to make things work and do things better, not make money. So I decided to try to improve the lot of humanity, not as a political do-gooder, but by actual technical devices used for the advantage of others."

So in 1927, with a new baby daughter, he withdrew into his Chicago "semi-slum" apartment and vowed "to give up speech until I had cleared my mind of other men's words. My wife spoke for me. For nearly two years I was silent. I didn't want to speak until I was sure that the words coming out of my mouth represented what *I* was really thinking, not the clichés we borrow from others like parrots. All the changes that came after I was thirty-two happened because I started thinking for myself.

"How do I account for my success? I've simply been doing things that needed to be done, things nobody else attended to. I set out to design equipment for a period fifty years ahead of time. I discovered if I could go fifty years ahead, everybody would be sure to leave me absolutely alone. Engineers called my designs absolutely impractical. But nobody looked on my work as a threat. Therefore it was allowed really to prosper as art or curiosity or amusement or whatever.

"People constantly tell me they're sorry my car wasn't a success because it didn't get into production. I was not trying to go into production, I was not trying to make money. Detroit was very interested, but the marketing system—things being built to fall apart—couldn't handle a really durable product. I was simply testing principles—were the cars safe and effective? And they were. So the car was a very great success."

Is he happy? "My dear, I'm sure you couldn't find a happier person." Buckminster Fuller exhales, making his hands into a steeple. "How would I describe myself? I don't try. I don't know what I am until I confirm it. We're all very mysterious."

MAY 11, 1975

Note: Buckminster Fuller died July 1, 1983.

J. P. DONLEAVY
Tales from the Graveyard

"I was fascinated to wake up this morning and look out the window to see a cemetery, a very elegant cemetery," marvels J. P. Donleavy, the celebrated American writer who lives in an Irish castle. "I have a lifelong fascination with cemeteries. The only job I ever had was working in one once. When I was sixteen. In Woodlawn Cemetery, in the Bronx."

Can it be? This veddy veddy genteel tweedy chap who says "awfully" and "one" instead of "very" and "I"? Who plays the harp and raises wolfhounds and cattle on his 180-acre estate? Who has bank accounts on various continents? ("I suppose I could count up a few pennies.") Who carries his own bottle of maple syrup in his suitcase? From the Bronx? "Indeed. Born in Brooklyn [fifty-three years ago]. Raised in the Bronx. Served in the American Navy," he offers in his splendidly ersatz if vaguely British accent. "I've written a piece I call 'My Romantic Bronx,' a marvelous description of one's background, and I can't get it published anywhere. Oh well, I imagine if it were Beverly Hills instead, it might have a wider appeal."

Each of J. P. Donleavy's eight novels records the rowdy romps of a ribald rascal. His first, *The Ginger Man* (1955), is a campus classic—"set in type in English thirty-three times," banned, bowdlerized, pirated, translated into twelve languages, "ten million sold," he claims, "the most influential, most imitated book of its generation." Later books (like *Schultz*, about an American theatrical producer abroad) are less profound, more profane. But Donleavy's creative immortality is assured: "One of the few truly great writers we have," gushed *The New Leader*.

"As a child," he recalls in his Philadelphia motel suite, "I was not allowed to eat white bread, soda pop, or ice cream. That alone could have made me an outsider in America." For starting a fraternity, he was expelled from Fordham Prep. He joined the Navy, then studied bacteriology and zoology at Trinity College in Dublin on the GI Bill. Living in Ireland with a "small stipend" from his family, he briefly became a painter. "The art world," he sniffs, "was one gigantic con game. Amazingly, I wasn't that unsuccessful."

Reaching inside his jacket, he retrieves a small yellow notebook and commences to inscribe in a fine spidery hand. "These [book promotion] tours don't have that much effect on me, because I'm still immersed. I notice everything around me." This trip, he's fond of prowling the corridors of mental hospitals and strolling through slums. "I don't look at the glamorous, pleasant aspects of American life. I look at what's appalling, sleazy, grimy, horrifying."

Writing, he says, is "turning your worst moments into money. Basically that is the story of being a writer. . . . I don't read novels at all. Novels are for entertainment, not really things that interest me. I read medical books. I'm still fascinated by medicine. Once you decide to become a novelist, stop reading altogether and all you do is write. It's an American notion, 'he's up at bat now, let's see what he can do.' That really doesn't apply to serious authorship at all. Your battle is not with other authors, your battle is with what you put on the paper."

Writing isn't a job, he says. Being a graveyard groundkeeper, cutting grass, was. "My father was a building inspector for the fire department, and a former florist. It just so happened he mentioned the job to me. I took it, and happily never missed a day. I was quite happy. I turned up regularly."

Wasn't he fond of sleeping among headstones? "Exaggeration. I used to sit in one or two cemeteries in England. One was a churchyard. Frequently I came in there.

"If you walk through graveyards, reading gravestones is like reading history. I'm always fascinated by the guy who builds the biggest mausoleum. He's probably not even famous. For example, the Hollywood cemetery I just visited, I took down the man's name who had the most pretentious mausoleum. Probably he was some very rich man. Very few people know of him, but he was a financier and must have been a very difficult stingy man. It was so large it must have cost millions to build. He is the only one in it. His brother died, and he wouldn't allow his brother to be put in this big mausoleum. The brother had to be buried in the ground nearby."

I say, J.P., old fellow, you seem fascinated by death. "Yes, I always have been. Death is the kind of thing that terminates life. Well, a lot of people don't believe that. But there are some lines I recall from my book *A Singular Man*. George Smith was building a giant mausoleum and someone says to him, 'What does it matter what happens to you when you die?'" he recites. "George says, 'It matters all the days you live.'

"I'm possibly one of the few authors in the entire world who has actually started his own cemetery [at his estate on the shores of Lough Owel]," he declares. "It's attractive, the idea of having a cemetery. This old friend of mine, an American whom I used as a model for one of my most famous characters, Kenneth O'Keefe in *The Ginger Man*, I promised to bury him there. He's a real living person. He has never married and has no family. Astonishingly, he's still alive. I find myself fascinated by him though I have already written about him three times.

"I was amazed to find in his passport, 'In case of accidental death, get in touch with J. P. Donleavy.' He came to visit me not so long ago, and I was amazed to see this. He literally does intend that I should take his body and ship it to my cemetery and bury him. Oh, there is nobody in my cemetery yet," he explains. "I plan only to make my cemetery big enough for about twenty people or so, only those close friends who haven't betrayed me.

"My revenge, you see, is being very much alive. So those people who haven't betrayed me will probably be buried there if they like, if they need a place. It's a very comforting thing if you think of it. I can say as an author, 'That man has served me very well as a character,' just having listened to him talk, and I'd like to take good care of him."

His attention strays to the highway below. "I think that is a funeral down there," he announces cheerfully. "There is a gray limousine and two black cars. See what I mean? Keep our eyes peeled. They all have a little red seal in their windshield. If you can follow them, they are going to turn right. Let's see, they've got two limousines and four cars, five cars, six cars, seven cars," he counts in childlike rapture, "eight, nine, ten, eleven, twelve cars."

Does he look out the window because he's shy? "No. Because I want to see what I can see. Thirteen, fourteen, fifteen cars." Has he planned his own funeral? "There was a point where I had, in fact. I was investigating having a mausoleum built in the same Bronx cemetery where I once worked. . . . Some newspaper in England got hold of the story and a lot of reporters showed up at the cemetery in New York to find out more about my plans for a mausoleum. I never did, obviously, then, for financial reasons, start building it; I guess I would have been able to afford it, but it was rather extravagant."

Will he concretize, uh, marbleize those plans now? "Being a farmer, I hate to see grass wasted. The Welsh, when they bury someone, cattle generally do graze over the graves. That doesn't bother me at all, the notion that one's grave would be used for grazing cattle," he says, then asks me, "Have you children? I'm just interested. It's rare to meet a woman nowadays who has children. I suppose one just doesn't see them around." He is genuinely curious upon meeting strangers. "I like talking about the lives of others more than I do particularly talking about myself. It's no consequence to me to hear myself talk. I'm not interested at all in self-discovery.

"Look, there goes the hearse we saw, delivering the body to the cemetery. There is another hearse, and another funeral, see? We're having a lot of action today. There are funeral cars with the red badges on the windshield," he murmurs. What does he feel, faced with such sad processions? "Nothing. Just interested. Not that I attend them. As Norman Vine says in *A*

Fairy Tale of New York, he says, 'Death is a pause in the life of others.' This indeed is the fact. You stop to think what was a fellow's life and what happened to him, it's sort of like having the whole story revealed to you."

Man's predicament as victim preoccupies J. P. Donleavy. "I think, yes. Anybody who has led any sort of life necessarily is a victim of sorts. That is part of living, you feed the earth. That is a biological truth.

"It all has turned out slightly strange," he muses. "I never thought I would end up being a farmer. This has surprised me, that *The Ginger Man* did indeed predict my own situation. Because that is what Sebastian Dangerfield [the protagonist] dreamed of, his inheritance in the world. I have really ended up exactly like Dangerfield, with a big estate and so forth." Does he sully his hands? "Yes, I do a lot, actually. I'm very good. A rarely accomplished man. An accomplished stone-mason. And I dig up stumps and ditches and I do all kinds of heavy work. Deliberately.

"Life is the thing that really kills me, although so far I'm surviving with flying colors," he says, going from headboard to nightstand in search of wood on which to knock. Undaunted, he settles for a lamp table. "I'm sure this is plastic." Has he an epitaph handy? "I suppose I did have something. What a pleasure it is always to read a gravestone when somebody puts something on it," J. P. Donleavy says softly. "Not something to do with me so much, but with words. One might have something like what Yeats had on his headstone, 'Beware of Horsemen Passing By,' something like that. Merely something attractive for the reading public."

DECEMBER 9, 1979

TOBY OLSON
The Real Reward of Writing

Someone is good at what he does, and he does it quietly, for the joy of doing it, and his friends praise him, and his wife loves him, and after twenty-five years a committee notices and gives him a $5,000 prize, and he gets interviewed, and he buys an answering machine, and his boss asks him to make a TV commercial, but he still does what he does, quietly, for the joy of doing it.

His name is Toby Olson, and writing is something he does, something he is. From his experiences, from "entering myself," in everyday words, he makes poems and stories—first his sixteen fine books of poetry published by small presses, then his two novels published by New Directions. *Seaview,* his amazingly beautiful second novel about a man, a woman, knowledge, pain, love, golf, cancer, a journey, death, and apocalypse, was pretty much ignored until it won literature's prestigious PEN/Faulkner Award earlier this year as the most distinguished work of American fiction of 1982. Ironic, when the book wasn't even reviewed by *The New York Times.*

Toby Olson came to Philadelphia in 1975 and directs Temple's creative writing program. He and his professor wife, Miriam, share a neat little house on a side street downtown near the Jewish Y, where he likes to swim. Summers he spends writing on Cape Cod. He has a calm, balanced confidence about him, but absolutely no conceit, no arrogance. Self-promotion is not his style. The word "masterpiece" makes him flinch; he can't say it aloud. He lives with his talent, comfortably; he knows what he can do, and he does it.

Finally, at forty-five, he's awarded and rewarded. "I did everything late," the red-bearded fellow says, laughing. "I got out of high school at a normal age, then I worked for a couple years with Reynolds Aluminum as an expediter in the metallurgical department. You know, it was a job you get off the street. Worked in a gas station for a couple of years, then I decided to go to California, where I had lived before. I went out there, and there were no jobs. It was the late fifties, and the job market was very depressed. And my hair got too long, and my car quit running. Didn't have a place to live, was staying with people. And I said, 'Well, let's join the Navy.' It was really that kind of thing."

He's not sure why, but he signed up for training as a surgical technician. "In really involved surgery, like brain surgery, you're the person in the soap operas whose hand comes out with the instruments and gives them to the doctor. They test you when you go in, which means you can go to a variety of schools. I could have had electronics, whatever. I don't know why I chose medical stuff. I have some inkling, but it's very psychoanalytic. It has to do with my father's illness, and the sense of being around sick people, and feeling comfortable with that. Also, feeling *uncomfortable*, but it was familiar, in a way."

Maybe wanting to make it better? "Oh, yeah. Absolutely. Yeah, but that's all in retrospect, you know what I mean? So I assisted at a lot of operations. Which was very good, because when I got out of the service, I worked full-time nights when I went to college and earned a salary by working in an emergency industrial medical clinic in Los Angeles."

What was he like as a child? "I was a very good boy. Well, it's clear to me, and I mean it's public for me with my first novel, *The Life of Jesus*, so I mean, I can speak about it, it's in there, but it's kind of veiled. I think that my childhood was really overwhelmingly influenced by my father's illness. You can hear just from the rundown of what happened in terms of times and places.

"When I was in third grade, my father was already quite ill with arthritis, and we moved to California for his health. He had worked at General Electric in Illinois, and then, as he got sick, he took on various jobs, ah, insurance salesman, then some home mail-order work when he couldn't leave the house. So my mother was working, supporting the family; I have a younger brother and sister, and my father at home sick. She started out working for Ball, they make mason jars. And her job was to put the cardboard dividers in the boxes, right, at the plant. I mean, we were not dirt poor, real poor. But she did have to work. And my father was at home," he repeats.

"I stayed there [in California] until I graduated from grammar school. Then he got sicker, so we moved to Arizona. While we were there he got very ill and went back to Illinois to stay with my grandmother where he went to a clinic for operations. Then I went back to Illinois, and he died when I was seventeen. And after he died, I really, you know, kind of went off. That's when I went into, ah, well, I was involved with a teenage gang . . ." he says. "And then—this again becomes of course psychoanalytic, but I think it's true—the trip became for me returning to all those places where things were better. That is to say, retracing my steps. I went back to California, spent a little time in Arizona again, kind of roamed around a lot. Went into the service really half-cocked, just joined up. Happily, it all worked out. . . ."

Did the Navy make a man of him? "I think so, sure. Yeah, it really did. I've come to see that in an awful lot of things I write, what happens is, first of all, a kind of fundamental nostalgic view of life. I mean, I'm really fascinated, much more interested in, I shouldn't say much more," he amends, "but *most* of what I write is about the past, and . . . a sense that there's an awful lot of what I see as waste in my past. We all feel that. I feel a sense of waste. And the writing becomes a kind of reclamation, you know. That somehow, by turning it into something hopefully significant, you make it more than waste, wasted material. You know, life material. . . ."

Starting college at age twenty-four after he left the Navy, he eventually got a B.A. from Occidental College and an M.A. from Long Island University. "It's funny," he muses. "The background I come from, Chicago suburbs, most of my relatives worked at the Western Electric Company. There was no sense, it was never suggested to me that I go to school, to college. I don't know quite why that was. It was just the expectation that we would go to work locally at Western Electric . . ." he says. "I was the first one to go to college of all my relations, actually—and I think that the pleasure my grandmother and mother took in that was a kind of pure pleasure, but it was because they didn't have these dreams. . . .

"It does strike me, and also, it's clear to me that it comes out in *Seaview* in various kinds of ways, and also in the first novel, is that this moving around, which I did a lot of, and a lot of schools, it can seem agonizing from the outside, and maybe it was. But there was also a sense of going to different places and different schools as a child and having a whole different set of friends and associations in those places, so that your life becomes very compartmentalized. There are these little nodes, and it's easy to become nostalgic about that, and it's easy to feel that as incredibly rich. Because there were all these little places, do you know?

"I was brought up in poetry with the stereotype, the early-twentieth-century one of the poet being apart and moody, and the candle and the garret and all that business. But I never was that way. I mean, I was never moody and hiding around at parties and looking grim. So my sense of . . . poetry [is] celebration. That poets should be the singers of the community and point out wonderful things that everybody should look at. Funny, wonderful, odd, sad, whatever. That's what it ought to be, it seems to me. I mean, that's what I'm most concerned with. Even though I deal a lot with death these days, it's really celebratory, as far as I'm concerned."

We talk about dreams. When he was a kid, one nightmare tortured him for years, until after his father died. "I don't quite remember the dream, but it had to do with a kind of irrevocable guilt. That is to say, there was something in the dream that I did that was so bad that I never could be forgiven for it. And I remember, I'm sure it had something to do with my father. . . . It got so extreme that I would wake up and not be able to really wake up for half an hour. Be roaming around the room. My mother would have to give me a cold shower, to kind of bring me out of it. And then all of a sudden it stopped. It stopped when I entered the service, as a matter of fact. . . .

"I was going to say something else. It's interesting you mentioned dreams. This isn't a dream, but it's like a dream. And the experience—I don't know if it's in *Seaview*; I've written about it in some poems, too—it's one of the most profound experiences in my life. I was visiting a dear old friend . . . and I stayed overnight at his house. He had been in the service in Japan. And the way I woke up was he had instructed his wife—this is a very male chauvinistic position—but he instructed his wife to do something that had happened to him in Japan.

"And that was to take a cup of tea, herbal tea, and to put it on the table at the side of the bed where I was sleeping. And as the steam came up off the tea, she blew the steam across my face. And I woke up. It was a scent that brought me awake. And to come awake with this, by scent, rather than sound, the transition between sleep and dream and waking, and then to turn and see someone's head there blowing this steam, you know, it was incredible. Because it was like a dream, you see," Toby Olson says. "The scent entered my consciousness, and it was like a dream, a dream of scent. And it was quite wonderful."

OCTOBER 23, 1983

MARGE PIERCY
Confessions of a Novelist

Marge Piercy, poet and novelist and radical, almost bled to death at eighteen from a self-induced abortion: "Working-class women my age, if you were to run a poll and get honest answers, I think you'd find an awful lot of us who did it our-selves. . . . The body count was very high."

She has a soft, musical voice, dark hair and even darker eyes, and an amazingly deft way of weaving together the personal and the political. Born in 1936, she grew up in Detroit, daughter of a Welsh father who worked for Westinghouse and a Lithuanian mother who read palms and told stories. She had a contradictory childhood—a tomboy nearly dying from German measles and rheumatic fever, beaten up in school for being a Jew, skinny and sickly and blue-skinned, given to fainting and seeking refuge in books; a troublemaker with a big mouth who later joined a teenage street gang and stole and fought and climbed up on the White Tower roof and threw things down the chimney until smoke poured out to get even with the guy who yelled at them and wouldn't let them hang out on the corner.

"I'm very driven, partly because . . . I have this sense of all these buried lives that are striving to come out through me to express themselves—my mother's life, my grandmother's life, the life of her sisters, the lives of some of my uncles, the family. All the people I've known, so many people I've known, who have a right to seeing their problems, their aspirations, their joys and fantasies and dangers and pleasures given the dignity that art lends when we see it in that form," the feminist says on a visit here to promote her latest novel, *Fly Away Home*, about a failing marriage clouded by a corruption of urban gentrification.

76

What is most dramatic to me about Marge Piercy is not just her deep public commitment to social change but her private struggle for self-definition: "I never thought of myself as a sexual pioneer. I was just very curious. . . . I mean, that's not true anymore," she says girlishly. In a way, her sexual odyssey from experimentation to conventionality mirrors the trajectory of the times, and until now she was reluctant to discuss it.

"I used to never give personal interviews because the people I lived with . . . don't really want me to talk about it. . . . Oh, I've lived all different kinds of ways. Well, I've lived communally. I've lived with three people, four people, five people. I've lived where you have almost a group marriage, ah, either in different households or the same households. . . .

"There was a long stable period of years where I had essentially two husbands," she reveals. "And I never talked about it, because I felt like it was the sort of thing, you know, I couldn't go around in the women's movement and they'd ask what do you do and I'd say, well, I have two husbands." She laughs. "You know, other people don't even have one husband, I have two? This is ridiculous. That was the time when everyone else was being gay, and I was living with two, two men." She laughs again.

"It seemed like not exactly the sort of thing that you wanted to suggest to other people. I mean, it's hard enough to find one man you can deal with. Yes, I've lived all different sorts of ways," she repeats. Interestingly, her first two husbands were scientists. "Well, we're talking about when I was in my twenties. Now we have to think our way back into that world. I think they seemed at that time somehow the keepers of this sort of arcane power, to me. That was the thing I didn't do. And they seemed to have a kind of energy that came from being on the cutting edge of knowledge. . . ."

Marge Piercy has been married three times. First, and faithfully, to a French physicist who neither drank wine nor chased women; she found his straightness stultifying. "Everyone had told me I was a bad woman, so I decided I'd be a good woman." Her second husband was a computer expert; their marriage was so wide open that they would live apart with others for years and had to make appointments to see each other. Her third and current husband is a writer fifteen years younger than she; they live on Cape Cod in blissful monogamy.

"I'm very happy in the relationship I'm in now. When monogamy works, it's awfully nice. It's simple. At the moment this works, and it's been working for four years, and I hope it will go on working. It really makes it easier at this point in time," she declares. "In 1972, if you were married, it was somehow harder to have relationships with other women, friendships. And friendships with other women are very important to me. I mean, it was when it almost began to be a battle with other women to have open relationships that I was willing to give [the relationships] up. To me, after a certain point it wasn't worth fighting the pressure against it.

"I think I have very strong survival instincts, and if things don't work, I try to find things that do work. I'm very deeply a pragmatist," she says. ". . . There was a lot of support through the middle to late sixties and early seventies for living in non-monogamous ways. But you have to be tremendously committed to it ideologically if you're doing it in our present society. And I'd found that it had begun to interfere with my relationships with women. That is, a lot of the women who I was dealing with and befriending and meeting politically and personally didn't understand the theoretical basis for it, and would imagine that I would somehow want to take their husbands or something"—she laughs—"or that I was somehow less to be trusted.

"So it became something that I found got in the way. Instead of being something that enabled one to deal more easily and intimately with other people and to form friendships, it was something that seemed more intrusive. It also would require a lot of energy to sustain it in the present society, where there's not a kind of movement support for it. And it isn't a priority to me in the same way that a lot of the political things I do are. I can't live unpolitically. It is something that can be sacrificed when the times don't support it and the general needs don't seem to call for it."

When did she decide to become monogamous? Was it when they met and were overpoweringly in love? "No, no. It was after we'd been involved for about, oh, I think three and a half years already in multiple relationships, and we just wanted to be together. And we were. And we liked it. And then we decided we would continue that way," she says.

How did she deal with insecurity and jealousy? "Oh, I tend to get jealous only when somebody is withholding from me something that I need, not when they're giving to other people." That's very politically advanced of her, I say. "It's not politically anything," she corrects me. "It's an emotional thing I'm talking about. If you're satisfied in a relationship, I don't think you go through that. But not everybody feels that way."

I ask her about being with a much younger man—she's forty-eight, he's thirty-three. "Well, as my mother said to me, the women in our family do much better with younger men. My mother was older than my father, and she said all the happy marriages in her family were always with men at least seven to ten years younger. She had no trouble dealing with it at all. She thought it was very natural," she replies.

Doesn't she worry about being so much older? "Sure," she admits. "I mean, I can get worried about that. I am an absolutely rococo worrier. I worry about planes. I worry about cars. I worry about hot, I worry about cold. I worry he's going to have a heart attack, he's running, he's running too much on the road, someone's going to run over him, a tourist is going to run him down on the road, he's going to fall in a pit and break his neck. He's going to eat warm custard and get ptomaine poisoning." She laughs. "The number of things I can worry about is just limitless."

But that specific worry—how does she deal with it? "I don't think in twenty years I'm going to be in a wheelchair and he's going to have to push me around," she says, laughing. "I think that you have to recognize that nowadays marriages you think are going to last anyhow, that have all the conventional things going for them, seem to fall apart in middle age anyhow. And I just hope things will work out. I think that's all you can ever do. You try to keep in touch."

Is she an intensely sexual person? "Yes. But I'm also intensely, ah, intimate. Now, intimacy is a very important value to me, and I'm not just using it as a synonym for sex. I mean communication. Talking. Like a lot of women, talking is extremely erotic to me, and also, just loving. I like to communicate. I like to communicate by talking. I also like to communicate by touch. And I don't mean sexual touch even there. Also, like a lot of women, I'm very touch-oriented. I pick up my cats all the time. I touch my plants. I pick up the dirt in my garden. I touch my friends. You know, I touch fruit. I touch objects." She laughs.

"I mean, if the society is unable to sell him on the images it advertises, of course he will remain loving toward me, if he's able to resist that. The society tries to sell you twelve-year-olds all the time—not even twenty-year-olds; you're too old at twenty. If he pays attention to the ads, he's going to chase twelve-year-olds, or ten-year-olds, or eight-year-olds, or seven-year-olds. It gets younger all the time. What you're being sold is a naked prepubescent body which has no breasts, no thighs, absolutely no lines, because it is neither used nor able to use itself much.

"The body of a mature woman—which was the goddess object of people for most of the time we've been people—is now an object of contempt. What did the goddess look like? A goddess was the body of a middle-aged woman. That's been the holy object of people for most of the time they've been people," Marge Piercy explains. "Well, it's got to come back."

SEPTEMBER 2, 1984

MARY HEMINGWAY
And Now She's Telling Her Story— at Least Some of It

"I've never been a public speaker, or a public anything, really. Except in the sense that Ernest was always being photographed with me alongside." Is it safe to say that widow Mary Hemingway has finally come into her own? "That's ridiculous," she snorts. "I was always into my own, ever since I was born."

Mary Welsh Hemingway, sixty-eight, fourth and final wife of the late Nobel Prize–winning writer, is not an easy woman to like. She's apt to respond to a question with "Oh, poop" or "Cripes" or "I haven't really thought about it" or the emptiest of nonreplies, "The answer's in my book." Though she rhapsodizes about the joys of interviewing penguins ("such charming, intelligent creatures"), chatting with me she has a brittle hauteur peculiar to pseudo-Britons or hotel bathroom maids. Our conversation threatens to become an exercise in acquired distaste.

Lately she has filled her life with concerts and ballet and cruises. Tonight she is going to see jai alai in Connecticut, and next week four Russian writers are coming for tea. We're in her sprawling Madison Avenue penthouse, and she's restlessly looking ahead to the dozen sandwiches she must make for her evening's jaunt. There is nothing soft about Mary Hemingway. Her white-blond hair, thickly mascaraed lashes, and silver-blue lids are janglingly offset by a dangling brown cigarette, harsh mannish voice, deeply lined face, and loud lime-green pantsuit that sabotages her petite, sprightly figure.

As a cheeky, chesty war correspondent for Time-Life in London during the blitz, Mary Hemingway blithely hobnobbed with the likes of H. G. Wells, Carl Sandburg, George Bernard

Shaw, Lord Beaverbrook. But she renounced all that—and her first husband—to marry Ernest. "No big deal," she shrugs. "It was more interesting to live with Ernest." The lusty hijinks of their "wild, crazy life" are now legend—bullfights in Spain, safaris in Africa, fishing in the Caribbean, hunting in Idaho, a nine-servant estate in Cuba, entertaining Gary Cooper and Sartre and Ava Gardner and Dali, and daiquiris, daiquiris, daiquiris.

She called him "Lamb" and he called her "Kitten," but their fifteen-year marriage was not exactly made in heaven. His tantrums traumatized two continents, and mostly Mary was "the whipping boy," selflessly pampering him despite spats during which he'd toss wine in her face or try to smash her typewriter. "You love someone," she sighs. Even he once consoled her: "You hired out to be tough, didn't you?" Mary's toughness received its ultimate test in July 1961 with Ernest's suicide by shotgun after months of paranoia, depression, and futile shock treatments. Since then she has become custodian of his literary legacy, editing his manuscripts and supervising posthumous publication of four books.

"Ernest and I lived for seventeen years under the same roof. Constantly. Which, uh, ought to certainly have given me some idea what kind of man he was," she says gruffly. "And in tranquillity, turbulence, joy, bad luck sometimes—a great variety of circumstances." Why, I wonder, didn't she combine home and career? "I was happy being a housewife, fisherwoman, hostess, housekeeper, gardener. I was not resentful. Nearly all the time I was contented. I got a lot of enjoyment from flower arrangement and looking after our cats and dogs and devising menus and cooking and designing very useful, very sensible furniture for our home." Did she mind typing his manuscripts? "Certainly not," she demurs. "We were never in competition as writers. He was the writer and husband and I was the housewife.

"He was not a genius in the house. He was a husband and he did his work. Other people claimed he was a genius. You know, that's all right if that's what they wanted to call him."

Was she in awe of him? "Not in the least. His purposes for me were being a good husband. If he wrote well, that was dandy." And was he a good husband? "It's impossible for me to say, because I don't know about other husbands," she hedges. Well, did he make her happy? "We had lovely times. . . . One of the more enchanting components of our life was our life in bed."

But. "Women always fell in love with Ernest because he was so good and sweet," she says. "He was an extremely attractive, enormously charming man. I certainly couldn't blame those other women for falling for him. It was the most natural thing in the world. He was a magnet. . . . But Ernest didn't have affairs," she huffs. "He had exchanges of compliments. He didn't have affairs. One of the reasons I feel quite certain— this is getting awfully personal—he slept with me. As a very good husband. In my bed. All the time. Every night. And aboard our boat as well. In Africa we shared a cot, sometimes just a little wider than this sofa. For fun. Our bodies liked each other.

"We were in constant communication," she continues, "eighteen hours a day. When we were both ill, we'd send six or eight letters a day to each other by the butler, carrying them from my bedroom to Ernest's bedroom. It was only when he was ill that he stayed in his own room, and I stayed in mine.

"We didn't have any heroes in our house. Except some of the cats were heroes," she nods. Their many cats were "love sponges." And now? "I don't have any animals at all. We had cats and adored them and they were a very important part of our lives, but one makes breaks with the past. . . . Somehow my character wouldn't fit in with so many ladies in this building who have those tiny whatever-they-are poodles. . . . I don't have time."

Though Ernest lavished an incredible amount of affection on his house pets, he persisted in game-hunting. "It does sound like a strange dichotomy," she agrees. "But I think Ernest would have changed if he were alive now; he would have boosted wildlife conservation. We were in Africa a long time ago, '53 and '54, and one saw up to ten thousand antelope wandering on a plain. It didn't feel so bad to knock off a couple. . . ."

She, at least, seemed a reluctant huntress. "I'm sure I missed a lot because I couldn't really bear hitting them." She clears her throat. "Because they were really too charming. He was delighted when I killed something cleanly. . . . But we weren't avid shooters; it was really seeing the animals as much. I don't think we could be considered," she gropes, "violent and obsessive shooters of animals."

Ironically, only after her husband's death did she publish her own book. "Well, I was too busy," she contends. "I always did pieces, one a year. Ernest was, at least he pretended, whether or not it was true, to be very proud: 'See what Miss Mary wrote.'" For *Cosmopolitan, Life, Look, Sports Illustrated, Vogue, Saturday Review.*

Her 537-page memoir of life with Papa, *How It Was*, is little more than a catalog of guest lists, weather reports, menus lifted from her diary. "*Time* magazine said I flunk in prose style," she seethes. "My prose style was gathered and taught to me by *Time* magazine more than anybody else. Who is this punk that says I flunk? His style isn't so great. Some jerk kid. I don't care about reviews at all, bad or good," she insists, then adds, "I have a pile over there. About two inches high, most of which are at least agreeable if not generous."

Heavy on the who-what-when, her book too often omits the how and the why. "I don't think of myself as a writer," she suggests. "I'm not ashamed of being a reporter. I think a good reporter is a respectable personage." Does she consider herself talented? "Certainly not. Just hardworking. Somebody once asked if I ever acquired Ernest's style. Well, anybody who has ever read my book knows it has nothing whatsoever to do with his style. That's absolute rubbish!"

Someday, she says, she wants to write short stories, a form Ernest excelled at. "The things I have in mind are totally different from anything he did," she stresses. "I did one which was published in a German magazine. American editors found it unacceptable, too far-out. I don't want to tell you too much, but it's about a woman who lives in a triplex apartment on Park Avenue with five husbands more or less all in the same place at the same time, all friends.

"I never thought of myself as a maverick. It's just that things happened to me that didn't happen to anybody else," she proclaims. "My childhood friends from Minnesota chose different careers than I did. It was all a matter of happenstance. . . . I don't remember doing anything special. I haven't gone up in balloons. I haven't jumped off cliffs with wings attached," she says grandly.

"Well, I *have* eaten live ants that you dig out of an ant hill in Africa. The trick is swallow 'em before they tickle your throat. I only tried that twice."

Some people might say her life-style with the Man from Macho was the quintessence of decadence. How does she respond to that? "I don't care," she trumpets. "Decadent? Eating lion meat? I thought it was original. Very interesting. Very few people do eat lion meat. It's quite good. We had it marinated, stewed. Tastes a lot like veal. Very, very delicate flavor, a little bit firmer.

"I never go over my life," Mary Hemingway says, laughing. "I don't have the faintest idea what the high points are."

JANUARY 16, 1977

CALVIN TRILLIN
Calvin Trillin Is Still Playing with His Food

"Health food makes me sick. All of it." Calvin Trillin, who is almost always hungry, or hilarious, or both, was a convincing portrait of temporary quease in tweed and paisley.

Trillin, forty-five, author of *American Fried, Floater* and *Alice, Let's Eat*, among others, has traversed the country in search of a decent meal or a toothsome story for *The New Yorker's* "U.S. Journal" since 1967. And here he was in Philadelphia, at the Athenaeum, the upper-crust private library on Washington Square, *not* to sample hoagies or scrapple or soft pretzels but to share a modest belch or two with us. "The smell in a health food store makes me sick. It smells a little like capsules that have been in the medicine chest since the Nixon-Humphrey campaign.

"And it is true," he continues his digestive divagations, "that I caused a scene in a Greenwich Village health food store when I shouted, 'Help, I have been trapped in a bottle of Coricidin.' And I can't stand all those salads with soy waste and stump paste and stuff like that." Stump paste? I'm not familiar with it. "They take the paste off tree stumps," he explains. "I don't know where they get them. God knows, that makes me just sick, like being on a very small plane in a storm makes me sick. So I stay away from it."

Can this be—the Happy Eater unhappy? Did he ever inadvertently sample some health food? "Yeah, that's what made me sick. So then that's why I quit. Oh, I had some kind of mung bean soy waste salad with toe food," he says, punning on "tofu." But does this pleasant, mild-mannered food really disagree with him?

"Yeah, it does, it makes me ill," he claims. "Well, of course, the other question is—if health food is so healthy, why do people who work in health food stores look so unhealthy? You walk into these health food stores and you see these guys with their pallid skin and wispy beards and they just look awful; you really want to dial 911 and get an ambulance there," he shrugs. "So I really was thinking, if soy waste is so good for you, why can't these guys grow a full beard? It's obvious it's not healthy for anybody. So now I feel a lot better at being a confirmed sausage eater than ever before."

There is something of the performer about Calvin Trillin— his quick wit, his delight with an audience, his fine timing, his nicely honed sense of self-deprecation, and indeed, unlike some of his ilk, he does not shy from TV talk shows. "It's often said that writers are much more comfortable in a room with their typewriters than not. I guess I am really not that way. If I hadn't ended up as a reporter, I wouldn't have been a poet or something. I probably would have been a lawyer. I never thought of writing as some sacred pursuit in a small room. I get lonely in a small room. I walk out. When Abigail, my oldest, would come to me and say, 'Tie my dolly's apron,' I was really glad to see her, to tie her dolly's apron. I think just the fact that I'm not absolutely horrified with public experience, which is what people expect from a writer, makes it seem that I'm more easily a performer than I really am."

Though the description "humorist" gives him indigestion, he admits: "I started writing about food as kind of comic relief. I couldn't write about a community controversy or a murder or something like that [constantly] because it was wearing me down. Then it turned out that it's easy to have a kind of persona in food writing which is not far from my true self—a cheerful glutton. And I must say, it's an awful lot easier for me to write about food, and eating, rather than write a piece about an argument in Denver on how to finance the symphony. And I guess I enjoy it almost as much as anything I write. . . ."

Tell us what it's really like working at *The New Yorker*. "Actually, I don't go there very much. I work almost completely at home. When I was at *The New Yorker*, I would walk around the halls, there were always all kinds of things on my desk that I hadn't touched in months, I found that I didn't get as much done, and also I didn't like it as much. I'd rather be home. I like where we live. We have a brownstone in the Village; I have a nice office there. I don't have to get dressed. I like being in the Village rather than midtown. I can get on my bike and go to Chinatown for lunch, or else if Alice is home we can have lunch together. It's just a lot nicer."

There are rumors that perfectly polished prose leaps from Calvin Trillin's fingertips. "I wish it were true." He laughs. "Unfortunately, it's not. I don't think perfectly polished prose leaps from anybody's typewriter. I do draft after draft. I think it's a real fallacy that people somehow get to believe that writing is some kind of magic. The more drafts you write, the better it is. Nobody who is serious about trying to write well turns in anything without draft after draft after draft. I have to work the same way everybody else does." Sigh.

"I also think that any writer, particularly of nonfiction, which is basically what I do, who thinks they are changing the world or are leaving something for posterity is probably in bad shape. . . . What am I trying to accomplish? I'm trying to get to the end of the piece usually, that's all. No, I think if I can give somebody a giggle on the Madison Avenue bus, that would be nice. But I don't have any thoughts about doing anything beyond that. I don't mean that I don't have any pride in it, but the thought that it is somehow written either for posterity or to change the world I think is just silly."

Don't think he's a curmudgeon. He sees himself as "cheerful, pleasant, thoughtful to a fault—oh, maybe not." He begins his day by making breakfast at 7 A.M. for his two young daughters, Abigail and Sarah. "I make my special recipe, scrambled eggs that stick to the pan every time. It's my only recipe. Oh no, I don't really cook at all. Sure, I can kind of keep us alive when Alice is not there. I can make meat loaf and broiled fish. I'm getting to the end of my repertoire."

He says he didn't marry Alice, his wife of sixteen years, because she was a good cook (which she is), or because she broadened his palate (which she did), but because "she, uh, knew the access routes to the city, how to get on the Grand Central Parkway, that sort of thing. Also, she told me she could spell 'occurred,' words like that I can't spell. This, however, turned out not to be true. Alice and I can't spell the same words. It's been a terrible problem."

What do they argue about? "How to spell 'occurred.' And 'separate.' We argue about 'separate.' We are both wrong usually in these things. Fortunately, now that Abigail is beginning to spell pretty well and Sarah is already an unusually good speller for our family, we have other sources. So when I yell out how to spell 'occurred' and Alice can never remember two *r*'s or one, sometimes Abigail will then yell from her room how to spell 'occurred,' which I couldn't tell you right now."

Calvin Trillin grew up in Kansas City, longing to be a cop or a cowboy or a fireman, loving to watch fires. "I was a well-behaved kid," he recalls. "But I wasn't like some novelist who comes from the Midwest that you read about who was sensitive, off by himself. I liked to ride my bike and play baseball. I wasn't off in a corner reading," he protests.

"My father most of his life, or most of my childhood," he amends, "was a grocer. By the time I was about ten, he had several grocery stores. Then he sold them all, because he never wanted to be in the business in the first place, he was always waiting to get out. Then for a while he had a restaurant, just an ordinary restaurant. It's hard to describe, a family restaurant. I've written about it, but even though I have written about it, I can never remember what the food tasted like, which I suppose basically must be some sort of commentary on the food itself.

"At lunch my father wrote poems on the menu, and I always thought that was why he wanted to be in the restaurant business, so he could have an outlet for his poetry. He wrote couplets, little rhyming couplets like 'Don't sigh, eat pie.' Then he'd rhyme 'pie' with a lot of things, like 'evening is nigh,' and 'Okay, Warden, I'm ready to fry, I've had my last piece of Mrs. Trillin's pie.' Yeah, I always thought his milieu was Burma Shave, and his inspiration."

Did his father's associations with food and writing inspire

him? "Not at all," he insists. "I never connected his having a restaurant—oh, he influenced me a lot, but not that way. . . . I suspect my father named me Calvin because he thought it might sound good at Yale. . . . He had read a book as a child called something like *Dink Stover at Yale*, and therefore I went to Yale. Pretty much, that is kind of how it happened, though it sounds odd. But I don't think what he *did* for a living had any particular influence on me, but the way he *was* did. . . ."

So, as a kid, did Calvin Trillin play with his food? "You'll have to ask Grandma, I don't know. I think I had the same kind of feelings about food as most kids. I liked hamburgers, and mashed potatoes, I would eat the usual things." When did his tastes become more adventurous? "I guess maybe in college. And then when I started to travel around the country, it was partly in self-defense. And then Alice has always been a big influence." He grins fondly. "It has a lot to do with Alice."

I offer him one last opportunity for biliousness and dyspepsia. Does he hate anything else? "You mean, besides health food? I hate the sort of food you get at political banquets, prime ribs with leaden vegetables, I hate that kind of institutional food," he confides. "And I don't like Stuffed Stuff with Heavy. That's what we call English gourmet cooking, where they stuff something with something else and then cover the scene of the crime with some awful heavy sauce. I can't think of any kind of ethnic food I don't like. I'm not crazy about Ethiopian bread," he muses, "but that's it. In general, I'll eat anything. How do I feel about eating things I know are bad for me? I feel fine about it," Calvin Trillin says, "as long as they taste good."

MAY 3, 1981

TIM O'BRIEN
"I Never Thought They'd Send Me to Fight"

"There's no question about what I value in my life—courage, imagination, love, and behaving bravely," famous writer Tim O'Brien, a brooding and Byronic thirty-three, had been telling a class at Temple University Center City.

Taking English courses scared him; he didn't know what metaphor was and he's still not sure, but going to war made a man of him, and a writer. His Vietnam novel, *Going After Cacciato*, a "walking away from war" story, won the 1978 National Book Award for fiction. Though he fears flying, he had indeed flown from his Cambridge home early that morning, teeth gritted through breakfast and lunch, so we talked in a downtown Philly restaurant while he had a ham and cheese omelette and two bloody Marys.

"I was a Phi Beta Kappa summa cum laude intellectual student-body president, all kinds of really hot things, and I was drafted immediately out of college. I was twenty-one. The myth was that that kind of person didn't go to Vietnam, that blacks and Hispanics and dumbos got drafted. I didn't think I'd have to go. I wasn't prepared for it at all," he confides, tweedy and intense.

During Army basic training, he came "really close" to deserting. "I had my shot [immunization] record, my passport ready. I had all my plans made. I was going to Canada. I had written my mom and dad to get all those documents from them, lying, saying I needed them to go to Vietnam. I had money. I had gone to the library and researched how to do it, where to go. I clipped out four or five articles on desertion, it was big then, this was 1968. There were names of organizations in France and Denmark and Sweden and Canada that would help you. So I had all that information. I was stationed in Fort Lewis, in Washington State, and Canada was only ninety miles away, I could get there in an hour and a half."

One Friday night, two weeks before he was scheduled to depart for Vietnam, he was on leave, packed and ready. "I had checked into a hotel in Seattle to think it over one more night, think about leaving my family and going into exile. I was sick at the time, violently ill; it later turned out to be pneumonia. I was up all night, vomiting and thinking and feeling so bad. There was fear, too. About leaving my whole history behind me, running away from everything I've ever known, America, my family, girlfriends, everything.

"Sometime during that night, I don't know when, I can't even remember, I just kind of switched onto automatic—go, succumb. It was like gravity pulling me into war, some kind of physical force, not a real emotional, rational decision. I thought the war was wrong, I hated it, I didn't want to die in an evil war. But I still went. That's what happens in life," he mutters. "I had to go. I valued the respect and love of my mom and dad. I valued my reputation. I also valued my conscience. I didn't want to be known as a deserter even to myself. I wasn't a flaming radical peacenik. I just thought, no way I'll be in the Army. I was going on to Harvard, I never took it seriously. It was the experience of being drawn like a sleepwalker into the war, then being confronted with the reality, which is never expected."

Even when he got to Vietnam, he assumed he'd be assigned to a typewriter. "I never thought they'd send me out to fight and be a real foot soldier. Even though I knew that was what I was trained for. So at each stage—getting drafted, in basic training when I decided to almost run—I thought something would save me from actually seeing the war face up. I was stunned when it happened. I was actually walking around in Vietnam, wearing funny hats, with a real rifle."

In basic training, he hadn't even paid attention to how to use his weapon. "I didn't know how to work it," he admits. "I didn't know how the bullets fired, I just hadn't listened in lectures. Oh, I had shot the thing three or four times. But when

I got to Vietnam, out in the field, and I had to defend myself with that thing, I had to ask other guys how. And I didn't know how many hand grenades to carry, exactly how long you had to hold them. I didn't know anything. I was never very mechanically inclined, anyway."

Throughout his fourteen months as a foot soldier he felt like a loner and detested the other men. "I thought they were awful a——, creeps and killers, some of them, tough guys, they didn't give a damn about fighting in an evil war. They were really unbelievable, they weren't educated. I felt totally out of place. It was like being at the stock car races with a bunch of hoods when you didn't know anything about stock car races and you didn't care and it seemed to you dumb, hicky, and stupid. Some guys, they knew how to work guns, they knew they were going, they were more open-minded. Not open-minded," he amends, "what's the word, they weren't deceiving themselves. They were able to adjust to Vietnam in a way I wasn't."

It wasn't just the shock of seeing people killed all around him, it was the thought of his own vulnerability. "Over and over, getting shot at, I'd think, My God, it's exactly as it is in the movies, ducking, that ricochet sound, bullets twanging, my God, they are real. The feeling of having a camera going over your shoulder, watching you, so you want to behave well and act right and don't cry while being shot at, don't run, you want to keep a good face and tell jokes when people are being killed, because it doesn't seem real, it's like you were in a movie, a very deadly movie, a real movie. It had a movie feel to it. You want to be as good as Bogie, as good as Gable. I don't know how that sounds to a woman," he almost apologizes.

In minor ways, he rebelled. "Some terrible things I should have rebelled against, I didn't; things that happened I should have taken legal action or turned people in for attempted murder, I didn't. . . . I could have been busted for turning in officers for attempted murder. By keeping your nose clean, you do bad things. . . . Little things, though, I often did, but do they count?" he muses.

"Like one day, after a week of walking through minefield

after minefield after minefield (we operated in the My Lai area where the massacre happened, and it was very heavily mined), very rarely if ever did we see the enemy," he explains, "and there was a sense of frustration building up after a week or two of losing a whole bunch of guys to the mines and never being able to take any revenge or shoot back. Well, we were walking along the paddy dike in single file, and almost spontaneously the men began shooting at a cow, a water buffalo. There was our whole company, maybe 140 of us, plugging this cow. You could see the meat jumping off it, but it just stood there, it didn't fall, all those rounds hitting it, hand grenades thrown at it, unbelievable. I remember shouting, 'Why are you doing this?' But that's a petty kind of thing."

Sometimes, he says, he'd overcompensate, as he calls it. "At times I got worse than those guys, just to get back at them. I remember one guy tried to grab my beer. He had been picking on me. I slugged him. I had him by the head and I was hitting him over and over and over. Broke his nose. I had never done anything like that before. That's not my personality. Afterward I thought to myself, 'That was over a beer?' But it really wasn't, it was over how much I hated him, how much he had hassled me. Those things happen in war, not in civilization, and then you realize that is not what being a man is, that's just animal stupidity."

Well, he made sergeant, didn't he, so he must have played somebody's game? "Anybody can make sergeant," he scoffs, "if you don't commit murder or get court-martialed. It's not that big a deal. If you behave normally, you'll make it. Actually, I hated the Army much worse than Vietnam. In the end, I extended my tour of duty in Vietnam so I could get out of the Army sooner. Really, the Army is a terrible, terrible thing, so I thought."

Once, though, Tim O'Brien had wanted to be a cowboy. This was back in his "happy-go-lucky," small-town Minnesota Methodist days. He was fond of football and baseball and "dumb physical things" until he discovered debate in high school. As a senior, he wrote sports stories for his hometown paper "just to make money," he insists, though years later, during his postwar, postgraduate days, he was a *Washington Post* intern and, briefly, a reporter. His father sold life insurance "but he could have been a writer. While he was based in a destroyer in the Pacific during World War II, he wrote some things and I think they were published in Philadelphia papers. His name? William O'Brien, same as mine, except I like my middle name, that is what I go by."

Like his father, Tim O'Brien broke into print in the service. While he was still a soldier, he sold *Playboy* a piece on land mines. "No question, I would not have become a writer without going to Vietnam. It gave me something to say. Because I didn't know about anything. I hadn't confronted anything important about myself. I majored in political science and philosophy [at Macalester College], went to graduate school [at Harvard] after Vietnam for my Ph.D. in government, thinking I'd be a scholar or maybe a politician someday.

"I didn't remember fear being a big part of my history until Vietnam. You know, I'm still looking for a book about Vietnam that is better than mine. I don't think of *Cacciato* as a war novel. Most of it doesn't take place in Vietnam, it takes place away from it. Flight is one of our main instincts. You're scared to death, you want to run." Has he ever secretly considered himself a coward? "I'm not sure what a coward is. That's why I write about it. That's the problem, it's hard to say.

"When I was in Vietnam, I was too frightened to write anything down, too scared to take the time to keep a journal, so I didn't do it. I didn't want to give myself any bad luck. I pictured my body being found with a journal," Tim O'Brien says, "and all this terrible stuff inside."

OCTOBER 26, 1980

RONA JAFFE
The Torture Academy Stretched Her Mind

"They gave me a hotel room with very loud wallpaper that looked like it was going to eat me, and the rug gave me vertigo! I decided I couldn't handle that. So I asked for a different room, and they gave me this one. I love it because it is sort of no color," says novelist Rona Jaffe, a fragile, doe-eyed beauty, swathed in silk and aglint with gold, who has always had the best of everything.

Indeed, the Brooklyn principal's daughter who went to the Dalton School and Radcliffe called her very first book *The Best of Everything*. That 1958 blockbuster about four single women in the big city catapulted her to celebrity at twenty-six. Now, ten books and twenty-three years later, it's *Mazes and Monsters*, about four college students ensnared in a dangerous fantasy game. "Mind if I get a glass of water?" she asks, ducking into the bathroom of her Bellevue Stratford suite.

"Why do I write?" She sighs. "I think it's the only way I can survive. It's the way I deal with my life. I've written all my life. I think that people who write . . . are born with one skin too few. Things really *hurt* them, and the input is so strong, they feel these things so strongly, that if you write, that's how you save yourself from having to deal with that *pain* of being aware of all these things that go on in people's minds and lives, and even in your own life.

"I used to think how wonderful it would be to go through life as a grapefruit." What's that? "That's a line from *The Best of Everything*, the girls they call the grapefruits, because when you cut them in half they were all in sections, and everything was padded just so and equal and there were no surprises. Well, I think if you are a grapefruit it's great, because then you don't have any of the pain. But if you have all that awareness, then writing is a terrific outlet. You express your feelings and you feel better."

More than merely sensitive, she is "funny and nice and shy and real and smart, and very professional and hardworking." She reveals that she likes to eat chocolate ice cream in bed, that she has failed at "cooking and shop, but I've never been married, so I didn't fail at that." When I say her ring looks like a wedding band, she thanks me. Is it? "No. I don't know why I said thank you. I guess I'm programmed."

Rona Jaffe is an incredibly youthful forty-nine who claims she wrote her first poem when she was two and a half. Does she remember the words? "Yeah. The first time somebody asked me what it is, little did I know it was going to be my most publicized work," cracks the author of *Class Reunion, The Other Woman, Family Secrets,* and *Mr. Right Is Dead.* "Okay, here it is: 'Said the snow to the cloud / I want to go down / to see the world. / So the cloud gave a push / and down went the snow / to the ground below.' Sweet," she deadpans.

"My mother wrote it down for me. Good grief, I wasn't writing at two and a half. My mother wrote it down, I dictated it to her, and she wrote it on a paper bag because she was in the kitchen at the time, which is where mothers were supposed to be, that's what they used to say. . . ." But wait. How does a toddler compose a poem? "I was an only child. My mother was at home all the time. She and my father had both been teachers. The house was full of books. I was always being read to. They didn't teach me to read, but my mother played word games with me. I talked very early. By nine months I had quite a vocabulary. Before I could even walk, I would sit in the carriage and chatter—people passing by thought there was a ventriloquist around. I started doing tongue twisters at two, I was very verbal. It was natural, I guess—all that stuff was being read to me. I knew what a poem was, and I knew how to make a rhyme, so I made one up."

Rona also made up a whole imaginary world with her best friend. "They said she was a bad influence on me. We had this game when we were seven called the Ritz-Top Torture Academy. That was a fancy girls' school, maybe it was coed, I can't remember. Well, in this imaginary place, all the 'students' were our parents and our teachers and our friends' mothers, everybody we were mad at. We would do this whole fantasy. One of us was Miss Ritz-Top and the other was Miss Plush-Bottom.

"We would say, 'Now we'll torture Alice's mother because she makes Alice eat prunes and buttermilk instead of candy.' It was like out of *The Perils of Pauline*, with the heroine tied to the tracks and the train came and she got rescued, or they strapped her to the buzz saw. Then we would do the victims' voices. We'd go"—she mimics in a high falsetto—"Eeek, eeek, no, oh help, please, help, please don't do that, please don't, please don't kill me, oh, eeek, please, oh no, no, no!'

"Then we would yell"—her voice deepens into a gruff roar—"'Yes, take that, there!' and we would make all these noises, too, and carry on. Meanwhile our mothers would be in the living room, having a nice conversation. 'Will you girls be quiet, what's all that commotion out there?' Then in our game we would put *them* on the railroad tracks. We would do that. We'd have this really nice time, we'd throw things, we'd get all our aggressions out, and that was it." She chuckles.

Quite the artistic prodigy, Rona graduated from high school at age fifteen, tempted by acting, painting, and writing. "I had to make a choice when I was young about what I wanted to be. I knew I was going to *do* something. I always knew that. When I was four, I wanted to be a journalist. I pictured myself in the jungle with a man photographer and we would be sort of boyfriend and girlfriend, we would be in like Tarzan country finding stories. Don't ask me why I picked the jungle.

"Or I was going to be a movie star and best friends with Shirley Temple and sit around the swimming pool eating tangerines, which I thought were just about the most exotic thing in the whole world because you could hardly ever get them. Then I found out Shirley Temple was older than I, which meant she would never be my friend. So I abandoned my plans to be a movie star.

"Also I was good at art. At Dalton I studied with [painter Rufino] Tamayo. He said I could be a good painter. Helen Frankenthaler was in my class, there were only three students. Imagine!" she marvels. "But I didn't want to be a painter. And it's a terrible thing to be an actress, you get rejected for bizarre things, like if you look wrong. Who wants to be rejected for that? It could really kill you. At least, it could give you an inferiority complex, telling you that you're too old or too fat or too short or too tall. Then also it's very hard to do your craft if you don't have an acting job, and those are scarce. But if you are a writer you can always write, even if you don't get published. Sure, it's horrible not being published, but you can still write, it's fulfilling."

Is it true she started sending short stories to *The New Yorker* when she was nine and once even trudged down there after getting a rejection slip? "Yes," she admits. "Isn't that pushy? But I *was* reading *The New Yorker* at nine. Anyway, I'd send them my stories and they'd send them right back the next day. I couldn't believe it, I had the feeling they just put it in a different envelope and returned it."

Didn't she know the trick of testing the editors to see if they were actually reading manuscripts by putting in a page upside down? "When I was an editor at Fawcett, writers used to do that all the time, or they'd put a hair on the page. That annoyed me. So I'd read the manuscript and leave the page upside down so they would think no one had read it," she says, laughing.

Why'd she do that? "I was a rotten kid. What did I know? I was a twenty-year-old editor. . . . But I just didn't spring up out of nowhere. It's not just a story of filing clerk makes good," says the ex-slush-pile queen who writes books. "My life has always been hard work." Did she ever find any great unsolicited manuscripts? "I kept wishing I would because it was just terrible, [the other editors] kept sending the stuff back, they didn't read it. . . . I took stuff home but I·never found anything."

Did she model herself after anyone? "No. I'd look at my teacher and I'd see this underpaid woman who only had two dresses and everybody made fun of her and called her an old maid. And I would think that I didn't want to be like that. Then I'd look at Emily Dickinson, or Elizabeth Barrett Browning, or any of those poets, they always seemed to be sick or a recluse locked in the house by a tyrannical father who was neurotic. I didn't want to be like that," she declares.

". . . I always wanted to be a writer, but I had a naïve idea of what a writer was. I loved F. Scott Fitzgerald, I read everything he wrote that I could get my hands on. I read that once he passed a jewelry store and saw a watch he wanted, so he wrote a short story, sold it, and then he bought the watch. It just seemed to me totally glamorous, to live hand to mouth." She laughs. "Every time you had to pay your rent, just write an article or a story. I thought that would be a nice life—you would have free time, you could do what you wanted. I just thought that would be the most prestigious, marvelous thing, to have something *published*, to have something to show my friends. 'Look, look, I published this!' *That* was the ultimate. I always knew I would be a writer, but I never conceived that this would happen to me. . . ."

Nearby, on the nightstand, beckons a box of choice Godiva chocolates. "That's a present from the hotel management. Because breakfast was late. I wanted it at seven, but that's not when they brought it. When I complained, they said they could only promise it sometime between seven and seven-thirty. Well then, I told them, I would order it half an hour earlier. The next day my breakfast was there on time"—Rona Jaffe smiles triumphantly—"and they sent the candy along with it."

DECEMBER 31, 1981

S. J. PERELMAN
He's "America's Lampoonist Laureate"

"I think humor in America has greatly declined and may disappear entirely," growls S. J. Perelman. Seated in a black leather chair, his feet by the radiator, he suggests, "It is not easy to satirize the absurd when the absurd has become official."

S. J. Perelman gives pomposity a good name. Give him a cliché and he takes a mile. *The New York Times*, which must know, labeled him "America's lampoonist laureate," and he's been variously dubbed "a satirical wielder of the acid pen," "one of today's greatest nonsense writers," "terrifyingly jocose." The titles of his pieces bear truest witness to his screwball wit. To wit: *A Child's Garden of Curses, The Ill-Tempered Clavichord, Road to Miltown, Malice in Wonderland, Acres and Pains, Chicken Inspector No. 23.*

The humor is missing today.

He does not want his conversation to be recorded, and he is not exactly overjoyed at being interviewed. He would have much preferred to continue affixing sticky tape to large cardboard cartons containing his possessions, so he could leave shortly on yet another globe-girdling journey to whet yet another book.

A cranky, erudite septuagenarian, Sidney Joseph Perelman wears a neat clipped mustache and the same oval steel-rimmed glasses he picked up in Paris in 1927. After selling his Bucks County retreat four years ago, resettling in London as a much-heralded "resident alien," then moving back to his loved/hated New York, he lives momentarily in a quietly elegant Manhattan hotel overlooking Gramercy Park. Soft-spoken though nasal, with a courtly command of exotic English, he is a small man seemingly surrounded by eyebrows. His red plaid shirt is probably a relic from his pastoral past.

The celebrated humorist and author of countless high-gloss, highbrow-comic *New Yorker* essays, books, films, and plays, does not seem to be in good humor. Owlishly doleful, he does not particularly care to discuss pretty girls, despite his reputation as a literary Lothario. He does not care to discuss dirty jokes, though he is considered a connoisseur of the genre. He does not care to discuss the Marx Brothers, for whom he ghosted gags during their "Horse Feathers" daze.

He describes his meticulously crafted writing style as "a mixture of all the trash I read as a child, all the clichés, criminal slang, liberal doses of Yiddish, and some of what I learned in school from impatient teachers.

"I have all the neuroses and prejudices we collect as we get older. I think spoken English is becoming corrupted, but that's nothing new," he humphs, and I decide to say only yes and no for the duration. "Current writing isn't too distinguished. By strict definition, a writer should be a reader. Young writers don't read enough these days." Before I can rush to the defense, he reminisces.

"On Fridays, growing up, I'd go to the Providence, Rhode Island, library and take out eleven books and spend the weekend sitting in the kitchen, my feet in the oven, munching cookies and reading trash." Trash? "That's right," he nods. "Adventures, detectives, romance. They help fertilize the brain, like mulch.

"I had been drawing pictures from infancy and wanted to be a cartoonist. I even drew cartoons in my father's drygoods store on the long cardboard strips around which the bolts of cotton were stored," he says. "After college I became a comic artist for some humor magazines. I'd write jokes that had nothing to do with my pictures, an intricate system of verbiage, founded on puns like 'I have Bright's disease, and he has mine!' Soon the captions of my drawings"—curiously morbid woodcuts—"got longer and longer. Finally they displaced the drawings entirely."

He's been a free-lance writer for fifty years. "Call it a license to starve," he jests. "But I work very slowly. I'm a bleeder. It's a good day when I get a page done. I think easy writing makes hard reading. Actually I find writing a very time-consuming, painful process. And when anyone introduces me as a humorist, I get somewhat nervous. There's something about the term that is a bit off-putting.

"Humor meant to be read—humorous writing—is passing out of existence. As a class this sort of writer is doomed. A person so impelled today usually ends up as part of a six-man joke-writing team."

Or in Hollywood. "The dream factory," he says with a flourish of his cigarette. "Hollywood is a dreary industrial town controlled by hoodlums of enormous wealth. I worked for all kinds of weird people. My late wife and I collaborated during the thirties. The studios had a profound respect for husband-and-wife teams, thought they were fashionable. They were under the impression they'd get double value—writing during the day, discussing the script in bed at night."

In 1957 S. J. Perelman received an Oscar for his screenplay of Mike Todd's epic extravaganza *Around the World in 80 Days.* Did he reject the "bourgeois bauble"? No. "I think everyone who receives an Oscar, even myself, is delighted. All those excited gurglings and gushes you see on the TV box were hardly what I felt, but I was pleased," he concedes gruffly.

"For some time I used my Oscar as a doorstop. When I tired of that I stored it in a drawer and forgot I had it. Each time I've opened the drawer, I have a sense of wonder and discovery anew." He grins. "You know, it would make a good weapon to protect oneself from muggers, though a bit heavy to carry around the streets of New York as a steady form of defense.

"I've lived in a number of places in my life and can't make up my mind which is the most agreeable. I enjoy travel so much, but I find most places after a lengthy stay turn out to have drawbacks. So" —he peers at me with his watery blue eyes—"the idea is to be a moving target. Then it's impossible for people to pick you off. But the Delaware Valley is really one of the loveliest sections in the world. After my wife died, I sold the hundred-acre farm in Erwinna, where we had lived for forty years, and went to London. Too much rural splendor—Bucks County summers were hot as Bangkok.

"So your next question automatically will be why did I leave England after saying I was there in perpetuity? I did stay for three years. But it wasn't favorable for my work. Too much gentility, civility, couth. Nothing at which to get irritated. Besides, the British never heard of bagels, definitely a flaw in their character.

"Actually I get quite homesick for Bucks. I keep an elderly, very cute MG stored in a barn there, perhaps as a subconscious pledge that I'll return. Occasionally I do visit," he admits. "I wrap my arms about the fenders and sob lovingly, causing the chrome to become rusty. But I definitely need New York for my work. It's detestable, dangerous, filthy—the city, I mean— corroding, more and more pestilential, twice-breathed air, and all. But there's a feeling of pulse around me. Everyone is busy. That's inspiring."

S. J. Perelman's thirst for geographic novelty and stimulating literary material has taken him on African safaris, in search of illicit sturgeon, and around the world in eighty days— shades of Jules Verne—by steamship, train, and lady elephant. "I was duplicating the exploits of Phileas Fogg one hundred years after Verne's fantasy. The trip was remarkably without incident," he says, shrugging. "We crossed the southern part of India by elephant. Highly uncomfortable. Though the elephant was dressed in very feminine garb—gilded tusks, ankle bells, pendant earrings, a little silver cap. She was very sweet, but . . ." Not his type.

The experience provoked several essays that eventually found their way into Perelman's latest book, *Vinegar Puss*, a title whose unfortunate origins I had been unwilling to speculate upon. All right, S. J., I do not want to ask this, but I must.

Any relation between you and the title? "It's an old expression," he explains patiently, "equivalent to sourpuss. Which is what I evolved after looking at a publicity photograph of myself.

"But I don't really see myself that way," S. J. Perelman disclaims. "Actually, I'm a fun-loving, sunny-tempered fellow." He chuckles. "I don't know what my enemies think."

MARCH 30, 1975

Note: S. J. Perelman died October 17, 1979.

SUSAN CHEEVER
It's All in the Family

"People ask me how it was growing up in my father's house—that's what everyone wants to hear about, life in the John Cheever household," says Susan Cheever, the famous novelist's daughter. "I had no idea there was any other way to grow up. I thought everything that happened was perfectly normal."

Inexplicably, Susan Cheever still has the round, rosy cheeks of a child and the easy, cozy, giggly manner of a girlhood confidante, though she is thirty-six. "I always thought I had a very normal childhood," she repeats over tea in her Fairmont suite on a recent visit. "I always thought that my father was just a normal suburban father. He wasn't very famous then. I never thought of Daddy being some strange genius, so that was very healthy for me. I was a very happy little girl, and this is something I don't really understand despite long, intense therapy. I was very happy until I was nine," she sighs. "Don't ask me why."

What does she mean, normal? "We moved around a lot. My father was always home, we didn't have any money for a long time. There is this famous story," she recalls, "how, mornings, Daddy would put on his one suit and go down in the elevator with the other men on their way to work. He'd get off in the basement of our apartment building, where we had a little storage cubicle. He'd take off his suit, hang it up, and then write in his undershorts. At lunchtime, he'd put on his suit, come back upstairs. Well, it just didn't occur to me till about a year ago what that indicated about him. I just thought that was what fathers *did*. Well, that's how you are, I was, as a child. Children are so uncritical."

Susan Cheever looks like her father "more and more, I'm afraid," she says, laughing. "That's terrible. Because my mother is beautiful, and my father is quite handsome . . . craggy. But I look like him and my brothers look like my mother. Daddy has snaggle teeth just like mine, there's this little place where they cross in front, that's just Cheever teeth."

Dental defects aside, he was a "terrific" father. "Well," she hastily amends, "as terrific as any father." Did he spank her? "Well, yes. This is a Cheever Story. The last time he tried to spank me, I was twelve, I ran and outran him. I jumped over the sofa and went through the bathroom and he couldn't catch me. We broke all that furniture, and that was the last time ever. Oh, I've forgotten [what I did]. Isn't that awful?"

One of her illustrious forebears founded the Boston Latin School. "There are all these stories, family stories, I never can think of them on cue. A lot of people have it, it's a sense of being special. It's also coming from Boston but having cast it off. In fact, *they* cast *us* off. What it means to be a Cheever is a good question. We've always been a family of interesting, brilliant failures. . . ."

Oh? "Very respectable. But about three generations back, the part of the family we call the Rich Cheevers—don't say that—say the Good, the Respectable Cheevers—had a falling out with the Disreputable Cheevers. Since then, my father's side has been sort of dissociated from the Bostonian respectability," says Susan Cheever, who grew up in Manhattan and Westchester.

Then she's from the raffish branch? "Absolutely." One would never know. "Well, we are desperately trying so you don't know." She chuckles. "This is the family myth, that we are *not* the Disreputable Cheevers. There's a lot of conflict in us. I think we all want to be the Respectable Cheevers but can't quite pull it off. My father's mother ran a gift shop, and his father, I think, ran a shoe factory, but after the Depression they lost everything and he just sort of became crazy."

Crazy? "He [her grandfather] read aloud Shakespeare to his cats, he drank too much, much too much. I never knew him.

I think he really *was* crazy, crazy enough that my father left home when he was sixteen. In my immediate family, there is a tremendous sense of what it means to be a Cheever, and when we think Cheever, we think Disreputable. It's a sense of specialness that is good and bad. It's not Rich People special-ness, but Intellectual specialness."

Yet this specialness brought a burden. "I don't like [a] kind of life [that's] based on other people's expectations of you. That you must do all this stuff. Like today I'm wearing a gray flannel suit because it doesn't bother people. They look and they don't say, 'Oh, a hippie.' . . . I want people to like me. . . . So I chose something I thought would not be offensive, something which would look organized, which I am not."

As John Cheever's only daughter, oldest of three children, what expectations did she face? "Growing up, I was miserably unhappy, because I was expected to be pretty, which I wasn't, and popular, which I wasn't. I was expected to be coordinated, which I wasn't, and to do well in school, which I didn't. I was a disaster all around as far as expectations were concerned."

Her parents were very nice about it, but very worried. "Wouldn't you have been? I mean, here they had this teenage good-for-nothing on their hands. They weren't mean about it," she murmurs. "I was headstrong, willful, disobedient, rebel-lious, contentious, negative, critical. I was bossy, I was aggres-sive, I was managerial." Sounds as if she should be our first woman President? "But I was miserable," she moans.

She had an "awful adolescence," refusing to bathe or cut her hair or stop reading comic books. She claims she once weighed ten pounds for every year of her age and had only one date before college and her first kiss at a decrepit nineteen.

Her teachers saw her as "lazy." Her parents, who knew she was "brilliant," started sending her to a therapist at eleven. "In a loving way, they thought I would be happier if I could lose weight, pull myself together, curl my hair, learn to use makeup, get coordinated, do well in school, have some dates. They were right, I would have been happier."

She had a "really bad time" in her three years at the elite

Masters School in Dobbs Ferry. "I was very unhappy. Athletics were very important, and the way you looked was very important. I just didn't fit in. I don't know how else to better put it. I stuffed the ballot box for the school election and they found out. . . . I was a terrible cutup, always in trouble. I didn't want to be naughty, I just couldn't help myself.

"I hoped in my wildest fantasies that I'd be loved. Then, for a short time, I wanted to be a writer, which is part of my wanting to be loved." But her teachers said her efforts were "terrible," so she put aside her notebooks and typewriter just like Daddy's, forgot "the outpourings of a lonely fifteen-year-old girl," and gave up literary ambitions for twenty years.

Instead, she had asthma. "That affected me dramatically. It was part of my whole inability to catch a ball, or run more than two feet. I was completely uncoordinated. Half the time, I was sick—no," she corrects herself, "not half the time. But it didn't help my ability to function that often I couldn't breathe. I was ashamed of that, and I felt I should hide it. So I worked out all these different ways to breathe.

"You sort of"—she demonstrates—"hunch your shoulders over so you won't have to gasp and wheeze, and you sort of lean over so you can breathe quietly. I can spot an asthmatic a mile away. It's very embarrassing. You feel so self-conscious. It's just another sign you don't fit in."

All her tormented teenage intensity went into reading—Dumas, Dickens, Hardy Boys, Archie Comics. Her heroines? "I loved Veronica in Archie Comics. She was an outsider who made it on the inside. And Nancy Drew. Still when I get into a tight situation, I'll say, 'Uh-oh, Ned, I hope you brought the flashlight.'"

When she got into Pembroke "by the skin of my teeth," she changed. "I figured out how to deal with people. It seems by an act of the will I changed myself. I realized you can't be an egg without the shell. Also, I based the change very much on two books, *The Red and the Black* and *Women in Love*. From Stendhal I got that people always want what they can't have. And from D. H. Lawrence I got that a woman can be fascinating, whole, autonomous, and still be sexy. I used these as how-to books," she exults.

Finally the boarding-school literary club reject has published her own first novel, *Looking for Work*. Reviews have been "definitely mixed," she notes, "wonderful and horrible." But not to worry, Warner Bros. has optioned it and *Redbook* is serializing it. Finally, after avoiding dynastic destiny, John Cheever's daughter, who has already taught English, made and sold macramé belts, been married and divorced, tried small-town newspaper reporting, and written for *Newsweek*, now wants to write novels for the rest of her life.

"I'm an outsider. I can never fit in," Susan Cheever says, smiling. "I don't even know what I'm fitting into now. I'm still trying to work it out."

MARCH 2, 1980

RITA MAE BROWN
Life in Rubyfruit Jungle

"This is going to sound dumb, but in seventh grade a turning point in my life was when I realized I couldn't go to West Point. I wanted to go there because I felt what a wonderful way to serve my country. That's very southern, you know. I wrote away and found I couldn't get in, and of course I was very upset."

Folks, meet Rita Mae Brown, who—though she has three short names and a spun-sugar drawl—was cheated out of being a Real Southerner by a cruel and minor accident of geography. "My mother, when she was pregnant, couldn't get herself over the Mason-Dixon Line. So I was born in Hanover, Pennsylvania, just nine or ten miles away on the wrong side. I can't believe it. But my heart is truly in the South. We moved to Florida when I was eleven, and the South has just left a more vivid impression on me. There's something about the South that creates writers."

It is not just dumb luck that Rita Mae Brown, thirty-three, has written a raucous and rowdy and irreverent and ever-so-earthy novel called *Rubyfruit Jungle*, which boasts one of the best female protagonists in recent literature. Sassy yet sapient Molly Bolt survives being poor, orphaned, and gay. "It's not about sex," Rita Mae Brown maintains, "it's about being resilient."

It is also about Rita Mae Brown. "A lot of it happened, believe me. I'm not that imaginative," she confides. "I always tell everyone I cleaned it up to get it published. Which causes a giggle. Which means I'm worse than Molly, I really am. She's a nice version of me. I'd hate to have me as a child." She smiles. "Sometimes I'm real nice and sometimes I'm a . . ."

Like her character Molly, Rita Mae Brown came to New York with $24.61 in her pocket. That was about ten years ago. She spent her first three nights in an abandoned car, then waitressed and slept on the floor of a cold-water flat. *Rubyfruit Jungle* was her first novel, and she eventually sold it for $1,000 to a small feminist press named Daughters, Inc. Seventy thousand copies later, word of mouth had made it an underground classic. First novels rarely sell more than 5,000 copies. Bantam cannily bought the book for $250,000. So far, 254,000 copies have been printed to sell for $1.95. Soon there will be a movie. Such is the higher math of paperback publishing.

Rita Mae Brown seems comfortable in her newfound affluence. She is wearing a monogrammed silk designer blouse, flowing scarf, slacks, gold chain earrings, gold chain necklace, gold chain bracelet, gold watch, Gucci shoes. "If I get money, I'm sure not going to walk around in rags," she says over stuffed filet of sole at a University City restaurant. "Like Sophie Tucker said, I've been poor and I've been rich and believe me, honey, rich is better."

Inevitably, Rita Mae Brown is the center of a growing cult. "People don't run after me when I walk down the street," she says, shrugging. Nevertheless, two women fans have named their car after her. She has female groupies camping out on her doorstep. She would prefer to "live a hundred years, write lots of books, and hope people get over calling me 'the lesbian author.'" They could also call her the political activist, the poet, the lecturer, the essayist, the screenwriter, and the wit. "Funny people are dangerous," she says. "They knock down barriers. It's hard to hate people when they're funny." Or: "I wanna tell you, honey, if Michelangelo were a heterosexual, the Sistine Chapel would have been painted basic white with a roller."

Rita Mae Brown spent several years in an orphanage near York, Pennsylvania, before being adopted by an Amish butcher and his wife. "When I was fifteen, he died, and that's when things got real bad. Mom and I were left with nothing. I can remember Mom making hambone soup for like three days in a row."

She can't recall "any one magic moment" when she realized she was gay. "I had lots of boyfriends in high school, lots of fun. But I never seemed to get enraptured like some of the other girls at slumber parties talking about Johnnnnnn," she mimics breathlessly. "I just thought it was such a waste, all this attention on this dolt. But of course in high school everyone is pretty dumb."

When she was sixteen, a schoolmate's father threatened to shoot her on sight—he had found his "daughter writing a love letter to me. They always assume somehow . . . I was the seductress. She got the whole thing going," she claims. "She was this cheerleader, oh yes, honey, she had white boots and blue pom-poms on, it was heaven."

Today, she says, she has "a lot of men friends. I don't have any horror stories to tell about men, I really don't. In the early days when I was with the women's movement, when people would say, oh, men are horrible, my boyfriend oppresses me, I didn't know what they were talking about. I just don't think a man can make me happy. . . .

"I told my mom in 1961—look how many years ago that was," she marvels. "She got real upset and carried on. I just left home, I was eighteen or nineteen. Well, it was real bad then. But we got back together in a couple years' time and now she's great.

"What happened to Mom is real interesting. She saw the daughters of friends who were desperately unhappy," she contends, somewhat simplistically. "I was the only one that was happy. I think that convinced my mother far more than any article or anything anyone could say. She just looked around and said hmmmm. So Mom has come slugging for gay rights.

"She's great, she's seventy-two. But when the book first came out, she threw it out in the garbage can, saying, 'I'm not like that woman in the book, you made that mother mean and everybody is going to think that mother is me.' I said, 'Oh, all little kids think of their parents as meaner than they are, don't worry about it.' Well, we had a lot of fights over the book.

"This is good, put this in," she enthuses. "I told her I've written another novel and she's the star. She said, 'Are you writing about this family again? I'm gonna give you hell. If I don't like it, I'm gonna sue. I'm gonna write my own book.' I said, 'Mother, this book will make a lot of money, I will buy you a house.'

"There was an excruciating pause. She reconsidered. She brought a scrapbook to the kitchen table, where she always held court and did just everything. 'Well,' she said, 'I better help you get your facts right,'" Rita Mae says, grinning. "And I bought her a car. I've supported her since I was twenty-two. I still don't have a car. I'm going to buy her whatever she wants. If my mother wants a mink coat, she is having it. Whatever the old lady wants, she is going to get."

Rita Mae says middle-class friends regard her as "a very primitive character. Because my speech is studded with bumblebees and grasshoppers. . . . I'm right there in 3-D reality. I don't think I've ever used words like 'paranoid' or 'life-style' or 'anxiety' or 'relate.' I don't think that way. I'm not that abstract. My speech is more immediate.

"Because I don't speak in psychological jargon—mushtalk that doesn't mean a damn thing—I'm really seen as some kind of throwback to Neanderthal woman,"she suggests. But that is an inaccurate portrayal. She doesn't watch any TV, so she can "keep my mind pure." She proselytizes for the joys of studying Latin. And she is unobtrusively well educated. "I have my Ph.D. [from the Institute of Policy Study in Washington, D. C.] in I don't know what you'd call it. I did my thesis on the relationship of art to politics," she says. "And I have an NYU cinematography degree. It's useless. You can't find work.

"Speaking middle-classese is like speaking French. I understand their language. I can do it. You can't get a Ph.D. without learning how to do that. But they can't speak my language. If I were to walk up to one of them and say, 'Honey, you are as black as the insides of a goat,' they'd think I was talking about race. They don't even know what that means," she says scornfully. But neither do I. "It means that you are having a very evil day. The South understands language. You should live there if you want to be a writer."

Not surprisingly, she disagrees with the notion that gay people "have had some kind of barren childhood." Why? "My [adoptive] parents loved me. They had a lot of love. They were married for thirty-six years before my dad died, and every Friday he'd bring her flowers. When there was a full moon, they'd go to the beach and hold hands. They were very romantic."

So it wasn't that she felt her parents had a rotten marriage? "Oh no. Their relationship was terrific. It was a wonderful model. I didn't know how good it was until I grew up and saw other parents' relationships. I grew up seeing that love could work."

And has *she* found love? "I think my friends love me." She pauses, trying not to be drowned out by the band playing "Feelings." "But not in the romantic sense. Like most writers I lead a pretty monastic life. Right now I have no lover. I don't even have time to look around. I don't know what's out there. I hope someday I'll get lucky like my mom did.

"I always tell people I'm a lesbian in name only," says Rita Mae Brown. "I'm too busy to practice what I preach."

NOVEMBER 20, 1977

CHARLES FULLER
He Grew Up with Words

The Pulitzer Prize–winning playwright, once hailed by the London *Times* as a possible savior of the theater, is innocently asked if he ever failed at anything. "Oh yes," he almost whispers, savoring my surprise, "English."

Charles Fuller's ninth play, A *Soldier's Play*, won a Pulitzer in 1982. It begins with a killing and ends with a confession, which is the reverse of most interviews hereabouts. On July 26 at the Walnut Street Theater, Charles Fuller's prize play will have its premiere in his hometown, where he grew up in the projects, went to night school, lived in North Philly until just a few years ago, and worked as a city housing inspector. Amiable, articulate, and unaffected by it all, he sits on a velvet couch in his living room, where the walls are wood and brick and the view through the back picture window is Pennypack Park and spectacular.

What does he mean, he failed English? "I was a *terrible* English student," he says, laughing heartily and unabashedly. "Are you kidding? I was awful." Why? He couldn't explicate those arcane Wallace Stevens poems? Neither could I. "No, not that. The business of placing commas and semicolons and things like that could drive me mad. I used to think it was just ridiculous." Oh, I see—that old bugbear, grammar. "I was always very bad at that sort of thing," he continues. But, he is told, that's not English; English is great literature, the art of writing. "Well, I learned that later," he says, laughing again. "But I wasn't, you know, the greatest English student.

"And I wasn't a very good student at Villanova, as I recall. I decided not to go to class for a while. I thought that the lives of people like Joseph Conrad, who had been on ships, and painters like Gauguin, who had wandered all over the world, would certainly prepare me much more for what I wanted to do than going to classes."

Having a printer for a father whetted his appetite to manipulate, if not master, the intricacies of language. "My father worked all day, every day of his life, and I would go and work with him on Saturdays. I used to set type for him. My father was in his way an artist with what he did. (He really wanted to be a violinist.) He used to print labels. And they were in three and four colors. Okay, so that each color on the label in those days had to be set separately, by a handpress. And he would bring the jobs home, and he would show us the labels.

"I was the oldest, and I guess I would take a little more care with it. I'm forty-four and I have two younger sisters. But he would show me the colors, and the fact that he had not put an extra mark on the paper, that the press had hit the paper so smoothly. And I would always look at his work, when he did letterheads and things like that, I'd always hold the sheet up to the light and look at it to find out how good a job it was, whether or not the ink was dried, whether or not it went through each letter, things like that. Words were always part of my life, very, very much part of my life."

He was, as a child, an outsider, though he would not like it to be said that way. He was always taller than everybody. He thinks he's stoop-shouldered because he was always worried about being so tall. He played basketball for a little while; he was "awful." He ran track "for a minute." He was probably very good at shooting pool. He wanted to play football, but he couldn't make the team; he was too thin. He was "very skinny, very skinny, very tall and skinny," he murmurs, "not a terribly athletic young man."

Despite this dearth of physical prowess, he was taught by his parents that he could do anything he wanted—anything he was smart enough to do he could do. He was never told there were places he couldn't go, ideas he could not think, things he could not have. His parents were the most confident people he ever knew. There were no limitations. They told him: The only limitations you have are the ones you make for yourself.

Though "we had a lot of books in our house, we were great

readers," he never knew there were black novelists until he saw the face of James Baldwin on a book in a drugstore. "I guess I was in high school. I was just fascinated, totally fascinated. I really didn't know there were black novelists. I went out and read his books, and I got very excited. It was the fifties, sometime when I was at Roman Catholic High."

Soon he decided to be a writer himself. "I had found a great deal of affection in the lives of writers, the lives of artists. I liked that life-style and the ability to think one's own thoughts and do something about that—whether it be to compose music or paint or write, but to be able to live one's life off one's ideas, to work on one's own steam, and not to have to think like everyone else to make a living, to live. And that was very early, very, very early," he says with a laugh, "*very* early."

"My father didn't think one could really make a living at writing. But if I thought I could really do it, if I learned enough about it, he was sure I would be a good writer. On the other hand, he said, because it is such a shaky kind of operation and risky at best, he suggested I go to school and study law and get my degree and at least have a foundation. If I wanted to write, he said, I could write after I have my life settled."

For a while he followed his father's wishes, labeling himself pre-law. Actually, he discloses, "I don't have a bachelor's degree. Oh no, I never graduated college. I found myself really wanting more to read all the books I could get my hands on, rather than going to class. So I spent a great deal of time in the library, ah, reading, reading, and reading everything I could get my hands on. I left Villanova, and went into the Army, where I continued to read."

He was stationed in Japan and Korea, and his service test scores were so high, "they said whatever I wanted to do I could," he says. Was it rough for him? "No, not really. Quite nice. I read a lot. I got a lot done. I wrote. I read everything I could," he says, laughing again. ". . . I ran the petroleum laboratory, but I won't say any more about it. . . . When I came back, I decided to go to night school at La Salle, because there was something in me that still felt, I suppose, some apprehension about being in the modern world without a degree." He had a year and a half to go. "I thought that finally I could get this problem out of my life, this business of being in the modern world without a degree from a university," he repeats. "So I decided I was going to do it."

There, while toiling days as a city housing inspector, he wrote his first play, *The Perfect Party*, which opened at Princeton's McCarter Theater. "And I knew thereafter that there was nothing else about this particular business that I liked so much, that I wanted to do so much, that I could ever learn at a university or a school. That you had to be there, to be really doing it, or I would be wasting a great deal of my life." So he left La Salle and has "been writing plays ever since."

Reading rave reviews all over the world "is very pleasant," he concedes cheerfully. But the critics have not always been kind. "I've had such bad reviews," he confides. "The worst thing ever said was I had written the worst play the critic had ever seen," he recalls with a laugh. "The play was a little ahead of its time."

He recently shuttled back and forth from Hollywood doing the screen adaptation of *A Soldier's Play*. Does he ever have moments of terror about what's next? "No. I've finally come to trust that I am a writer, that what I do is equal to what anyone does who is used to teaching, used to doctoring, or used to pulling out teeth, and so on, something you're just accustomed to doing. Not that you can equate writing with any of those things. But that is what I do to live. And it is reasonable that, having worked so long at reading and examining ideas, that a great part of me is steeped in a personal tradition of finding ideas to write about, things to create. So I don't think I'll ever run dry."

Gradually building his craft and writing play after play, he realized praise is ephemeral, applause is momentary. Did he ever get discouraged and wonder who's watching, anyway? "Oh, sure. But I think that like anything else, you either continue to self-start, or you self-destruct. I don't ever see myself as quote-unquote, famous. That's not me. . . . What I personally think of myself is much more lasting."

He is, he says, a history buff. He taught himself to play the flute. He likes being alone with his thoughts, quiet, walking around and reading, going to restaurants to sample "extraordinary food." He has a wife who is a nurse, and two teenage sons, one interested in engineering, the other football. His sense of humor is deep but generous.

"It's not true that anybody who writes is perfect, that we're not human somehow," he declares. "It's not true that there's something, some sort of gloss over us, that the writing somehow has made us less human. We are not things, we are people. We breathe. We get angry. We have the same kind of human problems everybody else has."

I can't help staring over his shoulder at a pair of squirrels skittering across his doorstep. "It's unusual here. You can hear the birds all day long. Yeah, they come up close to the house. All kinds of birds fly into the window. Every now and then, *bam*—they'll knock themselves out," Charles Fuller relates, "flying at their own image."

JULY 17, 1983

PAUL THEROUX
The English Girl and Other Adventures

Plaid slacks, tan turtleneck, brown hair still damp from the shower, dark glasses, wedding band. Wife and two kids at home. Hotel room in strange city. Appearance? Conventioneer. Reality? "Most people would agree, ah, that they lead secret lives, private lives. Most people have a double life. But it's the secret one, the hidden one, that's the real person. Writing, you see, gives you access to that secret life."

Paul Theroux, the Massachusetts shoe salesman's son who writes exotic tales of travel (*The Great Railway Bazaar*) and alienation (*Mosquito Coast*), is an alert, affable, attractive chap who spends his winters in London and his summers on Cape Cod. An extraordinarily fine, gifted author untrammeled by the demands of the marketplace, he's lived in Uganda, Singapore, and Rome, where he taught English, an odious enterprise he's spared now after a score of successful books.

Too often, interviewing a writer can be as exciting as watching grass grow—particularly when they growl, again and again, "It's in my book!" Not Paul Theroux. He is curious about his questioner: "Where do you live? . . . What time did you go to sleep last night? . . . And you're not normally an early riser? . . . Ordinarily I'd say that's terrible . . . it catches up with you . . . you get brain fatigue." About himself he is delightfully candid: "A lot of people think I'm a horse's ass, I'm sure, or I'm pompous, or not as funny as I think I am.

"I think writing tends to deny you a full life," he declares. "Writing is incompatible with everything. It's incompatible with having children, with having a job. You can't do everything. Virtually all you can do is cook meals. Cooking is a nice way to bring yourself down to earth once again. But apart from that, there's very little else you can do. It's difficult, it's very tiring. It's very hard. It's time-consuming. Um, it's why writers are such odd people, you know. There are very few writers who are not cranks in some way. I think most people would find just the process of writing odd—I think they would say, 'Why do you spend so much time doing it?'"

Paul Theroux recalls himself as a happy but solitary child ensconced in the bosom of a large family (six kids). His fantasies were both wholesome and phantasmagorical—the great outdoors and the nightmare vision. There was the "fresh-air fiend, emphasis on fiend," the kid in coonskin cap, the boy scout who would prowl forests, book or camera in one hand, gun in the other, shooting bottles and pretending he would become a fur trapper in Canada (where his ancestors came on Champlain's second voyage from France in the early seventeenth century). Then there was his icky ghoulish side, fueled by unspeakably evil horror comics that celebrated cannibalism, mutilation, murder, necrophilia, and other uncensored aberrations.

"A person can write well, yet still not have the temperament of being a writer," he continues. "And I think it's something that you have to discover, you know." While he talks, he plays with a large paper clip, as if he were making it into a TV antenna or a futuristic sculpture. "This paper clip? This is my pet paper clip. It can do a lot of things. It can sit, it can cling. It can fall on the floor. So let's leave him on the floor," he says as he drops it, a bit embarrassed at my scrutiny.

Does he hate being interviewed, is that why he's restless? "No, I don't mind being interviewed. But I, I, I tend to fidget," he admits. "I used to smoke. Probably I look like an ex-smoker to you, in the way that I'm toying with these things." Giving up his beloved pipe, he says, "is the best thing I've ever done." The man definitely lacks perspective.

I ask him about his travels, which include train rides across whole continents, and which he usually does alone, in contrast to his vacations. "Traveling is a solitary occupation, it's a very intense one. You look around, ah, I take a lot of notes. I spend nearly all the time looking and writing, eighteen hours a day. And if nothing is happening, I try to make it happen. And if I'm not meeting anyone, I go up to people and ask them questions, I mean, I try actively to seek people out. Now, I would never do that on a vacation. A vacation for me is the opposite of travel—it's fun, painless, lazy. Travel is different. It's not restful, it's very anxiety-making, and it's work."

Does he allow himself to be swept up by adventure? "You mean, somebody making a suggestion, 'A very strange occurrence took place over here, would you like to see it?' And I say, 'I was going to go to the museum, but no, I think I'll do that.' You mean," he asks me, "dropping everything? Yes, that does happen, and I do it. That's another reason you have to be alone. Because if you're with someone, and you're interested in something, you have to be ready to change your plans at a moment's notice. . . ."

But does he have adventures? "What do you call adventures? I call adventures a man saying, um . . ." He pauses to reflect. "I was in Madras once, Madras, India. And I was walking down the street. No, no, I got into a taxi. And I said to the driver, 'I'm hungry, I want to go to a restaurant.' And he said, 'Do you want to meet an English girl?' And I said, 'What kind of English girl?' This is in the middle of the night, in south India, the darkest strangest place, in an old rattling taxi. And the man at the wheel looked like a wolf, with these sort of wolfy teeth, vulpine teeth. 'Do you want to meet an English girl?' 'No,' I said, 'I'm hungry.'

"'Okay, all right,' he said, 'I'll take you to a restaurant.' And as we were driving along, I asked, 'What kind of English girl? Where is she?' 'You want to meet her?' he asked. And I said, 'Yes, no, yes, no.' Anyway, finally I said, 'Yes, I want to meet this English girl.' And he said, 'Nice English girl.' So I said, 'This is interesting.' And I was thinking, middle of the night, southern India, out in the country, I mean, he reversed the car, and we're on a bumpy road. I thought, this is amazing. Then he got out of town, and in the middle of nowhere—rice fields—he stopped the car and said, 'I'll be right back,' and slammed the door. And I was sitting in this car alone, and it was pitch dark, and I just saw little twinkling lights in the distance, and I thought, this guy is going to knife me and take my money and run.

"So I got out of the car and I was tiptoeing down the road, when he said, 'Sahib, come here!' So I followed him through this muddy thing, and I thought, now I'll get it, maybe I'll be pounced on. And I was still curious to know what was going on, because it wasn't happening the way I thought it would happen. Anyway, it was a brothel—he took me to a brothel where there were, oh, I don't know, about fifteen or twenty children. They were about twelve, thirteen years old. So I said, "Where's the English girl?' 'Oh,' he said, 'she's not here to-night.' So I said okay, and, well, I used that as my excuse to leave. What kind of English girl would be there? I wondered, you know, what would an English girl be doing there? And I thought it would be interesting, something to write about, and in the end I wrote about that experience. Is that what you mean by adventure?" Yes.

By contrast, his nonwriting life is sedate. He bicycles, sails, swims, and visits libraries. "I don't do any of those things well, but they give me pleasure," he says, grinning. His idea of rec-reation is reading a book about a termite community, or bird-watching. I've always thought birders, as they're called, were downright weird. What can he say? "Oh, it's fun, it's fun!" he exclaims. "It's identification, and if you're lucky, you see the birds *be-having*. You know, you see a ruddy turnstone actually turning over stones on the beach and looking for things under-neath. You just see birds doing what they would do. I mean, the way they eat, and the way they look."

Wouldn't he rather, as a writer, people-watch? "Yes, yes. But you don't need binoculars for people. And also, you don't al-ways get in the fresh air watching people. I mean, watching people is sort of a 3 A.M. activity, don't you think?" Does he have many close friends? "No, not many close friends, no. That's another thing that writers are denied. If they have a lot of friends, they don't write very much, I would say."

But his success has its own rewards. "With each book I've written, I've sold more copies. So I sell a lot of books now," he says matter-of-factly. "My first book sold very poorly, so poorly that they only printed a few copies, and now it retails for $200 a copy. It's a rare book. It's called *Waldo*, and yes, it's very, very scarce. So if you have $200, you can read it. And it's a very bad book, too," he says almost gleefully. "The people who pay $200 for it really deserve it. Why? Well, because that money doesn't go to me. That's just the scarcity value of the book. They're just buying an object, they're not buying something that you read. They're buying a dud!"

From reading *World's End*, a collection of his short stories, I get the impression his wife doesn't understand him. "No, no, no. Why do you say that? Because the stories are about marriage?" Kind of. "Unhappy marriages?" Kind of. That he's a man who's wandered afield from time to time. In his travels. "Ah, then you're confusing me with my characters."

Which happens, Paul Theroux allows—"but people shouldn't confuse me with my characters, because then they would be confusing me with a seventy-year-old woman photographer [*Picture Palace*], a fifty-year-old pimp in Singapore [*Saint Jack*], a mad scientist who goes to Honduras who is sort of bent on destroying his whole family [*Mosquito Coast*]. I mean, I would be put in jail if that were true. And I would belong in jail, I think," he chortles, "or a madhouse. They're responsible for themselves from now on, I mean, they have to look after themselves, these characters. Fortunately I'm just, I'm, am I middle-aged? I'm forty-one. I'm a forty-one-year-old bespectacled person, I'm just a bespectacled novelist who, ah, who dreamed all this up."

DECEMBER 19, 1982

MAXINE KUMIN
Ode on a Sad Childhood

So much depends on the great big red brick house with a white porch on Carpenter Lane in Germantown, where Maxine Kumin, the Pulitzer Prize–winning poet from Philadelphia, lived till she was seventeen and scribbled precious little ditties like: "Can it be that Spring is here? / Hark! Oh what is that I hear? / It cannot be, but yes it is. / The robins cheer!"

Then her name was Maxine Winokur and she roller-skated and went to Cheltenham High and Congregation Rodeph Shalom on Broad Street. But she would grow up to look and sound like a New Englander, wiry and strong-jawed. She would go to Radcliffe and marry a scientist from Harvard. She would publish seven volumes of poetry (collected in *Our Ground Time Here Will Be Brief*), four novels, twenty children's books, and a book each of short stories and essays.

She would be Library of Congress poetry consultant. When her three kids were grown, she and her energy specialist husband would move from Boston to a small New Hampshire town and a 200-acre farm they share with five horses, five cats, and a dog. There she writes, raises Scotch Highland cattle, rides, chops wood to heat her house, and when she must, shoots woodchucks with a .22.

"I should probably preface anything I say by saying it's a truism that behind every writer stands an unhappy childhood. Most of the things I remember are not exactly joyous," she tells me after her poetry reading at the Klein Branch of the Jewish Y's.

"My father was the biggest pawnbroker in the city of Philadelphia," she says. "This is what I remember being told." She found his shop at Nineteenth and Federal "scary . . . very alarming, formidable. But I was very little. It was so crowded on Friday nights that there was a policeman on duty to let people in and out of the shop," she recalls.

"I was a very, I think, lonely kid, very introspective. I felt very much at odds with my environment and my culture." Why? "Probably a genetic flaw. I can't really explain it. I was the youngest of four, so I think that isolated me. Also, I was sent out of the district to school. My father made my brothers all go to Germantown High, but he relented when I came along, because it was pretty tough. He let me go to Cheltenham—you could do that for two hundred dollars a year. I was living in a different neighborhood, so I really never made friends there. It was a long commute, a very long commute. And it was a very solitary time for me. I was just a real loner, taking my solace in books and writing and studying Latin, which I loved."

She edited her high school paper and yearbook and won some essay contests. "It was an embarrassment to win prizes. That was a way of being set aside, being different, being kind of a brain, which we used to call a *wonk*. I don't know what the term is now." Did she consider herself odd? "Yes, I did. To an alarming degree. And as an adolescent, it was a very great worry—how could I possibly turn out normal? Oh, I tried desperately . . . I tried to dress the normal part, but it didn't matter. I was still set aside. I was ostracized by my peculiar nature, and it was very painful."

To compensate, she had a rich fantasy life, "a very elaborate one, starting from trying to write a novel at a very tender age, I was eight, and after Chapter 3 I couldn't think of what to do with my characters, and it bothered me. I mean, I really felt like a quitter putting that aside. I felt guilty for years and years and years that I never finished it," she says. "It was heavily influenced by *The Bobbsey Twins*, let's put it that way." Was she the heroine? "There was some highly idealized little girl, and it had to do with horses and farms."

How does a city kid become enamored of pastoral things? "I don't really know. Probably some sort of a gene, a mutant gene that sprung up in my generation. I can't really explain it. I certainly was passionate as a very small child about the Fairmount Park Guard horses. And also, remember that when I was a child one saw a lot of horses, pulling carriages and garbage wagons. I think when I was about three I saw my first horse. My parents used to ride, and probably my earliest memory is being picked up and sat down in front of my father on a horse. Ah, that was at Valley Green in Wissahickon.

"Later, I'd ride through Carpenter's Woods into Fairmount Park along Wissahickon Creek. And I spent most of my childhood there. It was then considered perfectly safe and all right to roam around in those woods. Even then I was very oriented toward the trees and mosses and ferns and catching frogs."

For a while she wanted to be a doctor. "Well, I was so animal-oriented. I wanted to patch up everybody's wounds, animals and people. But I think I didn't like the gore," she says with a laugh. ". . . I felt alienated from my family because I was such a bookworm. I think I was a major disappointment in many ways to my mother, who had longed so for a girl that 'she went to the well four times to get me,' as I said in a poem. And then, instead of getting a little frilly fluffy girlchild, she got this large-size, sort of outsize, tomboyish, tough creature that also happened to be female, but only incidentally. And since the boys were doing all the fun things—playing football, running loose on their bicycles—it seemed to me a terrible misfortune and penance to have been born a girl. And I fought against it desperately for a long, long time. I was the center of my brothers' backyard football team for years.

"You know, I was an omnivorous reader, from a very tender age. I went to the Lovett Memorial Library on Germantown Avenue. I think any writer you talk to will have stories about going up to the librarian and respectfully asking to be permitted to take out extra books. Whatever it was, it was never enough, because I could read four books in an afternoon. I mean, isn't that what everybody did? I just *gobbled* books.

"And I remember not being permitted to stay up to read, and reading under the covers in bed with a flashlight. I did that for years. And being told that I would ruin my eyes that way. So, of course, I 'ruined' my eyes. That is, I have astigmatism, which I would have had regardless. But, oh, the books I read stealthily under the covers, in an era when children had the good sense to know what they should be afraid of, and that was the wrath of parents, which was more awesome than anything in my life. . . .

"I wasn't happy in Philadelphia, and I didn't want to go back. I wanted to start over. And in a sense going away to college *was* starting over for me. For the first time in my life I discovered there were lots of other people like me. . . .

"I think I was terribly, terribly moody as an adolescent. I had very dark moods. I was very depressed." Did she have therapy? "Yes. But not as a child, no. I went through psychoanalysis in my thirties. . . . What motivated me was I had tremendous anxiety about, oh, doing anything in public. Giving poetry readings was excruciatingly painful for me." Did the therapy affect her writing? "I think it freed me to write prose. It just made me more open, it made things more accessible for me. And it was far better than a Ph.D."

When did she finally relinquish her self-conscious quest for "normalcy"? "Once I was happily married, I no longer had to conform to anybody else's expectations." She looks normal now. "Well, what you see is a writer wearing her Gloria Grownup clothes put together by her fashion-conscious daughter. . . ."

This may be naïve, but how does a poet come to marry, and stay married (since 1946), to a scientist? "That's my prescription for a happy marriage—marry someone who doesn't do anything similar to what you do. We made a pact about thirty years ago that we would not put what we did on each other. Therefore, I never have to read his articles and paragraph them, or worry about the grammar, and he never has to read anything I'm working on. He reads things after they're published," she says. "It's a dinosaur marriage, to be married thirty-six years. People don't do that anymore, it just isn't done. But it pleases me very much. . . ."

Maxine Kumin is fifty-seven but could pass for ten years less. "Yeah," she accepts my compliment brusquely, "but look at my skin, look at my hands. These are country hands. These are hands that groom and tack and shovel. All the cream in the world won't help. This is not to be used in this article," she mutters. "We are not going to discuss my hands in your article!" She admits to a touch of pelvic arthritis that makes it harder to spend long hours in the saddle. "I don't like to spend a lot of time thinking how old I am, because it's frightening to realize how old you get to be. The thing is you never change, you know, the person inside the body doesn't change. I really don't look in the mirror very frequently. I try to avoid it. And if I'm weathering well, then it must have something to do with the fact that I lead a very physical life."

And a rather isolated one. Her nearest neighbor is half a mile away. "It wouldn't bother me, I could go a week without seeing anybody. I see myself as just kind of a New England character who's living off in the woods with her creatures. Not worrying, not minding at all being eccentric. I mean, if this is eccentricity, make the most of it. I feel much more at home in myself. Those concerns of that lost adolescent left me a long time ago. Now I'm loving this rather strange life I lead. . . .

"If you interview writers, you're going to hear the same sad story over and over. That's what's so fascinating to me. I have never met a writer who said to me, oh, I had a wonderfully happy average normal childhood and I had thousands of friends and I was a cheerleader and I was on this team or that," Maxine Kumin murmurs. "*Those* people don't turn out to be writers."

MAY 1, 1983

ART BUCHWALD
Can Humor Survive Analysis?

Here's Art Buchwald, specs, cigar, and all—looking like some tweedy, overgrown Muppet run amok—gently pushing away a large, lumbering dog with his foot before it bumps into him. Thus deflected, said canine lurches off. "This one's an old pal of mine. Mischief is blind and doesn't know where she's going half the time," he croaks.

The usual order of things is Art Buchwald getting into mischief, in print, for a living. My parents think he's funny, and so do a lot of other folks. But what I knew about Art Buchwald the man was scant.

He's one of the most successful humor columnists in the country; his stuff is carried by 550 newspapers, including this one. I knew he grew up in Queens, served in the Marines, went to USC on the GI Bill. I knew that, before moving to Washington in '62, he hung out in Paris for fourteen years with George Plimpton, Irwin Shaw, Theodore White, James Baldwin, John Huston, Gene Kelly, wrote for the *International Herald Tribune*, and was called "the most comic American observer of the European scene since Mark Twain." I knew James Thurber said he looked like Rudolph Valentino (and only learned later that he was kidding).

He doesn't mind praise? "No, I'm delighted with it, I can live with it," he tells me at a friend's home before a recent benefit here for the ACLU. "I've learned to deal with praise over the years. At the beginning I used to be embarrassed and think I didn't deserve it. Then I went into analysis and found out I deserved it. Before, I used to feel guilty about it. Now I enjoy it," he says. "Afterward I wasn't less funny. I was afraid they'd take away my humor, but they didn't.

"I probably am a perfect case for a psychiatrist. Because all these people that are doing things in show business and everything, ah, usually are people who are trying to make up for unhappy childhoods."

To get attention as a kid, he got laughs—and pretended he wasn't unhappy. "I never let anybody know what was really going on. Obviously, there was hurt and pain there. But I covered up very well, even for myself. So, whereas I always had a smile on my face and I always looked like I didn't have a care in the world, I guess I was hurting. And that's where you thrash things out in analysis. . . . People who have never been in it wouldn't understand it, and people who are in it understand it perfectly. There are successful ones and unsuccessful ones; I consider mine successful.

"When I was a kid, I had fantasies about what's really happened to me. My background is I was a foster child, I was in a series of foster homes.

"I was very much a loner, so I had a lot of time to fantasize. My fantasies were that all those people I knew then, someday I would show them, and they'd have to come to me, and they'd have to say they knew me. And they'd have to say, oh yes, I remember him well. I'd be driven up in a limousine saying well, here I am. Most of the people that I was trying to impress are dead. But the fantasies still remain in a strange way," he muses.

What did he mean? "Well, last year at the Kennedy Center I went out to do a monologue, and there was the President of the United States in the box, the entire Cabinet, and the entire establishment of the United States in the audience. And I thought about my father, who was a poor immigrant worker from somewhere in Eastern Europe, how he came to the U. S. and hadn't made it too well, he's passed away—but I thought to myself, boy, Dad, you're not gonna believe this! . . . I'm gonna stand in front of the President and make him laugh. You know, I was a little uptight about it, and that just relaxed me. Even in my fantasies as a kid I hadn't reached the point that I'd be walking out on a stage in front of fifteen, twenty million people—it was also on TV. So I call it a giggle, to myself, I sort of inwardly giggle about this whole thing."

Art Buchwald is a Jew married to a Catholic for thirty years. His earliest memory is being raised in a foster home by Seventh-Day Adventists. "I remember being lugged off to church on Saturday morning. And there was a lot of hellfire and damnation in that, a lot of sins I was very surprised at," he says with a laugh. Surprised at? "These Seventh-Day Adventists were very strong about, ah, no fun. No fun. And no meat, no fish. I was there six years. Um, there was a lot of it left in me, that stayed with me," he says, laughing again.

The most outrageous thing gentle, genial Art Buchwald did as a kid was running away from home at sixteen and joining the Marines. "And forging my father's name to the papers. I got a drunk to be my father to sign the papers," he reveals. "The thing that had the most influence on me as a kid was the Marine Corps."

Why did he join? "It was another romantic idea"—like his later move to Paris—"the uniform wasn't bad, and I saw all these Marine movies with John Wayne. Yeah, people are surprised; they don't see me as a marine. I *was* sort of a funny marine. Not in looks. If you were casting about for a movie, I was the guy who makes wisecracks. I was funny in the Marines, and that was a very painful thing. But it worked out fine, because the Marines really were a very big father image."

They made him into a man? "Yeah, they made me into a man, I think. I mean, at least they made me," he falters. "A lot of things I do today are based on the Marines. Sense of honor. Sense of feeling about your fellows. The Marines, if they don't kill people, is a fantastic organization, they're tremendous, what they do is do a job on you. They take a kid and completely brainwash him and then they rebuild him again. I mean, it's a fantastic thing to see. I went back twenty years later to Parris Island for *Life* magazine and saw it with my own eyes. You get four ex-marines in the room that are fifty, sixty years old, and their eyes still light up and they want to talk about it. For many of us, it was a tremendous experience. Because it is tough, the training is tough, but they make you ten feet tall at the end of it. And as I say, except for the killing part it's a great outfit. . . ."

Did he ever make peace with his father? "Oh yeah, but we were never close. He never understood me. He thought I was gonna end up badly. Everybody thinks a funny kid will end up badly, because he's against the establishment at a very early age," he says. "My father was very proud of me, but he would never tell me. He always told my [three older] sisters or he told somebody else, but he never told me. It was tough for him to admit he was wrong."

He flicks away cigar ashes that have settled on his chest, and continues considering his father. "Ummmm. He was a curtain manufacturer. Small. He had a loft and he had a lady that worked with him, and a man who helped him hang. He wasn't very rich." And his mother? "My mother died when I was born, right after I was born. So he put us in private homes until he couldn't afford it anymore, and then we were put in an orphanage and then we were put in foster homes. The first home we were all together, and then we were separated. Ah, counting the ones he paid for, we were in one, two, three, four, five, five homes."

Art Buchwald's emotional dislocation finally erupted in the early sixties, when he became depressed after moving to Washington from Paris. "I just felt completely useless, worthless. And I didn't understand it, because I had everything. So that's when I decided to straighten it out. It was a lot of stuff building up, and it just all came to a head. The psychiatrist said I had a mid-life crisis earlier than most people. But I squared myself away, and since then I've been very much at ease with myself. It was all probably triggered by the move back to the States. If I had stayed in Paris," he theorizes, "I could have hid it a lot longer.

"You deal with it either through booze, broads, or this way. And I wasn't big on booze, and I was, um, never too big on broads as far as messing around, so I took the third way out. . . ." You would think that people who are funny for money have uplifted personalities. "They're all depressives," he declares. "We're all manic-depressives of some sort." Does he still go up and down? "Ah, no, no extremes." Is he on lithium or vitamins? "No," he maintains. "We all pay a price, you know. Everybody thinks you've got it made, but that doesn't mean anything if you don't think you've got it made."

Despite commanding $12,500 fees for speaking, Art Buchwald still does not label himself a success. He admits he gets mad at "college professors who have never written a book" who give him bad reviews. His play *Sheep on the Runway* bombed in Philly years ago, and he still smarts at the local theater critic who sneered that he should stick to grinding out 600-word columns for the newspapers. He yearns for lasting literary accomplishments and acclaim, wishing he had written *Catch-22* or *Catcher in the Rye*, vowing he will try.

How does he think of himself? As a satirist? A humorist? A funny person? What's the proper terminology? "I don't put a name on it," he demurs. Well, what should we call him? "A survivor," Art Buchwald tells me, laughing. "Shall we end on that?"

Yes.

FEBRUARY 27, 1983

PAUL FUSSELL
In a Class by Himself

Alas, the world can barely keep apace of him—*here* he's this frivolous public buffoon, but *there* he's a very serious cultural historian, and it confuses people, it *does*, because they don't know how to cast him as a type. No, he likes that, he likes to keep shiftish and mobile, because he treasures his independence very powerfully, and he gets very Prufrock-like when he's formulated and pinned to the wall. He likes to keep, ah, like the Artful Dodger, ah, moving around, moving around.

Sixty-year-old writer/teacher/critic Paul Fussell is an arch, articulate, arrogant, argumentative chap who scurries about with a perpetual sneer in his voice and an indelible scowl on his face, because he's always noticing, noticing, noticing.

"I am a camera, virtually. I'm always noticing things around me. I learned this in the Army—if you're not alert, you'll get shot," he declares. "And you're listening constantly, you're looking, you're noticing the slightest anomaly as a hint that the enemy is near, you know, a broken twig or something. So you have to notice very accurately. So I'd say I notice a lot of things. It's part of what I do."

The exceptional essayist, recent recipient of a plum professorship at Penn, is the author of *Class, Siegfried Sassoon's Long Journey, The Boy Scout Handbook and Other Observations, Abroad: British Literary Traveling Between the Wars,* and his "Koran," the National Book Award–winning *Great War and Modern Memory.* Paul Fussell's earliest memory is of shaking the bars of his crib and yowling, "Let me out." He was, he recalls, an impatient child, fast-moving and impudent. Little has changed. Now he would say he's an elitist but not a snob. Perhaps he's a cynic, but he's not certain. On paper, he concedes, he can come across snotty, aristocratic, hostile, sharp, ill-tempered, but in actuality, he believes, he's nicer, more sympathetic than that.

He was the middle one of three children, his beginnings, he says, overprivileged but happy. His father was a corporation lawyer. He was born into the upper-middle class. His mother was a sort of clubwoman of the period. "Very respectable people, churchgoing, nondrinking. And I was that kind of person, too, until the war. And in the war I was a young infantry officer, and my whole life was changed by it. I left California, where I had grown up, and fled East, because I wanted to get away from the family and the whole atmosphere of piety and righteousness. In general, I've tried to turn myself into a non-Californian. Californians are optimistic, and I like to be not optimistic. That's part of my vision of the world."

Let's backtrack. Was he a curmudgeon in the cradle? "Probably, though I'm not now. That's a persona devised by journalism to sell [my] books, I would say. I've always been a critic, yes. One of my favorite characters in intellectual history is Flaubert, who, when he was a little boy, about five, used to keep a notebook in which he would write down, surreptitiously, secretly, the stupid things said by his parents' relatives, those moron aunts and uncles who would come up pompously saying things like 'Nothing wears like leather,' I mean, those clichés. And little Flaubert would nod and smile and then he would depart and write down these things. Well, I was very much like that as a kid," he reveals. "I didn't write them down, but I just sort of treasured them up. And I developed very early a sort of absurd view of the world, that the world is a very comic place."

He says he had an IQ of 160 as a child. Skipping two grades in grammar school, he was aware that some people were smarter, quicker, brighter, while some were slow and dumb. "That was my main distinction between people," he sniffs. "If I had been raised in New York near Carnegie Hall, I would have turned out to be an infant prodigy of the violin. I played the cello for years as a prodigy. I was always doing something that I taught myself—printing, photography, writing. . . . And I was brought up in an atmosphere where I suppose one felt kind of an obligation not to do things the easy way. I mean, it was assumed I would be a doctor or a lawyer or a professor or a judge or a senator or something. From the very start, it was assumed that I was supposed to be *somebody.*"

Was his childhood dull? "Oh no . . . just sort of empty. . . . I'd race yachts, I sailed . . . I went to dances and I took out girls and all that. But it just wasn't *about* anything. It was banal, it was shallow, it was Cal-i-for-nia, it was blond-boy-on-the-beach. . . . Yeah, I was very blond, and I was very tan, and I spent all summer at the beach racing yachts and swimming and surf-riding," he says, contradicting a self-portrait in one of his essays as a "fat and flabby" collegian who avoided "exposing my naked person." The war, he says, "suddenly made me very serious and suggested to me that there was something more to life than California."

Yes, he nearly died in World War II. "I was badly wounded, and I'm 40 percent disabled at the moment. A number of people were killed around me whom I liked very much, and it shook me up very badly. And I probably would have been killed if the Bomb hadn't gone off, the invasion of Japan which I was destined for. You see, I was a rifle platoon leader. I'm a very lucky man, because I survived; I shouldn't have. I was nineteen when I went in the Army, twenty-one when I was wounded. And so the whole end of my youth was involved with the Second World War, and I was badly shaken by it. And it's influenced everything I've done so far."

Before getting his Ph.D. from Harvard on the GI Bill, he spent four months in a French hospital recovering from his injuries. "My career as an ironist was really greatly forwarded by the fact that my leg wound got infected because somebody left a sponge in it and sewed it up. It was some incompetent Army surgeon," he contends. "So ever since then I've been noticing that people who pretend to be good at something very frequently are not. I mean, it's hard to go through an experience like that without developing an ironic sense, or a sense that people's claims to be wonderful are sometimes a little overstated."

He suggests that the war made him a social critic. "It made me see there's so much terribly wrong with the modern world, despite the modern world's fondness for praising itself and advertising how wonderful it is. The modern world is really an awful place, in my view—it's like hell," he declares, after a lengthy disquisition on the evils of the twentieth century. "This is the worst time since the thirteenth century—you know, the terrorism, brutality, contempt for human life. It's a very vicious place to live, this century."

Yet here he is, and live he must. He never had any doubts that he could do what he set out to do. Though when he was young he burned to be a poet, a novelist, a newspaperman, a literary immortal, he insists he always set out to do quite modest things. He expected he would be a professor of English, a schoolmaster, and then retire quietly and read books. "A professor of English, you know—that isn't like being Sartre—it's a fairly modest role in society, interpreting other people's ideas, other people's structures," he snorts.

Could he be an overqualified underachiever? "I don't know, because I don't know what more I could have achieved. Yeah," he concedes, "I suppose I am. . . . I've been very lazy intellectually about many things. Science, technology, I know nothing about them whatever. And in mathematics I'm appallingly dead. I'm very bad at analytic philosophy. Things that take real mental discipline, I shun them. And I shun them for what I'm good at, which is effects, fluency, presentation."

So he's dazzling us with his footwork? "Well, to a degree. Yeah. Yeah. And I recognize that intellectually I'm not as disciplined or as well trained as I should be. I'm very conscious of weakness there. I'm not an original thinker. I'm much more like a rhetorician, or a presenter, like an actor."

Whatever his shortcomings, he retains a superior mien. Naturally, he is almost always bored. "I can't stand movies, because they move at too slow a pace for me. The only thing I can deal with is letterpress. Television just drives me up the wall, because it's addressed to people with IQs of about eighty, and I sit there just pounding on the floor saying, let's go, come on, move ahead, I've got the point! I seldom watch anymore."

Has his intelligence impeded his encounters with the ordinary among us? "Not really, no, because one can pretend one doesn't have it, for the purpose of daily life, like dealing with the people at the garage, and so on. You learn protective coloration socially after a while, so you go on at other people's pace, even though you could go much faster. You're always racing inside, but you learn to control that, because there's nothing you can do about it."

His grown son and daughter think he's eccentric. "Why? Because I don't play golf," he says, chuckling. "And I don't play tennis. I don't play squash. I don't go on the standard weekends. I don't ski, I never have. I'd much rather read or write or talk. Skiing is turning off the mind, and that doesn't interest me. Yeah, look at all that big white expanse, and it's devoid of anything interesting. . . ."

Um, does he have any personal failings? "Oh, a vast number. Anger is the main one. Sloth. I mean, I could go through the Seven Deadly Sins, I've got them all. Yes, anger is very bad at the moment, because I get so annoyed at American society. . . . Ah, the worse things get, the happier I am. And I know it's awful, but that's how it is. I love being alive. I love talking and I love enjoying myself and I love eating and drinking and exercising. And I love being aware of things, even if what I'm aware of makes me angry. I'd rather be angry than dead, in other words. No, I'm not moody at all. No. I'm very cheerful, very optimistic. Yeah, it's one of the paradoxes, yeah, I think everything's terrible," Paul Fussell harrumphs, "and yet I just love being alive."

FEBRUARY 12, 1984

JUDITH MARTIN
She Concentrates on Manners; It's Too Late for Morals

"It's such a surprise to me that I have the *marvelous* advantage of being considered an eccentric just for wearing what my mother told me to wear—white gloves in summer."

Clutching her beloved white gloves, Miss Manners breezes in. With her tendrilly pompadour, peaches-and-cream complexion, and tidy middy dress, the *Washington Post* syndicated etiquette columnist otherwise known as Judith Martin looks charmingly Victorian and utterly anachronistic. But to call Miss Manners an etiquette columnist, even at her most maddeningly arch, is as bereft of sensibility, as barren of description, as horribly unsatisfactory as saying that marzipan is candy. There's a complex richness to her, a perfect melding of style and substance, satire and philosophy, advice and consent, design and destiny.

What we have here, Gentle Readers (as she would say), is a fascinating case of Author-as-Character, and she is decidedly endearing. Not content with being perhaps America's foremost and funniest authority on proper behavior from cradle to grave, she is also *Post* drama critic, author of *Miss Manners' Guide to Excruciatingly Correct Behavior* and novelist (*Gilbert*, a comedy of manners, is due next month). No wonder she once said she would trade places with Madame de Staël, a French writer in the Napoleonic era, "for her independence, her writing ability, her marvelous life with wonderful people of the age passing through her salon, her being the queen bee in both a literary and a political sense."

Judith Martin considers herself an aficionada of the history of civilization. Her life is a conservative paradigm. She's had the same employer for twenty-five years, the same husband for twenty-two years. She started at the *Post* as a copy girl while still in college. She's married to a doctor from Harvard—Robert Martin, now a researcher in biochemical genetics. Though "shy and bookish" early on, she gained poise as a child at grown-up parties when her mother would dispatch her to do "social duty"—to "rescue Mrs. So-and-so who was stranded because she spoke only Flemish."

Because her father was an economist for the United Nations, Judith became cosmopolitan by living in Washington and other great world cities. She wanted to be an archaeologist, though she says she had no patience and was sensitive to the sun; explaining this contradiction, she cites the "Yeatsian concept of the anti-self—he was shy, so he wanted to be a courtier.

"I forget what I was saying," she murmurs, momentarily distracted backstage at Channel 10's "Jane Whitney Show." Her résumé says she majored in Gracious Living at Wellesley—what's that? "That's a generational joke, you know. I find women of my age think that's funny, and women of your age don't know what we're talking about," she says with a laugh. "Wellesley was and is a very strict academic institution. When people used to ask me if I graduated in journalism, we would all be terribly insulted. That's a trade, right? But gracious living was a byword of that era, and it was a great joke at Wellesley, even then. We had teatime in the afternoon, and we wore skirts to dinner. And so I thought I would put it to good use. Actually my degree was in English literature, that wonderfully useful . . . preparation," she says, grinning.

"Am I a dreadfully rude person trying to break out of a rather genteel exterior? No. I mean, I took up etiquette because I have a tremendous love for form and tradition and politeness," she declares. ". . . How do I know etiquette? I have a head just crammed full of all this information, um, much of which nobody wants to know, I mean, all the little esoteric things. So I keep trying to trace how it got there. My excuse is that there are other people who have baseball statistics or the plots of minor operas in *their* heads, and this is what I have. . . ."

Formality was her grandmother's legacy. "She had two great problems in her life. One was that my great-aunt came in a couple consisting of three people, and my grandmother, who considered herself a great lady, kept pointing out that it threw her dinner party seating arrangements off *terribly*, and my aunt would just *have* to decide which gentleman she was bringing and come in a couple of two like everybody else. And the other thing Grandmother did was decide colored stones were vulgar, and got rid of whatever minor things she had in the way of rubies and sapphires, so I am not burdened with them today," she says with a laugh. "So does that give you an idea about my grandmother?"

Was her mother a tyrant for order and discipline? "Um, I suspect what you're really asking is did she run around like a maniac banging our little hands if we did the wrong thing at the dinner table? No, she's a very charming, quiet lady. But she is a teacher. In fact, we have teaching genes all over our family. She always used to say that everyone in our family, the minute you learn something, you can hardly wait to teach it to someone else. So in an unobtrusive way I guess she passed on everything her mother taught here."

Indeed, in photographs Miss Manners appears very severe, as if stiffened by whalebone. But in person she's very soft and warm and pretty. Three years ago, Miss Manners was "born" when Judith Martin was forty and tired of writing personal essays. "I got the term from Victorian and Edwardian etiquette books. There's a rule, which is no longer in effect, that you were supposed to leave something on your plate. . . . The rule was always phrased 'Leave something for Miss Manners.' That used to stand out at me. One day I thought, well now, there's a living. I can go and eat all the leftovers of the rich kids." She laughs. "And so I made myself Miss Manners."

Does she catch herself issuing unsolicited pronouncements at social occasions? "If I do, I hope my husband will slap me smartly a couple of times. There's nothing ruder than giving advice nobody asked for." Is she always a perfect lady? "Well, I certainly try." I apologize for interrupting here with my next question. "You mean, I was about to spill the beans and tell you all the rotten things I've done?" she teases. "No such luck." One reason her marriage has lasted, she says, is that "I've always taken the position, as has he, that we are not socially responsible for each other. If I make a fool of myself, he doesn't have to be embarrassed, and vice versa.

"I believe in politeness in the home. . . . I think it's easier to insult your friends; at least, it's easier to get a new set than it is to get a new family. We don't fight. We went up to his twenty-fifth [college] reunion, and I said, 'I think you'd better introduce me as your second wife, because people will think you have no initiative.' Well, people think they're being very deep and very honest and analyzing one another and critiquing each other. I don't think that's helpful. I think the answer to 'How bad was I last night, dear?' is 'Why, I thought you were charming!'"

Why is it that Miss Manners addresses herself to manners, not morals? "Well, because I have enough trouble with the manners," she says, laughing. "I do not wish to be in the position of making the great moral judgments of the age. . . . I think it is a very difficult moral time, and people are struggling with a lot of changing ideas of morality. If I could just get them to be polite to one another while they do that, I will be satisfied. Let Ann Landers tell them not to sleep with each other. They're not going to listen, so I could hope that they will listen to me say don't call each other names. It's a more modest ambition, shall we say."

If she were ruler of the world, what would she do? "I'd make you a marchioness. Would you like that?" she replies immediately. No—what I meant was how would she change the world? ". . . The natural thing would be to say I'd mandate good manners. But, you know, in Puritan times, questions of manners *were* a matter of law. I mean, you could get jailed for making faces or calling people names. So that system has been tried and it really wasn't too terrific. I don't know that I'd make any significant changes along those lines. . . ."

If you label her Victorian, she doesn't mind—as long as you

know what it means. "There's a great misreading of Victorian history. The popular idea, for instance, that the Victorians had never discovered sex leaves us with a few genealogical questions about how we got here. My experience is that the only things that the Victorians didn't do that we do was talk about it all at the dinner table. So if that is meant as what a poor, narrow, deprived life I lead, I reject the notion. . . ."

What does Miss Manners think about adultery? "Ah, for whom?" For married people? "I'm sure some of them have a marvelous time," she says with a laugh, "and I'm sure some of them have a dreadful time." For herself, then? "What Miss Manners thinks about her own private life is that ladies don't discuss such things." All right, then, has she known, and suffered, embarrassment? "I decided fairly early in life that I would give up certain emotions—guilt, jealousy, boredom, and embarrassment. Four big fat wastes of time. Which is not to say that you shouldn't be ashamed of yourself if you've done something wrong. But I'm talking about this unspecified guilt. I think that's a big, tiresome bore.

"So I simply do not get embarrassed. I'm not saying that I haven't had outrageous accidents, but I refuse to be embarrassed by them." We coax her to elucidate. "Oh, once I was sitting in a real nice restaurant, on a banquette, and I stuck a fork into a very tough duck, which took off from my plate. Actually I'm not the heroine of the story, the gentleman in the next booth is. I sat there a little dumbfounded for a minute, because a duck had never flown off my plate before. And a man came around and said, 'Pardon me, madame, is this your duck?' And I said, 'Why, yes, I do believe it is.' And he gave it back to me. He was charming. I got my duck back a little worse for wear, but everybody lived happily ever after."

SEPTEMBER 12, 1982

JOHN BARTH
Can This Be Our Best Writer?

"I have only three things worth saying," warns novelist John Barth, whose fiction is as florid as his disposition is drab.

Can this be "the Rudolf Nureyev of prose"? Our "comic genius of the highest order"? "The best writer of fiction we have, and one of the best we've ever had"? Is this the mind that snagged the National Book Award? Or, as Peggy Lee once lamented, "Is That All There Is?"

Churlishly cryptic, elusively erudite, John Barth, at forty-six, has come home to teach creative writing at his alma mater, Johns Hopkins University. A ruddy, balding man with a Fuller brush of a mustache, he wears black-rimmed glasses, gray crew-neck, corduroys, and work boots and seems to talk simultaneously through his pigeon-beak nose and clenched lips.

John Barth is fascinated with the technology of storytelling, the physics of fiction. He transforms daily life into flamboyant mythology and mythology into domestic comedy. His novels are perpetual-notion machines—big, bawdy, boisterous visitations of wit, self-parody, slapstick, manic satire, esoteric puns, and multiple anachronisms. In *Giles Goat-Boy* the world is a collection of university campuses and the "hero" is sired by a computer out of a virgin—so much for theology and academia. In *The Sot-Weed Factor* colonial Maryland is the backdrop for a tale of Pocahontas so blue Boccaccio would blush. In *Chimera*, his prizewinner, he created a far-out equation of writer's block and sexual impotence.

But meeting John Barth is, at best, anticlimactic. He's deadpan, slightly stuffy, and very much in a hurry. Like a good student, he repeats each question word for word, and answers at interminable length. "I've rather prided myself on leading a rather transparent life," he says, bristling a bit when I ask him about rumors of his eccentricity. "That bothers me, because I've tried to be as inconspicuous and colorless as possible." I'd say he succeeded admirably. "I'm a homebody," he drones, "and while no doubt my ego is as large as the next, I'm very uncomfortable around writers whose egos and life-styles are a prominent part of their fiction, like Mailer and Hemingway. There's no authorial swashbuckling for me," he declares. The personality of John Barth has nothing to do with his fiction. "On the other hand, recluses make me nervous," he complains. "To fly too inconspicuously from interviews and any kind of public appearances—like J. D. Salinger does—that makes me nervous, too," he repeats. "If you have to expend more and more energy to belligerently and artificially preserve your privacy, that can turn into an artistically dangerous kind of crankiness. It can be as preoccupying as self-promotion, and you must be harder and harder to live with.

"I did not find it unpleasant when nobody was paying very much attention to my books," he says. "Certainly I found it more pleasant when they began to. Not just economically but for reasons of simple gratification. The kind of writer I like best is, when he begins to attract some kind of attention, he doesn't fly from it. Too ardently to flee can be just as vain as too ardently to pursue."

Even in ordinary conversation, whatever that is, John Barth is so arch and convoluted his real meaning is often difficult to decipher. How did he feel about winning the coveted National Book Award? "I take prizes with exactly this much seriousness," he says expansively. "My definition of a worthwhile literary prize is that now and then one will be awarded to a writer *despite* the fact that he deserves it. If I were God, designing society," he intones, "I think I would put prizes in it for artists, dear me.

"Let me tell you how I write." He leans forward. "I've been writing for a quarter century now, and my output remains rather steady. I work on one project at a time, until it's completed, whether that takes a month like some of my stories, or seven years like some of my novels. I've never been able to think about the next thing I'm going to write while I'm writing."

Has he ever used stimulants? "I used to use chemicals"—he pauses—"but that frightens me now. I was younger then, and a healthy growing person can stand a certain amount of chemical abuse. I found that over very long book projects, what got lost for me was a basic element of suspense, for I planned carefully and knew where the story was going, so after the third year of composing I was tired of it.

"But a certain number of sentences had to be manufactured with a certain amount of energy and incidental inspiration. I found every two hours I'd lose my alertness and get drowsy and felt myself falling asleep over my own manuscripts, since I knew how the story was going to end. So my doctor prescribed Dexamil," he says, "I think it was an amphetamine and a tranquilizer. I'm not very sophisticated about chemicals," he insists, "but that's what I believe it is."

Nevertheless John Barth maintains his basic orientation is "antichemical." "Never mind the dangers for people doing things like driving," he says sternly. "In the Air Force they'd give these things to pilots who flew a mission, came back safely, and then missed the end of the runway. But for people sitting at desks doing what I was doing, the danger is that under the influence of amphetamines, so many things seem interesting to do that you're very likely to fritter away your time changing snow tires on your car or write seven other books.

"Anyway, to be a novelist is a stupefying kind of discipline," he sighs. "Now I keep alert by leading a healthier kind of life, I work shorter times than I used to, and I'm readier to turn away from what I'm doing to do other things, like exercise, sailing, skiing, going to bed earlier. That's right," he cracks, "I've become wholesome.

"My gift seems not to make very complicated things simple," he says, explaining what is already apparent, "but to make quite simple things fairly complicated. I like complication"—

he nods—"I like it for sporting reasons. You don't come to my books as you could come to *Jaws*. The reader of my book has likely cut his teeth on, you know, the giants of twentieth-century fiction—Proust, Joyce, Mann, Faulkner. So at my age, the most complicated task I can set myself is the task of becoming much simpler.

"I want my next book to be simple, but I'm afraid it won't be. I want it to be short, but I'm afraid it won't be. I want it to be finished, but it's not. I want it to delight people who don't have any terribly special literary training, but maybe it won't. No, I haven't retrenched in defining my audience, but perhaps I've changed my notion of what I wish it could be. I don't want to limit my audience to a tinier and tinier elite.

"I still like plot in fiction the same way I like melody in music," says Barth, whose boyhood idols were Stan Kenton and Duke Ellington. As a young professor, he played drums in neighborhood jazz combos, and he once attended the prestigious Juilliard School of Music. "I was going to be an orchestrator," he recalls. "What I found out in about two weeks there was that I was a talented amateur. But I believe that ambition to be an orchestrator, rather than a composer or performer, is significant. For often I feel about my writing that what I do is in the nature of orchestration. I'm happiest taking a narrative or classical myth and then orchestrating—arranging and reworking—to my purpose."

He once threatened to write a story about all the stories he had ever read, ten thousand stories in one. "That's a graduate student's nightmare," he sighs. "I remember as a student realizing how naïve, how unsophisticated I was about literature, and resolving I would read all the short stories ever published. So I tried. How far did I get? As far as realizing they were being published much faster than I could ever consume them. But I certainly did read hundreds, perhaps thousands," he considers.

"But I'm a dreadfully slow reader. I read *The New York Times* at the same rate I'd read T. S. Eliot's poems. I find I can't read any faster than I would read out loud, it's a habit so ingrained," he confesses. "I absolutely can't skim."

Heavens! At that rate it might take John Barth twenty years to read one of his own 800-page books.

FEBRUARY 22, 1976

SHIRLEY CONRAN
She Wrote a Book She Won't Let Her Own Mother Read

"They've been making a fuss about me in England and in Europe for a long time now. Somebody in America last year said to me, he didn't know I'd written this book, he said, you know, I think you're the sort of person who could easily be famous. And I said, well, if I want to be famous, all I have to do is catch a plane to London."

By the time you read this, Shirley Conran, the witty, perceptive British writer, may already be famous here. "This book" is *Lace*, her first novel, a steamy excursion into female sexuality. ("I got so cross with men getting it wrong," she says. "I got cross with D. H. Lawrence. I got cross with Ernest Hemingway.") Simon and Schuster says it purchased the book for a staggering sum while it was still in rough draft, and soon you will follow the fortunes of her four fortyish heroines in an ABC miniseries as well.

So it is that Shirley Conran, middle-aged feminist, former newspaper editor and TV personality, founder of a fabric firm, author of *Superwoman*, a clever guide to household management, and mother of Lady Di's favorite dress designer, is sitting in the New York office of her high-powered agent (who has also represented such hot literary properties as Spiro Agnew and Chuck Barris). Smoothing her red silk dress down over her ample, curvy hips, Shirley assures me her book is "charmingly romantic." Ah yes. The book, clearly destined for best-sellerdom, contains on page 281 a singularly romantic scene involving a man, a woman, and a goldfish. Small wonder she won't let her own mother read it.

But before you dismiss Shirley Conran as a smarmy matron on the commercial make, before you subject her to an onslaught of knowing winks and leers, listen. She's an original: "Really, when I look my most sophisticated is wearing a bathing hat for diving, because then I look bald as an egg. . . ." And: "I very much distrust the state of being in love. I think it's rather like being drunk, that you don't see things clearly." Listen as she tells how she's painted in Casablanca and gone in a Greyhound bus across America, how she's lived in a French country farmhouse and a five-story London brownstone, how she now makes her home in a Monte Carlo flat—"straight ahead to go skiing, turn left to go sunbathing, turn right to go to the Italian Riviera." Listen.

"Well, there's such a lot to tell," she says. ". . . I remember my first fur coat. It was white ermine. I was about two, and I remember stroking this downy little thing." Was her father well off? "Yes. He was a dry cleaner. It amazes me that in England nobody believes that. You know what I mean? Who shows off about their father being a dry cleaner? It wasn't as if I was saying my father was a duke, you know?

"When my father married my mother, he was considered to have married beneath him. And his mother, who was a retired headmistress—do you say headmistress over here?—well, she used to absolutely terrify my mother. And when she died, she left my father a lot of land and farms and things. And he turned to my mother, and this was very typical of him, and said, well, Mum was never very nice to you, and you always tried to be nice to her, so we're going to sell it all up and buy jewelry for you. And one morning they took a shopping trip to the best jewelers in London, and they came back and my mother was dripping with diamonds. And that was it. He spent the whole lot on her."

Though she grew up with maids and gardeners and housekeepers, she says she was a worried child. "Well, the war was going on, and we kept on being evacuated, and I had to look after the other children. It was a worrying time. You know, you worried about your father getting blown to bits. In fact, my sister and I were machine-gunned once. And I was most indignant. Most indignant." Was she also bloody? "Oh no, they missed us, inefficient Germans. But I was just indignant!" she repeats. "How dare they? And we were bombed out twice. But really we were very lucky because we didn't have anybody in our immediate family killed.

"My parents were not very good at their timing during the war. Whenever they thought it was safe to bring us back, they brought us back, whereupon the Battle of Britain would start. And we lived right next to the airport from which the pilots went out. So it was pretty noisy around there. Whenever it was calm, they sent us away, and whenever they brought us back, battles started again. . . . I think if I had been older, it would have been romantic fun. I think I would have enjoyed the war."

She attributes her achievements largely to attending St. Paul's Girls School in London, which, she says, "trains the elite women of England. We had been trained to work by ourselves and never waste a minute and just get on with things. They told us to get it right the first time. You might just as well get it right the first time as the second time. No dummy runs. Give it a bit of forethought." But a subsequent finishing school in Switzerland "was very bad for me," she says, laughing. "I mean, it encouraged laziness and sloth, and I must say, I took to laziness and sloth like a duck to water. I did absolutely nothing for a year except eat cream cakes and chocolates and tea. And in retrospect, I was vexed to know that I wasted this time. But in fact, I still have friends I made when I was there. My first boyfriend, who I met when I was there, still phones me up for half an hour every Tuesday wherever I am in the world.

"I believe it's just as tough to start at the top as the bottom," she declares, "so you might as well start at the top. I'm the eldest of six, and we're a very close family. And three of us became millionaires and three of us married millionaires. I did both. But I think this happened more or less by accident. I mean, I think one doesn't go into something to make money. You go into something to do it right, you see. I mean, if I was interested only in making money, I wouldn't have sweated so over being a designer and being a journalist. I would have probably gone in the dry-cleaning business like my daddy. We all know that dry cleaning costs a fortune. But do you see the point?"

Yes. At twenty-three, after studying sculpture in art school, she married Terence Conran, who would become one of the world's most successful design tycoons. That marriage ended in divorce, as did another. She has become a millionaire in her own right through business investments. "I was going to have a face-lift with some of the money from my book, but I couldn't spare the time. I once said to my son, Jasper, who is obviously very conscious of these things, when he was sixteen and we were doing the dishes together, I said casually out of the blue, 'I'm relying on you to tell me when I need a face-lift.' And we went on chattering away. About half an hour later, he looked up at the ceiling, turned bright red, and said, 'Now.' 'What do you mean, now?' I asked. And he just said in an agonized voice, 'Now!' So I burst into tears. That was about ten years ago. Now I look forward to having a second sort of shot at things."

What she wanted most as a child really had nothing to do with money. "We weren't spoiled. We couldn't be, because there was a war on. I always wanted a bicycle. And a coconut. And a banana. A banana was all we wanted in the war. There was no oranges, no ice cream, nothing. After a banana, what I really wanted was actually very naughty. It was joining up invisible people to the local lending library, so I could take out extra books. I read my way around the library, book by book. I read Saki and Oscar Wilde and Evelyn Waugh when I was thirteen. . . ."

"I don't think I really care too much about money," she muses. "There was a certain time in my life that was awful, feeling that my children"—sons now twenty-six and twenty-two—"were penalized because I didn't have enough money" as a single parent. "I think you feel the lack of it more genuinely if you've got children. I mean, anybody can live without mink and pearls. I mean, it isn't very difficult. People have asked me, what are you going to spend it on? The answer is,

I'm probably not going to spend it. Because I'm already living the way I want to live. Which has nothing to do with having X amount of money or twice that amount. . . .

"I'm more than anything for people doing what they like doing, and not doing what they don't like doing. That's the basic pitch of my life. . . . I really don't want to have on my tombstone the inscription 'She was a good duster,' you know. I really would rather get out there and write best-seller books or go around the world or ride a camel across the Sahara than stay home and vacuum. And it is possible. And you don't have to be aggressive to do it, you know. You just have to decide you want to," Shirley Conran says, "and then take a deep breath, hold your nose, and jump in at the deep end."

AUGUST 29, 1982

MIGUEL PIÑERO
Failure as a Criminal, Success as an Artist

"Don't worry, I won't steal your tape recorder, and all you guys walking down dark alleys are safe, too," says the small young man with sad eyes and drooping mustache. He puffs out his bush with a comb and pirouettes in front of a mirror reflecting a cluttered apartment at Fourth and Bainbridge, then continues.

"Look, I don't know what I've done that's dangerous. I'm really tired of this whole 'Puerto Rican ex-con drug addict' thing. That's gone. I'm tired of seeing it in print. I'm more than that," complains twenty-nine-year-old Miguel Piñero, "America's most celebrated new playwright." Certainly he has more than his share of labels to bear: ex-burglar, ex-shoplifter, ex–heroin addict, ex–drug dealer, ex–gang leader, have I forgotten any?

Oh yes. Miguel Piñero is celebrated—or damned—as "the first Puerto Rican from the streets of New York to write a play that established itself in a major Manhattan theater." *Short Eyes*, which received the New York Critics Circle and Obie awards, brutally re-creates the cellblock murder of a child molester.

One of the most visible things Miguel Piñero has done since moving to Philly earlier this year is play God. That is, God a.k.a. an attendant in Bruce Jay Friedman's *Steambath*, at a café theater in South Street. "That was fun," he says remotely, as if he couldn't care less. "Anyway, as a writer I play God all the time." Yeah. A God who's spent seven years behind bars. A God who's been busted "seven or eight times" on charges ranging from armed robbery to obscenity. A notion of God not inappropriate for the era.

"This is the new Miguel Piñero," he proclaims, sipping a Budweiser and sitting back in a tapestry chair. "I used to be known as a liar," he's said, and "I've always been a loudmouth. Nowadays, if I have twenty dollars in my pocket, it doesn't go for drugs. I take care of essentials—rent, typewriter ribbon, paper, keeping the machine clean. And this isn't the way I used to dress. I used to dress 'outlaw'—dirty all the time. I'm dressing like this from now on," he says, pointing to his clean white undershirt and navy polyester slacks.

Once a month he reports to his parole officer. In between, Miguel Piñero's perfecting his artistic hustle—"starting grassroots theater projects" for the Puerto Rican community, holding acting and poetry workshops, and trying to bring his friend and mentor, influential producer Joe Papp, to Philadelphia.

Miguel Piñero is a wiry five foot seven and alternates between describing himself as "tall, dark, handsome, debonair" and "short, ugly, and fat." He likes to think of himself as a Renaissance man. What qualifies him for that inflated epithet? "The fact that I decide to call myself that," he says pugnaciously, squelching any further argument. Since his 1973 release from Sing Sing, he's edited an anthology of young Puerto Rican poets, written almost a dozen plays, performed with a prisoner theater group, and appeared in a forthcoming Dick Shawn flick.

"Look, I can always go back to New York if I want to—it's only two hours away," he says, cracking his knuckles. But New York was dangerous; he claims he had suffered "four stabbings and five shootings," because they thought he was rich. It must have been strange to suddenly find himself on the receiving end of crime as well as the giving end. "When I first got here," he recalls, "I grabbed a furnished room in North Philly, and I got ripped off. My typewriter, a TV, a record player, and a leather coat that was given to me as a present," he says regretfully. "The guy left me his coat—it's over there.

"I like Mozart," he says abruptly, putting on a record and waiting for me to challenge him. "I have me a nice beer, a good joint, my head is mellow, I got a play working over there in my typewriter, I listen to Mozart, and I can just see all these characters running around in my head. Right now I see a girl preparing herself for a visit from two guys.

"Sometimes I'll be writing, like a character I got now, Pan-ama Smith, suddenly I'm ready to go onto something else but I can't, he has something else very heavy to say. That's the only thing that frustrates me, when they're arguing in my head and the dialogue goes so fast I can't get my fingers to move that fast and the keys all get stuck and I end up beating the typewriter." He snaps his fingers and makes a series of machine-destroying noises. "I broke three typewriters that way.

"The play that Joe Papp's doing in New York now, *The Sun Always Shines for the Cool*, took me four days to write because it was just coming out of me real fast, all those characters moving around. It usually takes maybe five or six days," he announces.

With just a seventh grade education and his first "brush with the law" at nine or ten, how did he develop his extraordinary verbal skills? "Duh?" he deadpans. "When I was about thir-teen, I started writing letters for guys in jail: 'My dearest, my darling, as I sit here looking at your picture, taking pen in hand, my heart is full of thoughts of you.'" He laughs. "You know, it was a form letter.

"And I read lots of Marvel Comics. That's how I picked up dialogue. Have you read the new Superman-Spiderman comic book? It's really great, man, Clark Kent is shouting, 'Where's the phone booth, where's the phone booth,' and the new mod-ern phone booths are just a shelf on the wall!"

Miguel Piñero never apologizes for his past. Most of his crimes, he insists, "were against property, not people." But he did mug people. "Yeah, but I never hurt nobody," he claims. "I had a nice way of doing it. If I came up to you in a dark alley, you would be scared to death, right? But if you're stand-ing at a bus stop and I come up wearing a suit and sneakers, very conservative, you wouldn't expect it, and when I was done I'd say, 'Have a nice night.'"

Radical chic is still with us, and the same people that placed him behind bars are inviting him to their cocktail parties. "Mostly they want to hear dramatic things, what it was like going into a big bank and maybe shooting it out, stuff like that. But I don't want to talk about that," he says quietly.

Does he see himself as a successful artist or a failed criminal? "Oh, wow!" he sighs. "A successful artist. Because being a criminal is an art, too. Let me show you something," he says, bringing out a plaque hand-painted with the following quote: 'I never intended to be anything but a gangster but I was such a lousy criminal I decided to be a creative person.'

"After *Short Eyes*, I went through a lot of changes. Suddenly you're expected not to create but produce like a factory. I have . . . poetry being published, and one poem from that period has a line: 'suicide / is the most sincere form of self-criticism.'

"I found myself contemplating different types of suicide. You know, a good OD; overdose is a good way to go. Right after Tennessee Williams wrote *A Streetcar Named Desire* he went to Mexico and I guess that's where I got the idea to visit Mexico. I spent two weeks with the Yaqui Indians and learned a lot about myself. I learned I liked myself too much to criticize myself so heavy. And I also went to look for [ex-convict/playwright] Jean Genet in Africa. I went all over, to France, and was told he was in Morocco or Tangiers, but I couldn't find him. I thought he could give me something. I've always learned from people who have lived that way."

I ask Miguel Piñero about prison experiences with sex. "Well, you live in a homosexual environment," he hedges. "My experiences were limited. Yeah, I had a kid I used to be with," he admits gruffly. "Sort of like a lover. When I was on Riker's Island for four years and we were both seventeen. He was a clerk and I was captain of the clothes box. We were together all the time.

"Finally we fell in love. I was willing to give my life for him and he was willing to give his for me. I don't know whether it was our upbringing, you know, being Puerto Rican macho and all that, but we never got into a sexual thing," he says, "though we had plenty opportunity always being together. It was weird.

It was a real love affair I had with this dude," he says pensively, then jumps up abruptly and shouts.

"You know why I carry this cross?" Miguel Piñero brandishes a silver crucifix. "It repels overzealous psychiatrists, priests, Jesus freaks, cops. When they start spouting off I hold up my cross and say, 'Back, back!' You gotta keep it in your pocket, ready, like a weapon," he instructs, bugging his eyes in mock horror.

Obviously the amulet doesn't work against journalists.

APRIL 4, 1976

BETTY FRIEDAN
"I'm Not Any Beauty Contest Winner," Says Feminism's Matriarch Emerita

"I like men. We're not all braless man-haters," Betty Friedan exclaims in a throaty Tallulah voice, silver-coin earrings tinkling. "I like a lot of men. I love some. And I don't think the others are all that horrible as a class. Listen, you really gotta go soon 'cause I must pack. Did the cleaner bring my dress back yet?"

From a royal-blue couch in her Lincoln Center high-rise, Betty Friedan, matriarch emerita of the modern women's movement, holds court. A departing *Newsday* writer wonders if the former founding president of NOW, draped in a tenty polka-dot dress, will dare to sample Saint Laurent's "new" ethnic couture. She is leaving, momentarily, for an East Hampton weekend. It is controlled chaos.

On the wall is an idealized portrait of Betty Friedan as a handsome, raven-haired young woman. But at fifty-five she is pleasantly, earthily imperfect. There's a run creeping down her stocking, her leg is skinned, and when she plumps a pillow, dust comes out in a cloud. Salt-and-pepper hair softly frames her tanned Hermione Gingold face, her mouth carefully outlined in, yes, pink lipstick. Black sandals set off slim ankles. She is exuberantly energetic.

In 1963 Betty Friedan published what became the bible of women's lib, or at least its Old Testament. *The Feminine Mystique* changed millions of lives, most dramatically her own. The "New York housewife who wrote her book on her dining room table," who had a maid to help with her three children and an ad-exec hubby, has been a divorcée for the past seven years. She says "the movement" has strayed too far from its original "martyred housewife" constituency to concentrate on such peripheral issues as vaginal orgasm and lesbian politics. Recently she wrote her second book, a historical memoir, *It Changed My Life*. Unlike her more radical "sisters," Betty Friedan will discuss "the sex-role revolution" with anyone who will listen, or read—at the U.S. Air Force Academy, in *True* magazine, at an exclusive Philadelphia men's club, even at the Vatican, where she once handed Pope Paul a women's equality symbol, saying, "Here's a different kind of cross."

She has always been provocative. "As a fifth-grader back in Peoria," she recalls, "I organized the Baddy-Baddy Club. When I gave a signal, everyone dropped their books on the floor. There was a substitute teacher we didn't like and we drove this teacher mad, mad, mad." She claps with glee. "I was summoned to the principal's office, and he said I had great capacity for leadership, I must use it for good, not evil," she mimics. "Under dire threat we disbanded, and formed a new club, and yes, we played kissing games."

But she had a lonely adolescence. "I was Jewish and didn't get into a sorority. I felt very rejected and would go read poetry on a tombstone in a graveyard, and do the Emily Dickinson bit much more than I felt like doing. I read an awful lot. Escape. I'm not all that much introverted, you know," she sighs. "I guess I would have liked to be an actress, had I been prettier."

Doesn't she have an IQ of "nearly 200"? "Well, it's horrible that I knew this. I didn't realize how high it was. Either 180 or something above. I tell you, there are certain dumb things that are ingrained. Part of me wanted to be kittenish and, you know, taken care of," she admits. "I was smarter than most of the boys, the first and only girl that took physics. I was very bad in mechanics, though. The football team did all my experiments and I did all their math. So when I was valedictorian, the football team cheered.

"But to this day I am absolutely a moron about electric fuses and dishwashers and wires and washing machines, any kind of machine a competent woman should know about. I have no idea what to do if something breaks," confesses Friedan, who graduated from Smith summa cum laude in psychology.

"And you've heard that horrible, ignominious story about the typewriter." She shudders. "I haven't typed for thirteen years. For some reason, after writing the first chapter of *The Feminine Mystique*, I handwrote the rest and I liked what I wrote. I haven't touched the typewriter since, and my handwriting is so bad. I typed all through my newspaper and magazine days, but I'm just not good mechanically," she insists. "I give it to a typist. Fiction writers do that, good novelists. Uh, this is strictly a literary phenomenon. I'm so embarrassed. Listen, let's not make too much of this.

"'Cause I'm kicking myself now. It's like not driving. It's an imprisoning thing not to drive," she says. If there is a woman who would want to get somewhere under her own steam, I imagine it would be Betty Friedan. "I hate driving. I stopped as soon as we moved back into the city. Now I should start again. I was never good. I drove too slow." And talked? "That's the trouble, see. No, please, I know men are like that too. I have a funny kind of mind, and I'm not very mechanical. Also I have some excuse, my right eye and my left eye are discrepant. But I swore this summer I'd try. Then I became the eccentric lady on the yellow bicycle. Actually, I was thinking of getting an electrified golf cart and putting a fringed awning on top," she quips.

I ask her about her twenty-two years as a wife. "Uh, about my marriage." She hesitates. "It isn't so much that I don't want to talk about it. It's that my ex, if he's mentioned by name, gets infuriated and threatens to sue. He has a fit when I discuss him. But I'm not against marriage," she stresses. "When we were first married and I earned more than he did, that embarrassed me so much that sometimes I, uh, felt so peculiar about it I'd lose my purse. It was so stupid, an unconscious thing, always feeling guilty about the money I earned. I wouldn't lose my purse now!"

Why is she called hard to get along with? "I'm called a lot of things," she agrees. Like middle-of-the-road, hopelessly bourgeois, namby-pamby, heterosexist. "I plead guilty." She smiles patiently. "Some women hate my guts. I have enemies. What's so strange about that? For different reasons, both Gloria [Steinem] and Bella [Abzug] wanted to get rid of me." Betty Friedan denies published reports that she was jealous of Gloria Steinem's "blond, pretty" looks.

"The image of me given in the press is of some big monstrous ugly woman and they always make that contrast between me and Gloria. Actually, I'm not nearly as cool, calculated, and steely as she is," she coos. It has been said that Friedan pioneered and Steinem beautified, that Friedan was the battering ram that made it possible for Steinem to be graceful.

"Look, I'm very human and I've got my share of feelings. I'm not any beauty contest winner. I use my hands when I talk. My mouth is always open. It is possible to take a picture of me where I look like a monster," she says. "I get so sick of people coming up to me and saying I don't look like my pictures, and finally I realized they were saying I am not nearly as ugly and jowly and grotesque as they thought I was. Yes, they say, you really should do something about those pictures. Nobody wants to be ugly, but I don't feel I am. How would you react?" Her brown eyes challenge me.

"In a sense, I am the conscience of the women's movement," she announces as she walks to her bedroom to begin packing. "I can't be controlled. I can't be manipulated. I can't be co-opted. The women know that. The women also know if I think something is really wrong, really dangerous, I'll say so. And I'll say it loud and clear and I don't care what names I'm called. I'm not afraid to speak the truth. And they can trust me. Some women would like me to drop dead, would like to push me out, because I still have a very powerful influence.

"As I look back now, I should have fought harder," she says, echoing earlier regrets that she wasn't adept at power games and she couldn't manipulate. "I didn't, and I didn't win. I was outfoxed and outmaneuvered. I shouldn't have slunk away. I wasn't ready to die and move out. I mean, time and time again I've started an organization and then bowed out. I didn't care that much about controlling it.

"Probably I am a great woman, do you know that? I don't know how I got that way." She tosses her head and laughs.

"The combination of my problems and my strengths. My brains and my passion and my energy and my frustrations and my superb education and"—she catches her breath—"my skills and my causes.

"Somehow or other I've used it all, finally, in a way that enabled women to change their lives. I used all the pain and all the joy to go beyond myself, to serve others. It's more marvelous and exhilarating than being on talk shows," she bubbles.

"Oh, you never know what to take on this stupid weekend," Betty Friedan complains, running back and forth between two closets and cramming brightly colored dress after dress into an already bulging overnight bag. "The trouble is, I'm going to get sweaty."

OCTOBER 3, 1976

TOM McHALE
"The World's Worst Irishman"

"I'm the world's worst Irishman. I can't write if I drink. Four or five scotches and I get absolutely lousy, tired, and witless very quickly." Ladies and gentlemen, it's Tom McHale, "one of this country's more brilliant young writers of serious fiction"—or so they say, safely sipping chablis in his Bellevue suite and trying not to sound witless.

Here he is, clean-cut, athletic Tom McHale—a ringer for Robert Kennedy—who at thirty-two has made a literary career out of skewering his mother church's supposed crimes against childhood—"hypocrisy, regimentation, and intolerance." The same Tom McHale, late of Temple (pre-med), Penn (creative writing), and the Department of Public Assistance (caseworker), whose first two savagely comic novels, *Principato* and *Farragan's Retreat*, are set in Philadelphia streets teeming with gangsters and superpatriots, boozers and bullies.

Tom McHale, I discover, really reads better than he talks. With his close-cropped brown hair and blue eyes offset by a pigeon-gray turtleneck and tan corduroy slacks, he reminds me of a tweedy book-jacket model. You know, someone rented from the William Morris Agency to pose prettily for photos who—*surprise*—suddenly finds himself stuck with giving an interview; so he does, dutifully but dully.

He's made all the right moves for a writer. Paris and Spain, bankrolled by a "doting old aunt." The University of Iowa's "literary finishing school" on Philip Roth's say-so. Rustic New England retreats, a National Book Award nomination, and this year a Guggenheim Fellowship which feeds him, so he only has to teach one day a week in Boston.

"I wrote"—he underscores the word with a bite of shrimp—"in the beginning to exorcise certain personal demons. Now I

166

write because I don't know what else to do. Besides"—he grins—"I have mortgages, places in Boston and Vermont. I guess it's true, though, that you are a born writer in the sense that you wouldn't do anything else. And except for violent physical things like building walls and repairing cars, there's not really anything else I want to do."

Three years ago Tom McHale was compared to heavies like Philip Roth and Joseph Heller. Has he borne out that promise? "No." He laughs, balancing his glass on his knee. "I was bemused when they said that. Did I find it burdensome to live up to? No, because there's nothing I *have* to live up to, no sense in me that I must be at a certain place at a certain time doing a certain thing."

Right now McHale faces a dilemma. "When my earlier books used an Irish Catholic Philadelphia family framework, critics suggested, 'Maybe he's purged his venom and can move on to something new.' I think I have used them up, and I'm either mellowing or taking another look at the whole tradition. But when I did move on to something else in my third book, *Alinsky's Diamond*, they were disappointed, saying it was unfamiliar terrain, that I should stick to what I know.

"Now I'm kinda superstitious about using the word 'Philadelphia.' I'm thinking of sticking it in for luck in every book. It's curious"—he crunches a cracker—"but Philadelphia wasn't mentioned anywhere in *Alinsky*, about an international diamond intrigue. I wonder if I had given them something just a little bit familiar, the book might have succeeded better," he speculates.

"I always start with a bizarre idea and a very simple plot, and I expect to finish it in five months and walk away with another check. But then I get terribly bogged down and uncertain about what I'm doing, and my characters begin to grow on me. I drink loads of coffee and usually lose twenty pounds at a shot when I'm writing.

"I think it's fair to say, though a lot of writers won't admit it"—he looks up at the crystal chandelier—"that you're fulfilling your own fantasies through your characters, that you're always the protagonist in a faceted way. I write about men

seeking balance, stability, amid the madness that often surrounds them."

Someone said facetiously, I tell him, that the Irish either
fight or write. "I fight, too." He laughs, flexing a skinned finger. "I got a new car, a Citroën, and it's my think tank. I like
to take long fifty-mile drives and think about my writing, especially if I come to a snag at the typewriter. The only problem
is, since I've gotten this car, I've noticed it antagonizes certain
people who might be easily threatened by an expensive French
sports car.

"I was coming back home to Boston the other week and a
guy in a new Mercedes convertible was right on my back,
flashing his lights, beeping, tailgating me for miles. I tried to
let him pass, but he wouldn't. When we stopped at a toll
booth, I got out of the car, boiling mad, and went back to see
what was happening. This real greaser, a middle-aged guy with
a silly cap, gets out of the other car.

"I nailed him right there and broke my hand. Glass hands,"
he says ruefully. "I knocked him into his car, and the girl he
was with—I guess he had been trying to impress her—started
screaming." Who was McHale trying to impress? "No one. I
was just trying to get home," he says, leveling. "I can't remember the last time I was in a fight."

Of course it all goes back to his youth. "Now I better watch
what I say." He grins, shifting in his chair. "I grew up in a small
Pennsylvania town near Scranton named Avoca—two thousand people. My father worked in the post office. I went to
parochial schools and a Jesuit high school. Everybody in town
seemed Catholic, pro–Joe McCarthy, and very patriotic. I
can't remember the things that made my stomach grind. I'm
trying to cloud the issue, but everything is a blur.

"We almost lived in a theocracy. I can't tell you how many
funerals and viewings I've been to in my life. Grotesque. We
learned by rote and no one was tempted to think. Of course, I
became well disciplined, and that's helped me as a writer," he
concedes. "But I felt the regimentation was kind of absurd and
began to be interested in ideas that weren't looked on favorably

in school. I began to read ravenously—James Joyce, Balzac, Tolstoy.

"I never knew an un-Catholic until as a teenager I worked summers as a waiter in the Poconos at a Jewish resort called Tamamint. I learned who Lenny Bruce was." He laughs, munching on a shrimp. "What a great thing to learn at a time like that. Obviously I was attracted to him because he was irreverent. It never dawned on me that he was Jewish. When I met Jews, I didn't know they were Jews and I certainly never knew blacks till I came to Philadelphia to attend Temple. It's incredible."

He abandoned his childhood dreams of becoming a doctor after getting a biochemistry degree from Temple in '63. "It annoyed me that I was doing it for money and security. I realized I just wanted to bum around for a while, not take a job or go to grad school, just get the hell out of the States. I had introduced two Israelis to each other, and went over for their wedding. I ended up staying a year and a half, living and working on a kibbutz. There were," he jokes, "no Irish Catholics around. I was suddenly safe among all those Jews."

Is he bitter? Does he feel maimed or scarred? "No, I'm actually very happy about what happened. If I hadn't gone through that childhood that messed me up, I'd be terribly afraid that I'd wake up at forty and do myself in out of absolute despair and disillusionment. But having experienced that anguish at an earlier age has helped considerably because I'm able to set out and define my goals and where I want to go and not be the victim of an inertia, a predictability." He gets up, picks up his bags. I'm afraid he'll leave me in mid-sentence.

Who's the strangest person he's ever met? I ask Tom McHale on a whim, trying to catch his attention, before he leaves for the airport limousine waiting downstairs.

He muses for a minute, then answers, "Me."

DECEMBER 15, 1974

Note: Tom McHale committed suicide March 30, 1982.

JEAN SHEPHERD
What's Jean Shepherd Got Against Woody Allen?

When I was this kid in a small New Jersey town, after it was supposed to be bedtime, I'd listen to the radio in the dark, so my mother would think I was asleep. If I wasn't listening to the Yankees, or a strange kind of music where the notes didn't exactly follow each other, I'd be listening to Jean Shepherd, a late-night storyteller who moved me so powerfully with his words that I grew up wanting to be a writer.

WOR, his New York radio station, had such a strong signal that it carried Jean Shepherd's flat midwestern voice with his sardonic, offbeat, intellectual musings to maybe twenty states around midnight, so he affected my friends Matt and Steve and Bonnie and Walt and Joe and Bobby and Buzz the same way. There we were, countless kids all over America, going to school with dark circles under our eyes from staying up late to listen to Jean Shepherd on the sly.

It was heady, hooking our imaginations to his. We Believed him. He Knew Something. He was our voice, the voice of small-town America, a voice raised more in regret than in relish, a voice reviving memory after memory of How It Really Was, a voice raving about "creeping meatballism" or rhapsodizing about his mother's meat loaf or recounting the remarkable mishaps of his friends Farkas and Schwartz, a voice that elliptically removed us from Innocence to Experience, a voice that ruminated on the mysteries of Existence, and shrugged.

"Dear Jean Shepherd," I wrote to him when I was sixteen in the final fan letter of my life, a letter he never answered, "when I grow up, I want to marry a man just like you." And so, when I am grown-up and a writer, and Jean Shepherd has grown older and put his stories into books and on TV, we finally meet in the Park Avenue offices of his publisher (A *Fistful of Fig Newtons; Wanda Hickey's Night of Golden Memories; In God We Trust: All Others Pay Cash*). The Voice is much bigger than the bonsai plant his agent/producer/lady friend places on the table; once the bonsai expected to be very big, but with gradual pruning it has been trimmed down to permanent miniature size, and that is why it is possible for an entire yew tree to fit in a teacup, but that has nothing to do with Jean Shepherd—or does it?

Jean Shepherd does not quite resemble the possessor of a $100,000 income, a Maine cabin, a Florida condo, a Delaware Water Gap retreat, and his own airplane as much as a carny barker trying to con you into a game of chance with a cracked frying pan for a prize. From his blue leisure suit whose fibers never graced a living thing to his spiky hair and thin beard matted by body oils or bad air, to the silver sand dollar pendant he wears over a shirt gaping open between the buttons, to the Styrofoam cup of coffee he holds, he is slightly seedy.

"I'm one of the great underground performers. In spite of the fact I have millions of fans," he proclaims, "I can't imagine why [someone] wouldn't know about me. . . . I've had three best-sellers, I've published forty-eight stories in *Playboy*. Critics have done papers on me. I've influenced more kids. I've done thousands of shows at colleges. I've been on the Carson show many times and on the Merv Griffin show. I've had my own television series for years on PBS. And yet [some people] never heard of me. Now you're understanding the nature of twentieth-century fame. It's one of those things you accept as a fact of life, like the rain. Is the rain frustrating? No, it's just *there*. . . .

"See, I was part of the whole beat, hip movement. And it's very difficult to explain, I was part of that whole crowd. I came up—friends of mine at the time were people like Mailer and, ah, Jules Feiffer, this is, the whole Village crowd. I was really kind of one of the centers of it. In fact, I was a character in Jack Kerouac's *On the Road*. I'm the Angel-Headed Hippie, the guy they're always listening to on the radio. Did you ever read the book?" Yes—twenty years ago. "But I'm saying that was a whole *movement*, and it brought in almost everything we've got today, as far as art is concerned. The kind of acting that Dustin Hoffman does. It had great ramifications all the way down the line."

Does he see himself as great? "That's something I can't answer. How can I say that? I'm not Woody Allen, who would say no or yes. . . ." How would he explain Jean Shepherd to a Martian anthropologist? "How would you?" he says, laughing. "I couldn't. I don't think the individual can. It would be like asking, ah, Thomas Wolfe, do you see yourself as a gargantuan, unbelievably talented, totally undisciplined, ah—" He pauses. Genius? "Genius?" He laughs again. "How could he answer that?"

Son of a dairy office manager who moonlighted as a cartoonist, Jean Shepherd grew up in Hammond, Indiana, and Chicago. He began in radio as a teenage actor for syndicated serials, playing Billy Fairfield in "Jack Armstrong." He can still sing every word of every verse of the theme song of "Little Orphan Annie" and other children's radio shows of the thirties, yet today he dismisses radio as a "huckster medium." After installing radar in North Africa for the Army, he attended a string of colleges on the GI Bill, studying engineering, psychology, liberal arts, and drama without graduating; he calls himself an early dropout. He's worked as a steel company mail boy, a sports car salesman, a factory laborer. His legendary WOR radio show ran on and off from 1956 to 1977, though he insists it started in 1959.

Like many people who have yet to achieve their ultimate, he's touchy about his age. "People assume that I'm a lot older than I am. Because everybody believes he was a kid when he listened to me." How old *is* he? "It doesn't matter." Well, I read he was born in either 1922, 1923, or 1925. "Actually, it was '29," he claims. "Look it up in, if you really want to look it up, look it up in Who's Who," which says '29. "What I'm gonna say here, though, I don't want age written about, if you can help it. I know you're going to put it in, so it's all right. And I'm gonna say to you, you know why I don't? Because it doesn't matter how old Robert Redford is. . . . What difference does it make, let's say, how old Cheever, ah, Updike is when he writes a short story? It's serious. *I'm* serious. And all these things just cloud—" He breaks off. I'm just trying to fix on the truth. "Well, truth—truth about what? Truth about my work?" Yes.

"Well," he continues, "nobody asks me about my work." I did. "No, not much." Then I'll ask more. "No, when you say work, ah, have you read any of my stuff?" Sure. "Well, a lot of people haven't. Many people come to me and they'll interview me and it turns out all they did was be a radio listener. . . . An artist doesn't want people to be involved with him, he wants people to be involved with his work. Well, his work, period. Nobody ever asked me how I create a story. They say to me things like when I was a kid I listened to you. Well, that's like saying, ah, to J. D. Salinger, when I was a kid I read you, and then you don't say any more after that. . . . Nobody hardly ever talks about my work, they talk about me.

"Well, that doesn't irritate me, but it makes me wonder whether or not they ever heard me seriously." He seems to have total recall. "No, not at all. I'm a storyteller. My stuff seems like memory. It isn't. I will see something happen the afternoon of a show and create a story about it, but I will put it in the past. Are you listening to me," he says, laughing. So he was spinning short stories on the air? "Well, I was, yes!" he exclaims. "In fact, that's what McLuhan said. If you're curious, you can look it up in *Understanding Media*. . . . He paralleled me with James Joyce. And he's right. But you're— it would take somebody with the kind of insight that a Mc-Luhan would have to discern that. . . ." How did he evolve his method? "Well, it happened gradually. That's a difficult question, almost impossible to answer. That'd be like asking Picasso how he evolved his technique. He couldn't tell you, it just seemed natural for him to do that," he declares.

". . . My mother never asked me what are you gonna be

when you grow up, that was never asked once in my house. My father could have cared less. I never thought about it. See, that's an eastern thing. That's why a movie like *Fame* would be absolutely incomprehensible to somebody in Indiana. It's a make-it attitude. You know, the title of the film says 'fame,' it doesn't say 'art,'" he says, laughing. "It says 'fame.' They don't give a damn what the hell they do to get famous. They *want* to be famous. In other words, fame is the end product of what you're going at, not a good performance or great art or a great play. A *successful* play is what you write," he sneers.

"That's epitomized to me in the plays of Neil Simon, to me the classic non-plays of our time. He doesn't know anything about the real world, he knows only about the make-believe world. All his people are involved in make-believe things." Does *he* know about the real world? "Well, I grew up in a steel town. You have to damn well know about the real world. If you didn't, for Christ sake, you wouldn't live ten minutes. And I'm not saying this as an example of superiority. There's just two kinds of worlds. That's why I can't really sit through a Woody Allen movie. He seems to live mostly in the world of fantasy. Well, I never had fantasies. No. Not the kind, gee, I wish I could have a date with Ursula Andress. Well, I'd go *get* a date with Ursula Andress," he says, laughing again. "And that's the end of it.

"I think we're tremendously affected artistically by the very earliest things. Like, take a Woody Allen. He seems to be only affected by movies. I never went to the movies, they did not interest me. I, I never had romantic fantasies about, ah, Humphrey Bogart. See, I came from the Midwest, where movies and musicals were just distant mutterings on the horizon. See, I've enjoyed life. Really. Literally. And as a kid I always thought writing was meant to be funny. I was absolutely fanatic about reading P. G. Wodehouse. How's that for an influence?

"Now, I don't know what would have happened to me had I been, let's say nine or ten, and read *War and Peace*. I think that's why lots of kids grow up and their literature is so full of the kvetch, you know, life is hard, life is tragic, because so many novels are written like that. So if you're ten and read Vonnegut, you'll grow up thinking life is bad news. But if you grow up reading Shepherd, you'll come away thinking life is basically a giant joke, life is an endless shaggy dog story. It always seems like any minute now we're gonna solve it"—Jean Shepherd grins—"any minute now."

Hurry.

JANUARY 9, 1983

ALEXANDRA SHEEDY
She Just Wants to Be Famous

"I want to write a hundred books by the time I die, and the last one is going to be an autobiography of my life," declares freckled, brown-eyed Alexandra Sheedy, who at thirteen is one of America's youngest living novelists. "I want to be a star ballerina and I want to be an actress and I want to sing and be in a Broadway play and I want to do a million different things," she adds with a toss of her long honey-brown hair.

Whew! Already Ally Sheedy's biography is longer than mine. She's danced at Lincoln Center with the American Ballet Theatre. She's appeared on "The Merv Griffin Show" and "To Tell the Truth." She's published a movie review in *The Village Voice* and an article on her parents' separation called "My Mother Screams, Does Yours?" in *Ms.* She's been interviewed by *The New York Times, People, The National Enquirer.*

"Why are people making a fuss over me? I'm a young writer and that's unusual. But that's not why they published my book. They published it because it was good," she insists. Ally's book, *She Was Nice to Mice,* currently in its fourth printing, details the misadventures of a literary mouse at the court of Queen Elizabeth I, who seems to have a curious penchant for the furry creatures.

Innocent enough to be unaware of dictionary definitions for words like "jaded" and "neurotic," yet sophisticated enough to discuss $3,500 advances and trust funds, Ally Sheedy is at that delightfully sunny midpoint between little-girl charm and big-girl sensuality. Sitting on a green-flowered Victorian couch in her mother's sprawling, book-crammed Upper West Side Manhattan apartment complete with candy vending machine and huge papier-mâché mouse head, Ally's wearing a faded blue denim skirt and an orange T-shirt decorated by a bright yellow bunny.

"Gee, you have a lot of questions," she chirps, sneaking a peek at my list. "I just read half of them upside down. Is this the next one?" Ally Sheedy is an interview pro. Even today. Despite ordinary domestic distractions like her mother pounding away on a typewriter or shouting over the phone and her eight-year-old brother crawling around the room like a giant green blanket-wrapped caterpillar.

"Some people who interview me say, 'Exactly how much help did you receive on the book,' or, um, 'Did your mother write that book?' and it's hard to convince them, you know. It's true that I wrote it. I can't believe it when they ask those questions. It really bothers me." I notice she looks slightly sad. "No," she demurs, "I was just thinking. I go off and think a lot, I like to think.

"One thing that gets me very angry," she repeats, "is when I hear that they don't think I wrote the book or they think my mother wrote it for me. It's absolutely not true," she says fiercely, "because I really worked hard, it was something I really wanted to do, and I just can't stand it when people say I didn't do it. I wrote out the pages in longhand and then my mother typed them out and gave me two carbons. I paid her one dollar a page, same as she pays *her* typist, 'cause that was not part of her normal motherly duties. She was like a reader of the book, and if she got mixed up, if she came to a word that made no sense or a sentence that led away from the original story, we'd discuss it, and I'd dictate the words that had to be changed," she explains carefully.

But her mother *is* a literary agent. "She's *my* agent, too. She has sixty-two clients," Ally says proudly, "and I'm one. She treats me the same way she does any other client, not because I'm her child. I pay her a fee, I think 15 percent, she gets what all agents get, and," she insists, "she didn't help me write the book or anything like that."

Though Ally's publisher loftily claims the book was inspired by Virginia Woolf's *Flush*, a dog's perspective on poets Robert and Elizabeth Barrett Browning, Ally never actually read it. A real-life model for several incidents in the book was Ally's dear departed pet hamster Samantha, who lived behind the living room bookcase to periodically emerge and pilfer sourballs from the hard candy dish and who occasionally nestled at night in Mrs. Sheedy's hair.

"My mother and I have a great deal in common," Ally asserts. "Well, we both like to write. She influenced me, I think, because she is a writer. One reason I really like to write is because I could always hear her clacking away at the typewriter, so it was almost a natural thing for me to write, also. Not because she forced me." Ally Sheedy's been writing since the ripe old age of six, "long, intricate stories" about princesses and a defecting Russian dancer and a sea gull with a broken leg.

Mrs. Sheedy, an anxious, pigtailed woman in her late thirties who was the daughter of a Philadelphia shopkeeper, has written a book called *It's Alright to Hate Your Kids*. "No, I don't feel any different about her because of that title," Ally says. "Tell her," Mrs. Sheedy interjects, "about my book on Jewish women." "Quiet," Ally implores. "Anyway, she always gets that in. My mother always writes books, I guess she's written three or four, and she's writing another called *It's Alright to Hate Your Parents*."

Ally's parents have been separated for five years. "*Everyone's* parents at school are," she says, playing with her tiny turquoise ring. "They all go back and forth from house to house. I live half the week at my father's and half the week at my mother's," she sighs. "At first it was hard to adjust to, you're going here and you're going there and you have to remember the address and the phone number and it seems like your room is in a strange place. But I'm used to it now."

What, I wonder, was the happiest part of her childhood? "This is *still* my childhood." She laughs. "I'm still having a good time." Alexandra Sheedy's creativity extends to devising unusual children's games. "I've made up a game about an orphanage, where a lot of kids are treated really badly. You know, the classic story. I play the headmistress." She giggles. "I put the kids to heavy work, they don't eat at all, they barely sleep, and I brand them, ha, ha. Of course, I really don't," she chides me. "Oh, we really have a great time. I'm very mean to them if they escape." What does this tell us about the secret recesses of her personality? "It's not me, it's just there's nobody else who wants to be headmistress. I don't either, but I made up the game and it's easier to play that kind of part. I don't mind, I play witches sometimes, too."

What about her younger brother and sister—how do they react to Ally's fame? "They're both jealous and both proud. My sister Megan—she's eleven—is trying to write a book, too. And my brother Patrick said, 'What's all this fuss about? She's only Ally Sheedy.' But last summer they had my book in a shop where we were staying on Fire Island. My brother went in, picked up the book, and kind of shoved it under some man's nose, saying, 'My sister wrote this,' and the man said, 'Hmmmmmm,' and my brother said, 'See, her picture's right here on the back of the book.'

"I *always* wanted to be famous," she admits, "but I didn't quite know what I wanted to be. I had always seen movie stars. I wanted to be really well known. Doesn't everybody when they're young? I still do. It wasn't something my mother told me. Even after I die, I want my name referred to. But," she says scornfully, "I don't want to be famous just for writing books. I don't want to be famous just because I was a great film star. I want to be famous because I did this, did this, did this, did this. I want to be famous because I've done a lot of things I'm good at.

"My mother's always saying she's not a stage mother and she doesn't get fame off her children. And she *is* an agent and she *does* write herself. So we have a big joke about how she'll be known as 'Ally Sheedy's Mother' instead of me being known as 'Charlotte Sheedy's Daughter.' But I'm not a stage daughter either," she sniffs.

I suggest to Ally Sheedy that she's been extraordinarily lucky.

"Lucky to get a book published? Yeah, I sure am." From the kitchen her mother shrills, "You're lucky to have me for a mother."

"Oh," Ally laughs, and says ever so sweetly, "I'm lucky to have an agent for a mother." Then, taking a deep breath, she instantaneously switches from literary patter to child's plaint and yells, "Hey, Ma, now can I have a Mallomar?"

OCTOBER 26, 1975

*E*LDRIDGE CLEAVER
The New Passion of Eldridge Cleaver

Everything American the Radical reviled—even baseball and hot dogs. He raped America's women, cursed its men, defaced its buildings, broke into its homes, stole its property, sold drugs to its children, repudiated its politics, defied its laws, denied its Deity, defiled its prisons, shot at its police, and fled its borders. Trading stays in San Quentin, Folsom, and Soledad for asylum in Cuba, China, and the Soviet Union, the Radical went into a long exile. His son was born in Algeria, his daughter in North Korea. His "codpiece" theories for redesigning pants to free male genitals from the restrictive confines of conventional clothing originated in the South of France. As he wrote in *Soul on Ice*, his impassioned 1968 manifesto that sold millions, he was "extremist by nature."

"Even when I make collect or person-to-person phone calls, the operator asks me, are you *the* Eldridge Cleaver?" he says now. The question is, *which* Eldridge Cleaver? The fiendishly brilliant ex-Black Panther minister of information? The chic ideological chameleon who published essays in *Esquire* and *Mademoiselle*? Meet the Radical at Mid-life. This Eldridge Cleaver has replaced revolutionary rhetoric with civics-textbook platitudes on good citizenship. Rejecting communism and embracing democracy, he prattles about this country's needing a "new consensus," a "new majority." There is an American flag pin in his lapel, and a semblance of humility to his speech. He looks like a minister now, gray and vaguely distinguished, and he tells of finding God while contemplating suicide abroad; it is a poignant tale. He wants to run for mayor of a city he once terrorized, and he has even reconciled with capitalism: "I used to hate money. Now it means a lot to me. I need $250,000 to run for mayor of Oakland. And millions for my fantasies.

"I don't know how to describe myself," muses the Radical at Mid-life. Neither do I. Born in 1935 in Little Rock, son of a jazz musician-waiter, Eldridge Cleaver grew up in the Los Angeles ghetto wanting to be a lawyer or an economist. These hopes were dashed when he was arrested at eighteen holding "a shopping bag of marijuana, a shopping bag of love." Now, while we chat, he forgoes sugar in his coffee and ignores a plate of tempting cookies. Later, revealing he's diabetic, he rails against the evils of sugar, a "dangerous" substance he wants outlawed. Do yesterday's left-wing crazies become today's pillars of respectability? Someday he'd like to record an album of songs. "Eldridge Cleaver sing the blues?" he parries. "No. Oldies but goodies, maybe. I'm not a blues person, you know. But I would predict the record would be a best-seller. . . . I'm a great promoter."

Whatever his momentary stripes, "quiet, bashful, shy, naïve" ol' Eldridge Cleaver is still destined to outrage someone out there. These days he exploits a free enterprise system that allows ex-criminals to repent publicly—and lucratively—on the campus lecture circuit. Interestingly, his current speaking tour of twenty-five colleges is arranged by an educational arm of the Unification Church. Though Eldridge Cleaver denies he's a Moonie—*or* a CIA agent, FBI pawn, turncoat, traitor, liar, or wife beater, for that matter—our interview takes place near Penn and Drexel in a communal house with various Moon devotees, mostly young men in suits, milling about, preparing for a banquet with Cleaver that evening. While no one harangues me, they are too earnest, too attentive, too helpful, too polite, a row of gingerbread men from the same cookie cutter.

Can Cleaver make a living by lecturing? "Well, unfortunately, it's just not enough. I mean, I don't do it often enough to be able to live solely off that. So it contributes to my living." What else does he do to support himself? "I make flowerpots," he declares, wiping his glasses with a handkerchief. "I make designer flowerpots out of cement and stone." Really. "All right!" he says, grinning. How did he get into that? "Ah, I used to build walls, you know, when I was younger. I studied masonry; I used to be sort of a brickmason. And I think being in prison a lot gave me a fascination with cement.

"Most of the time, when you think of a prison, you think of steel bars. But actually what confines people is cement. The bars are usually on the front of the cell, but the rest of the cell is all cement," he explains. "And many times solitary confinement is made out of cement. So that I used to really be amazed at the nature of cement, that it was at once both supple and very strong. It's as supple as water and as strong as steel. And I used to write poetry about cement. I used to hate cement, because it was killing me, it was confining me.

"Then, working with cement as a mason, I studied the properties of cement, how cement was made. And I used to build these brick walls with stones. And these were always large stones. And I used to go to riverbeds and gather the stones. And I always noticed that there are some very beautiful shapes of stones you find. And the shapes recur—whether it's teeny stones or large stones, you ran across the same shapes. And there'd be all these beautiful stones that were so small you couldn't use them on the walls, and they weren't good for anything.

"And just one day, ah, I was looking at a bonsai plant, and I thought, what a beautiful plant to be in such a lousy, ugly flowerpot. If you notice these kinds of flowerpots, you find people with beautiful homes and lousy flowerpots. I've studied botany and horticulture, floriculture. Um, I've had a commercial point of view." This was in prison? "Well, no. I went to a college, to a community college in 1980. I just started making the flowerpots just a few years ago. But when I took this course in botany and horticulture, they gave a survey of job opportunities in the field, and it was saturated with people. And the only area where nothing was being done was flowerpots.

"There's no recognizable brand name in flowerpots," he exults. "And so I saw this bonsai plant, and I remembered those small stones, and I was thinking what this plant would look good in. And I just got a flash—a miniature wall built around that plant would be beautiful. So I built my first flowerpot for this bonsai plant, and it was beautiful. So I just really started making flowerpots and selling them. So that's really my passion," he confides. "If you ask me what I prefer to do, I prefer to make flowerpots. And, ah, I hope someday to be able to do it on a consistent commercial basis."

I tell him I write poetry, but I also like to work with my hands; it's a kind of meditation. "Yes, it is, exactly. My first writing was also poetry; I don't know if there's a relationship, but I do like to work with my hands. And I think it's regrettable when you can't do anything with your hands, when you can't make something," he murmurs. How does he sell his pots? "Just through word of mouth. People who know people, ah, order them from me. I've got orders now. I've got a collection in a house in Berkeley, where this lady shows them to people and then they order them.

"I make them in jags, you know. I have a kind of a portable kit with my tools in it that I take around. And different parts of the country you find different kinds of stone. And, ah, I make things in place, structured on the spot, I call it. Sometimes people might want a little wall built or a little planter built in a certain space but that would be impractical to build somewhere and transport. So I do that. I bounce around like that, and, ah, when I have nothing to do, I make a planter or something, a little wall or a series of flowerpots, to fit their particular location.

"I had a little workshop in the back that had been a greenhouse, this was at the house I had with my family," until his wife got a scholarship to Yale last fall. "But now I've really gotten it down. You know, the way we handle cement gives you a bad image of cement. Because a construction site is always so sloppy, cement everywhere. But actually cement, working with cement, can be a very clean process. And when I first started doing it, I had cement everywhere. But now I could work right in this room and never get any on the floor, you know, because I have the right instruments and the right understanding of it. And so, literally, I can do it anywhere. That's why I say I have a little portable kit that contains my tools and a few pigments for coloring and a couple of ingredients of that type. And I can do it anywhere."

Why did he study botany? "Actually, what made me take those particular courses was spiritual. Because, to me, the beauty of flowers, the organization of plants, leaves, trees—these things speak more profoundly and loudly of the hand of the Creator than do the words of men. So, to me, ah, when I see all these symmetrical shapes—little stars and little hearts and triangles in flowers and plants—there's no way in the world that I could think that they came about accidentally. They seem very specifically designed; then it's perpetuated through a genetic code.

"And I use plants and flowers a lot when I'm trying to, ah, convince someone that there's a God. I use them successfully like that. So, ah, I had some free time, and I had the ability to go to the school; it didn't cost anything. So I wanted to know more about plants, and so I took these botany courses. And I worked with tree surgeons. My interest in plants and flowers was already there. . . . I just took the courses to become more familiar."

Did I read that Eldridge Cleaver demonstrated how to prepare barbecued spareribs on TV recently? "No," he gently corrects me, "that was Bobby Seale." I apologize for confusing him with his fellow former Panther. "Bobby Seale is writing a cookbook called *Barbecuing with Bobby*," he offers. My, what different paths people take. "Well," he agrees, "we all have these different things in our lives, you know what I mean? Different attitudes. And we came together in a desperate moment, and then the moment having passed, we went our separate ways."

NOVEMBER 21, 1982

*J*UDY BLUME
Growing Up with Sex

There is less than a hundred pounds to Judy Blume, with her dark wispy hair and her swirly adobe-colored skirt and turquoise shirt, and she seems far too fragile to bear having been branded the Jacqueline Susann of children's literature, or the national expert on the sexual feelings of teenagers, or the godmother of upscale adolescent realism.

And she certainly seems far too well bred, as a New Jersey dentist's daughter once married to a lawyer and then to a physicist, to have written kids' books that mention s-e-x and death and divorce and playground cruelty and scoliosis, books some people call a scatological soft-porn, *cinéma vérité* view of childhood, puberty, and growing up, books that are considered contemporary or frank or dirty or objectionable or sickening or too much trouble for libraries because of the right-wing protests they inspire.

"Oh dear . . . where did you find those things? . . . Oh, that's ridiculous," laughs the forty-six-year-old author of more than a dozen polished, popular, prize-winning children's books and two steamy adult novels, the latest of which, *Smart Women*, starts in a hot tub.

I know Judy Blume is somebody's mother, but it's hard to imagine that she's twice divorced with two college-age children, because she still seems—and sounds—so girlish. "Oh, my voice. I hate my voice. I would love it to be lower. I don't like to hear it. If I had time and energy, I would take voice lessons."

Is she, as her detractors suggest, obsessed by bodily functions? "Am I? I don't think so. But I think sexuality is a very important part of my life. . . . And oh, menstruation I wrote about because it was such an important part of my life." And nose-picking? "Yeah, but . . . [I'm] remembering life in the fifth grade. . . . I write about real life as I see it. Everybody has problems. Everybody has ups and downs. I don't think my books are controversial. It's only to those who consider real-life issues controversial," she declares.

Yet throughout the interview she seems preoccupied with her physical condition. "Oh, oh, I have to watch out for gulping air," she says over an omelet and endive salad in her suite at the Four Seasons. "People who laugh and talk while they're eating and swallowing air blow up with it. And it's very uncomfortable. And it happens mainly to vivacious women who are having a very good time at mealtimes"—she laughs—"and laughing and gulping. No, I don't pass out. Don't worry, I don't pass out. But I get very uncomfortable."

I hope she doesn't pass out, because I can't do CPR. "You can't?" she says apprehensively. No. "Well, you *know* how," she says. No, I don't. Does she? "I took a course. My son is an EMT. An emergency medical technician. So I took a one-day course," she says. ". . . My editor worries about me, because she thinks I'm too thin. This is how I am, no matter what I eat. And she worries, so she says, 'You have to eat.' So I say, 'Then you have to tell them to plan the book tour with time to eat.'"

She's not anorectic, is she? "Oh God, no. I love to eat. But I just burn it up. I just never gain weight. I'm a very healthy eater. I have always eaten three times a day. I eat *well* three times a day. But I have never been a snacker. . . I have to eat lunch or I get weak. . . .

"My children tell me," she says, laughing, "that I come from a family who rewarded illness. And it is certainly true. It was a very big thing in our family. During the early years of my [first] marriage, I was sick all the time. I just had one thing after another after another after another, until my first book was published. I mean, I had everything you could think of . . . stomach pains . . . I always had allergies. Eczema. I was an eczema baby.

"And my father died when I was twenty-one, suddenly, right before I was married. And the first year of my marriage I was covered from head to toe with hives and itches and rashes and I was just a mess. I have a rash on my neck right now, and I'm convinced it's from this book tour."

Could she talk to her mother growing up? "No. I wouldn't have known how." She laughs. "Because the parent has to make the child feel comfortable from the earliest ages on. I can absolutely remember standing in my kitchen asking where babies came from, and nobody told me. . . . What I remember was this sense of adults sharing a knowing look and then turning to me and saying something like 'The stork brings them.' I mean, I'm not sure that anybody even said that to me.

"So I looked it up under 'sex,' in my World Book Encyclopedia. And I was terribly disappointed. It all had to do with plants. And there were color pictures with plastic overlays. Vague, very unsatisfactory. When I was ten, my father took me on his lap. That was how I knew I was going to hear something important. My father also is the one who told me about my period. But he told me in a strange way. We had been visiting relatives, and my cousin, who was quite a bit older, wasn't feeling well that day. And I kept asking, 'What's wrong, what's wrong?' And she kept saying, 'You'll find out when you're thirteen.' And all the way home in the car—this was from Long Island to New Jersey—I kept asking, 'What will I find out when I'm thirteen?' And when I got home, my father told me about menstruation, but in a way that had to do with the moon." She laughs again. "It led me to believe that every time the moon was full, women all over the world had their periods. I thought it was a pretty exciting thing.

"And then when I was ten, he took me on his lap and was going to give me the lecture about how babies are made. He said, 'I think it's time for you to know.' But I already knew. I don't know how I knew, but I said I already knew that. And I also was embarrassed by it then. I mean I was embarrassed that he was going to tell me this and I already knew it. But I had a girlfriend who had a book about menstruation, and we would read it together. And I don't know how much we got from it, but at least it was a book, I mean, it was something."

It wasn't that little pamphlet, was it? "'Growing Up and Liking It'? I *wrote* one of those. Years and years ago. I wrote a revision of it, yes. My name never appeared. . . . I was a new writer. After one of my books they came to me. It was so exciting. They paid me $5,000 to write it. And I wrote it in my own way. I wrote it in a series of letters from one child to another child. I can't remember too much about it, but there were three girls who were friends, and one moved away. They wrote back and forth about bodily changes and development and getting their periods and asking each other questions," she murmurs.

"What I remember most is that one of the girls had gerbils. And they would write about the gerbils. And some male executive . . . changes the gerbils to kittens, to a cat who had kittens. I have no idea why they did that. I don't know if they're still sending that booklet out. But it was wonderful fun."

She returns to the more serious matter of considering her image. "I mean, the media can't avoid labeling. I suppose that's what it is. The *People* magazine syndrome—who got me to dance on the ledge of my terrace. Tap-dance. I love tap-dancing. It makes me feel good. For an hour every day, my mind is only on my tap-dancing. I'm competing only with myself. I had never tap-danced in my life until I started a year ago last fall."

Why? That's odd, isn't it? "But I love to dance. And I've always liked to dance. And I always loved the idea of tap-dancing. But when I grew up, um, nice little Jewish girls in New Jersey took ballet and toe. And I loved that. And I lost touch with my love of dancing over the years when I was supposed to be grown up, before we knew about fitness and all that. And when I'm in Santa Fe [where she has a house], I do Jazzercise because I think it's wonderful. But in New York [where she has an apartment], I don't even know why, I wanted to tap-dance. And I found out there's a studio just two blocks away. And the classes are filled with dancers twenty years younger than me. There are sometimes famous actors and actresses who want to learn to tap-dance. . . . I have my little goals, to be able to do a double pullback before I'm fifty." She laughs.

What do her books tell us about her? "That I'm very emotional. That I think out of pain comes humor. I don't know, I'm making this up." She laughs. "I mean, I hope this is true. That we go through some really tough times, but we can come through it. What do you think?" I tell her she reminds me of another famous writer I have interviewed. "Am I like her?" Judy Blume says, puzzled. "She's so . . . bizarre."

JUNE 17, 1984

E. L. DOCTOROW

Ragtime's *E. L. Doctorow Hits Some Sour Notes*

"I'm usually uncomfortable in situations such as this one," chortles author E. L. Doctorow, whose celebrated fourth novel, *Ragtime*, is now a $25 million movie. "But you are asking good questions. Actually you haven't asked any of the questions I expected you to ask."

Thus titillated, I succumb to speculation—just what are those predictable queries? "I'm not going to tell you. They are just the ones I'm tired of answering," he mutters. Then he relents: "Okay, the things now I'm really tired of answering are: 'When is the movie coming out? What was your involvement in it? Did you have anything to do with the film? What do you think of the film?' That's one set of questions. What else? Oh, I'll think of some others later," he says during a visit to Temple Center City.

Ol' E. L. is obviously at his best behind a typewriter ("When I'm not writing, I don't think") or in front of a class ("It's actually comforting to go through a great book and find flaws; perfect novels have always worried the hell out of me"). Beneath his grizzled erudition and attendant wit waits a hint of crankiness. He is both bear and teddy bear, formal and casual. A navy crew-neck sweater with a huge hole in the elbow sits unassumingly atop finely creased gray flannel slacks, crisp oxford-cloth shirt, high-gloss shoes.

Doctorow is a glossy writer. In *Ragtime* he mixed history with invention, real and imaginary people, Wasps and Jews and blacks and rich and poor, famous and obscure, to create a poignant turn-of-the-century kaleidoscope that left him obscure no more. His involvement with the movie was, in a word, unfortunate. Doctorow's thousand-page scenario for *Ragtime* was junked when producer Dino De Laurentiis replaced director Robert Altman with Miloš Forman, who brought in dramatist Michael Welles, who wrote the final screenplay, which took considerable liberties with Doctorow's work.

So, E. L., why do you dislike interviews? "If you're the subject, it's not your form. You don't have control over it. See, I deal with words, and I don't like"—he falters—"I like to compose and organize them for the effects I want. But when you are being interviewed, you are in someone else's hands. It's *their* form, in *their* hands. And so you find words in the paper and they are your words, but it's nothing you have done."

Then what would he like to tell us? "What would I say? I'd have to think about it. See, I never thought about that. Updike does that—he interviewed himself. That's a little precious for my tastes. I guess I'd probably create a fictional interview. In other words, the self I would be interviewing would be a fictional creation. That's how I have always felt about interviews. When I was taking journalism at Bronx High School of Science—you know this story, I have told it around enough—we had to do an interview for class. I handed in an interview with the stage director at Carnegie Hall. And Teacher liked the interview and wanted to use it in the school newspaper." But she couldn't print it because he had made it up.

He grew up in the same Bronx neighborhood he later chose for the childhood hero of his prizewinning 1971 novel *The Book of Daniel*. His mother was a pianist, and his father had a store that sold records and musical instruments. What was he like as a child? "I was a—uh, um, I read enormously. I spent a great deal of my time reading. But I also liked to play ball, go out in the schoolyard. And, uh, uh, I didn't have that many friends; uh, I was content to be by myself a good deal of the time.

"The Bronx in the thirties was an interesting place. There were a lot of things happening on the streets, and I was attentive to them. It seemed to me that more visibly crazy people were out on the streets than now. People weren't tranquilized as much; you'd see a lot of strange freakish things on the street that you don't see now," he says. "People with macrocephalic conditions, dwarfs and retarded people, spastics and beggars and peddlers and nuts. Plus a lot of derelicts wandering around in the thirties, what we call street people now, people who rummage through garbage cans, bag ladies, bag men. I was very sensitive to all that, and watched it very closely. It was interesting."

I ask him to elaborate on his "solitary" childhood. "I don't want to mislead you," he protests. "I mean, it was an active life. I had friends. I was in a gang. I remember getting my nose broken in a sandlot football game trying to play quarterback. So I was not a recluse. I used to go out and get into trouble of one sort or another. There was a gang that used to invade our territory and hold knives up to our"—he breaks off—"take our money away. I had a good, normal childhood," he says, laughing. "What were you going to do? They were bigger and you didn't want to get knifed for fifteen cents. However, I did swear vengeance."

He didn't start writing until he was eleven or twelve. "Actually, I thought of myself as a writer for many years before that. But I never felt it necessary to actually write anything," he declares. "I think I was in about the third grade when I first wanted to be a writer. There was a lot leading me that way— all the books I was reading, books available in my home, which was a generally bookish environment, and my grandparents and my parents and my older brother.

"Somehow I must have gotten some kind of positive response for whatever I did that was very . . . verbally adept. So by the third grade I said, 'That's what I am, I'm a writer.' I liked the identity and did not feel it was necessary to prove it for a number of years by actually writing anything. That's a very good way to become anything. Just imagine you are, and eventually it will take."

Enter Poe. "In junior high I started to write imitation Edgar Allan Poe stories. I knew I had been named after a writer, my first name being Edgar. I believed my parents named me after him. Many years later I told my mother, 'You realize you named me after a necrophiliac drug addict alcoholic sado-masochistic latent homosexual?'" He laughs. "She said, 'Oh, Edgar, stop your fooling.'" When was that? "Probably in my late thirties." He chuckles. "See, I actually read all of Poe; I was crazy about Poe as a boy. I read everything he wrote, and only later did I read about *him*. My God, I said, he really had trouble. Yeah . . . the whole thing about marrying this thirteen-year-old girl, his cousin, a level of morbidity brought on by drink and drugs. Just about every hang-up you could think of."

So why call yourself E. L.—to downplay Poe's sinister influence? "I use initials simply because it seemed just to go better with the name Doctorow, which would be difficult enough for someone to master without adding Edgar to it. So initials seemed easier. That is a decision I made as a teenager about the way I would be known. A lot of writers I admire did that—D. H. Lawrence, F. Dostoevsky, T. S. Eliot, W. Shakespeare." He laughs. "One makes a lot of crucial decisions at a very young age."

E. L. Doctorow majored in philosophy at Kenyon College, wrote several plays as a graduate student at Columbia, spent two years in the Army, then worked as an airline reservation clerk and a script reader for Columbia Pictures. Then he became an editor in book publishing, kept getting promoted, and when he had sold two of his own novels, quit to write full-time. So, at fifty, has he accumulated any of Poe's excesses? "Well, I'm not a necrophiliac, and I drink moderately. I don't do drugs. Certainly [the pattern of life] follows Flaubert's advice—live quietly in some sort of stable way. But I didn't know I was following his advice. I got married very young and I have three children and I am sort of a family person. . . . I wish I had some good clear stereotypical image, like a rowdy. If I was really self-destructive and got into heavy scrapes and made the gossip columns, it would probably be very good for book sales. But unfortunately I'm not disposed that way."

Yet his daily rhythms are not serene. "Listen, I have had so many crises I can't count them. The writer's life is daily crisis. Very great ups and downs. And, uh, I—uh, if one comes along of the kind you are speaking about [mid-life crisis], I'll let you know." Is he moody? "Oh yes. I'm in a good mood now. If you think this is bad, you should see me in a bad mood."

Does he get badly depressed? "I would like to qualify as a full-blown manic-depressive," he proclaims. "Because any state that is really realized would be very productive for a writer. I have written coming off a terrible sense of desolation about what I have done, and despaired that I would ever accomplish what I'm setting out to do. By sort of hitting rock bottom, I have found whatever it is I've needed to do the work as it should be done. So that could be very valuable. I wouldn't even call it a depression, it's more desolate than that. There's nothing mental about it, it's attached to something quite specific, words on the page that aren't working. . . ."

Speaking of desolation, has he spent much time in Hollywood? "Hollywood? You're jumping around very quickly," he chides me. I am? Then jump along. "Then I'd be in *your* rhythm, not mine. I'm a plodder, not a jumper. Now, what is it you asked? I have been there. You mean, did I work there? Never. I walked down Sunset Boulevard. I stayed once at the Beverly Hills Hotel. I had breakfast in the Polo Lounge." He laughs. "Actually I saw [that] all those people from New York in the thirties had moved out to California—the derelicts, the bag ladies, the macrocephalics.

". . . I have very conflicted feelings about movies. See, if there was a real energy crisis, movies are sort of energy-intensive, and the theaters would have to be shut down. Then we could read each other's poems in front of big bonfires. Can't you foresee . . . a bunch of people sitting around the fire and someone telling a story about the old days? I don't know what's coming; how do I know? But certainly my sense of danger has risen, what with military weapons and neutron bombs. It's very worrisome. None of us can bear to think of it more than twenty seconds, but it's there."

Does he feel he's ever failed at anything important? "Yes. It's personal," he says firmly. "Hey, I don't have to answer every question just because it's asked. What is there to say after we mention the neutron bomb? That's the curtain line."

JANUARY 3, 1982

SONIA SANCHEZ
The Muse Used to Stutter

"My father said he'd teach me two things—how to play a good game of poker and how to drink bourbon. But I don't mess with the body. I write under the influence of the idea, the high from that idea. That's the joy that propels me."

In a white cubicle on the eleventh floor of a gray marble tower, where Temple University's concrete campus confronts the North Philly ghetto, sits Sonia Sanchez, writer, teacher, vegetarian, author of ten books of poems, plays, short stories. Though she is forty-four, one is fooled into forgetting it by her braids, freckles, bangle bracelets, blue jeans, khaki bush jacket with hacked-off sleeves.

And when one sees Sonia Sanchez perform her poetry, which means she sings, hums, chants, grunts, and claps out words gutty yet tender, one is fooled into forgetting she once almost forsook speech. "I stuttered as a child," she confides, "and it's a very difficult kind of thing to try to communicate and be a stutterer. People, even your own family, don't have patience. So I became somewhat withdrawn, and I started to write at a very young age. I remember I began to write little messages instead of talking. I didn't know it at the time, but I was writing poetry.

"My communiqués to people became, like, little poems. For some reason it just came out in funny little verses. It was quite amusing on some levels, but I took writing seriously even as a child, because it was my way of communicating. They'd smile and they heard what I said, even though it was written. And they enjoyed it. I guess you could say I write in order to live. For me, writing makes things *be*."

She devised other vocal survival techniques. "If I were reading aloud, the stuttering would be much more pronounced, okay? Say I came across a long word. That meant, as a kid, I had to stop and break the word down into syllables. So, in stopping, or even when the teacher told me what the word was, it didn't matter, it still set off the stutters. So for years I would come across certain words and I would just simplify them. I'd get to a word and I would give a synonym that was much simpler"—she snaps her fingers—"just like that. So I wouldn't set the stuttering off."

Now she speaks fluidly, melodiously. "Well, the stuttering stayed with me for years, all the way up until high school. As a consequence, quite often I really didn't say a lot in my classes. And when I had to give speeches, I was just petrified, because I knew I would stutter through a speech and people would get bored or laugh.

"It's funny trying to say how you cure things," she reflects. "Because I'm not so sure you cure a thing as much as it becomes cured. I remember having to give a talk in class, and I rehearsed and practiced for the longest time. Then I'd say it in the sanctity of my home to my sister, and through most of it I didn't stutter, it was very good.

"But I knew when I'd actually get up in front of the class later on, I would just fall apart. So what I did is this. I said to myself, maybe I can control this via pain," she explains. "Maybe this sounds peculiar, but I stuck my fingernails into the palms of my hands as I talked." She demonstrates. "And at the onset of the slightest stutter that I felt emanating from any place in my body, I'd dig my nails into my hand a little bit more.

"And I mean I actually, you know," she falters, "I mean I really just did it very hard," she says, visibly moved at the memory. "When I finished my speech, I was really bleeding. But from that point on, I never, I never stuttered again. The fascinating thing, though, is that I still heard stutters in my mind. See, stutterers can stop stuttering. But it's like when you get up and give talks and whatever, you still hear stutters in your head, even though you're not stuttering out loud."

The first time she read her work to an audience, "I think it was in a school in Harlem, I changed my mind and decided I wasn't going to do it. But they called my name, and they pushed me onstage. So you're facing an audience and you can't very well stand there like a dummy and say nothing. So I walked out and I was furious. I kept thinking I'm gonna stutter, stutter, stutter, stutter, stutter.

"I remember distinctly that people were very noisy and I remember wondering how they were gonna hear me. So what I started to do, and I kept doing it for years, is that I started to move. I started to move. So they quieted down and began to watch and follow me. Afterward I went up to some other poets I knew and I asked how I was. Fine, they said, wondering what the hell's going on with me. Nonononono I said, how *was* I? You were great, they said.

"They thought it was ego, but what I was asking was what I was too ashamed to ask: Did I stutter? But I didn't ask that, you see, I couldn't bring myself to ask that. They kept saying you were fine, but I heard the stutter back there in my head." She frowns. "So anyone who stutters, it's not just removing yourself from the actual physical thing, but also the emotional attachment to stuttering that stays with you. And it took me years to feel good about talking out loud and not hearing those stutters inside my head. One day I woke and they were finally gone."

Did her teachers mistake her difficulty in speaking for mental dullness? "Always, always. I said very little in the classroom, and when I did, it was not too clear. It came out fast and hesitant. I remember once taking an exam and getting a very good grade. And I remember the teacher looking at me after giving out the grades and moving me up front, 'cause she figured I was cheating.

"Many teachers, if you don't speak out in class, they assume the very quiet student is very dull, or not bright. Which is a big lie. People never know why you don't speak out in class. It's really tragic, it's really tragic," she fumes.

Yet her grades were so exceptional she entered college at sixteen. "I got out of high school early. They skipped me. I'll never forget walking into my first class at Hunter College and hearing, 'My God, they are letting babies in.' I remember leaving school that day and going to a barber because I knew I was not going to go back with long hair that made me look like a little kiddie-kiddie. I was always teased, I was always asked how old I was. I really wanted to say nineteen. So I was kind of by myself until I learned to play bridge. Then I developed more important concerns," she says, alluding to her black activism.

Though Sonia Sanchez lectures on "The Poet as the Whore of the University," she makes her living in academia, and because she is outspoken, she moves around. "Oh, have I ever." She grins. "That's what happens when you teach black studies. I was 'political.'" She came to Philadelphia after San Francisco, Pittsburgh, New York City, Amherst. Last year she was at Penn.

"I have never hated white people, you know. I have never hated anyone. This country gives me 'inspiration.' Put inspiration in quotes. There are so many things that are incorrect about America that one has got to comment on it, to set it right. I'm not about wallowing in it, I'm about rectifying it. I'm definitely black, and I certainly have dignity.

"Look, you came to a poetry reading of mine. Well, someone else came to one of the same readings and said I was arrogant. And I'm not an arrogant person. But I'm not within the mold," she declares. "Sometimes what I'm saying gets misconstrued. I've said straight words to people, but because of the way I've said those straight words, they get taken very wrong, they offend."

Her philosophy of race is unflinchingly direct. "Simply, you've got to deal with me. Look, you know, I can like you, or I can dislike you. And if I dislike you, it doesn't mean because you're white or you dislike me because I'm black. But because I don't like you at all, damn it, I just don't like you, and I want that choice."

Her initial awareness of being black was "a destructive . . . hurting thing." "We used to play with these little white kids back in Alabama. One day they said, 'We can't come out and play with you, we can't, 'cause you're a nigger.' So I went inside and asked my grandmother what was a nigger. And she said, 'That's what you are.' That's how I learned I was black. And I always urge people to be the first ones to tell their children who they are, so it isn't a negative experience."

Divorced, Sonia Sanchez is raising ten-year-old twin sons herself. "My mother died when I was one. I have no remembrance of her. Period. She died in childbirth. I was born in Birmingham and we came North for freedom," she says sarcastically. "I really grew up in New York City. My father was a teacher in the South. I was very much alone.

"If I ever had heroes, heroines, it was when I was older, and they came from the library," Sonia Sanchez says, laughing, " 'cause I used to live in the library. I used to read two or three books a day. All kinds. It didn't matter. And what I first wanted to be was a lawyer. 'Cause in spite of my stutters, I could always outtalk anyone."

OCTOBER 29, 1978

ALLEN GINSBERG
Still Howling After All These Years

"I was gay," says Allen Ginsberg, parthenogenic progenitor of the Beat Generation, "and Kerouac was a big football player I had a crush on. He liked my goofy innocence, my shyness, my physical underdevelopment, my vulnerability. He liked me for myself, for my stupidity, for my awkwardness. It was like being given permission to be myself."

We're dealing with heavy-duty cultural history here, how a bunch of fellas in the fifties began talking and thinking and acting and writing, not crazy, but different, Allen Ginsberg and Jack Kerouac and William S. Burroughs and Neal Cassady and Gary Snyder and all the others, the drinking, the drugs, the ecstatic mystical visions, the celebrations of sensory excess, the late-night lunatic hip/bop discoveries that led to a whole new jazzy literature twisting intellect inside out and backward, a talky literature turning cerebration on its rear, a dumbing up and a smartening down, Cosmic Significance, and back when it all began, Allen Ginsberg was "just a skinny timid Jewish intellectual from New Jersey scared to go too far out."

But Allen Ginsberg, underground saint and mainstream misfit, son of a Paterson poet and English teacher, Columbia grad and erstwhile journalist, would go very far out indeed. He would write "Howl," a profane denunciation of materialism lamenting the best minds of his generation "destroyed by madness staring hysterical naked . . ." and he became our Whitman, our national conscience, while Jack Kerouac would write *On the Road* and become our Pied Piper of rootlessness. So far out did Allen Ginsberg go that he bumped into himself and came back in. His drug experiments following his 1960 trip to South America were repudiated when he later visited oriental holy men. He began to meditate, to accompany performances of his poetry with thumb cymbals and chants of "Om."

So it was that the explosive Blakean mysticism that briefly blasted Ginsberg into a mental hospital (like his mother, Naomi, before him) was supplanted by back-to-basics Buddhism tranquillity celebrating the "ordinary mind" and the delights of mundanity. Despite the controversial content of his poetry, Ginsberg went on to receive the 1974 National Book Award and be elected to the American Academy of Arts and Letters. He writes, he says, because of "some sense of divine mission I had when I was a kid. Some adolescent fantasy of go out and save the world."

"Um," he says, pausing for words, wiping his runny nose on a red bandanna, punctuating his sentences with coughs. He is fighting the bronchitis he picked up the previous week at an international poetry conclave in Managua where he met fellow bards Yvgeny Yevtushenko and Ernesto Cardenal to draft a manifesto praising Nicaragua's "revolutionary experiment." What brought Ginsberg to Philadelphia—along with his longtime companion, ponytailed Peter Orlovsky—was a benefit concert and workshop for Dharmadhatu, the Buddhist study and meditation center.

In ordinary conversation, Allen Ginsberg does not curse, yet his poems vault out at you with their vehement violation of the niceties of the language. But he is still a coruscating critic of American government, using emotionally charged words like "genocide," "paranoia," "tyranny." He mentions the assassination of a Latin American poet, and I ask whether *he's* ever been tempted to assassinate anyone. "No, I have a different mode," he tells me at Dharmadhatu on Sansom Street. "Yeah. Well, I mean, I've been attempting to assassinate myself and anybody I can think of in the universe. But everybody has, I think, thought of that at one time or another. I'll kill my mother," he singsongs, "I'll kill my father, I'll kill my President, I'll kill myself, I'll kill my brother, I'll kill my lover, I'll kill everybody in Africa, I'll kill everybody in India, I'll kill everybody in Asia." He laughs, pleased at his own spontaneous creation. "I'm sure we've all thought of everything. As well as making love to all of them. As well as forgetting about them all. But . . . I would be too much of a coward to go assassinating anybody. I never get that angry long enough."

The eighties version of this Bohemian dinosaur is still bearded with the same yarmulke-shaped bald pate, but otherwise gone surface-straight in tweed jacket, paisley tie, and gray flannel slacks. Does this ersatz college professor style mean *he's* changed? "No. I decided that the United States was so crazy . . . that it was a dangerous situation. And if I altered my appearance and said exactly the same thing, or even more trenchant criticism, maybe people would be less distracted by my appearance and listen to what was being said."

Which is somewhat the case. "However, it's posed other problems. Because then the journalistic stereotype is oh, this guy's mellowed now, he's changed; he's renouncing his former allegiances. Which was the *Time* magazine, *People* magazine interpretation immediately." What's the truth? "There is no *truth*," he declares. "Looking for the truth in a situation like that is looking for a piece of air with a magnifying glass." Then he hasn't mellowed? "I never was unmellow. I never thought I was unmellow."

Does he like that word? "No. Never did. It sounds like it's an ultra-hippie word, man, this is so mellow, meaning people lying around and sniffing cocaine and doing nothing, playing with themselves. Or it's an ultrareactionary word, well, he was a rebel when he was young, but now he's mellowed like us, and he's making $50,000 a year, and he doesn't have to care. So when it's used those ways I don't like it. . . ."

What was he like as a child? "Shy. Self-conscious. I thought I was ugly. Ah, completely virginal. I was afraid people would notice I was awkward. Like everybody. Most kids are like that. However, at seventeen, Kerouac got me to understand that my very shyness and awkwardness was really cute, sexy, intelligent, and charming. Because if you are an older person and look at somebody who's young and shy and awkward, it's really totally sexy, totally attractive. You're not talking to an accumulated layer of disillusionments, cynicisms, and defenses." Does that mean now he's romantically interested in much younger men? "Yes. Precisely." How young? "Oh, anywhere from fourteen to forty, fourteen to thirty-five, I'd say. Two months old to forty-five." When did he begin to sense he was different? "Very, very early. Around seven, eight, or nine." Did he feel like an outsider? "No, it was having a crush on kids my own age, slightly older, maybe a year older, who seemed more competent in the world and who could protect me, I thought. But I wasn't able to admit or express my feelings very easily for fear of being rejected. And nobody else talked about that, or felt like that, I thought. Then I had a fantasy of having a magic spell. And me and my boyfriend had a magic spell when I was eight, and we could have palaces and moats and torture dungeons and servants."

My mother, unaware of Allen Ginsberg's sexual preference, saw him on TV and urged me to marry him, he was so intelligent and well spoken. Now I tell him this. "When will we get married?" he replies. "Let's see, it's a quarter to twelve. *He* wants to get married." He indicates Peter Orlovsky. "He's got a girlfriend, a fiancée." Well, congratulations. "Them wedding bells is breaking up that old gang of mine," he mugs. "We've been together since 1954, twenty-seven–twenty-eight years." They've had a very unusual, durable friendship. "Some kind of magic. Like everything else, I think it's just trust." Well, what will the wedding do to their relationship? "Increase the range of trust." Peter always liked women, too, didn't he? "Always. He's heterosexual. He likes girls. I've had relations [with women], I've had girlfriends, too. How old are you now? I'm fifty-five. That's not too far apart."

Again he coughs, and I inquire about his health. "Well, right now I feel like I'm falling apart at the seams, because I got bronchitis and I've been in an airplane. But basically good, I think. . . . Oh, I'm feeling a little bit weak, or distracted. Because both travel, and spaceout from travel, and spaceout from giving up smoking, and sleepiness from bronchitis, so I feel slightly scatterbrained. I'm not up to what I should be doing. . . . I'm falling asleep on my feet right now. I'd love to go to bed. Forever," he teases. "My mind is falling apart. . . . From not smoking. I was smoking two packs a day and felt like there was a spike in my chest. Have you ever quit smoking?" he asks. No, I say, I quit sucking my thumb, though. "You know what it felt like, then, the first couple of days?"

Hard to imagine, perhaps, but Allen Ginsberg is doing rock 'n' roll in his latest assault on the establishment. His lyrics, of course, are politically oriented, and considering the precarious state of the world, it's really his version of the blues. He accompanies himself on the harmonium. Bob Dylan, he says, taught him chord progressions, he toured with Dylan's Rolling Thunder Revue, John Hammond recorded him, and he actually carries a tune rather gracefully. But it was his poetry records that endeared him to John Lennon. "I spent a lot of time with John and Yoko in the seventies. Not a lot of time," he amends. "But working with them occasionally, jamming with Lennon. He was very friendly. I got the biggest thrill, finally, after knowing him since 1965, about 1978 I visited them in the Dakota.

"And Lennon had said he always wondered what I did, but then he was listening to the radio and he heard this tremendous poem, this *voice*, and he thought it was Dylan at first. And then at the end it said Allen Ginsberg reciting 'Howl.' 'I can't read,' he said, 'I can read but I don't pick it up, it's all auditory for me.' But once he heard that he said, 'Oh, so that's what you've been doing. I thought you were some guy hanging around the margins all along. I always saw you around, but I finally understood what you were doing, and it was great. Do you have any other records?' It's funny." Ginsberg laughs. "Oh, I was just so happy he finally got the point."

All right. What does he want to be when he grows up? "When I grow up, I want to be a professional meditator." Each day he does meditate, emptying his mind and concentrating on the flow of his breath. "I'd like to sit [meditate] for a thousand days, go off on a thousand-day retreat. At the rate I'm going, I'm going so slow, I'll be ninety. I've done a lot of things, but never that, become a hermit. Once a year I go away for a week and sit for eight to ten hours a day, meditating. It's like dying," Allen Ginsberg says, blowing his nose, "and then coming back."

MARCH 14, 1982

ROBERT BLY
"Why Do I Write? Why Do You Take a Shower?"

"What did you want to talk about?" poet Robert Bly begins kindly enough.

He's one of America's leading poets, isn't he? "Hmmmmm. Who says so?" Well, in 1968 he won a prestigious National Book Award and since 1958 he's been publishing an important poetry magazine that started out as *The Fifties* and is now *The Eighties*. Let's just agree that he is. "No, I don't consider myself such," he demurs in his slight Norwegian lilt. "I never think about it. Even Frost said a poet should never use the word 'poet' about himself, because it's a praise word," the Minnesota farmer's son tells me at the Yellow Springs Fellowship for the Arts. Robert Bly prefers being known as "a person who writes poetry. Whether I'm a poet, that is yet to be seen."

Yet he affects a bardic mantle. For years he lived on a family farm where he didn't have to pay rent. Now he lives in the Minnesota woods and writes about the land and the mysteries of its people. Small towns in the Midwest are very boring, he says—there's nothing to do but write poetry, so he does. Three months out of each year he goes on tour. His poetry readings are not just Performances, they are Events. Like some lute-strumming courtier of yore, he will accompany his poems with dulcimer, don masks, discourse on Myths or Fairy Tales or the Unconscious or the Great Mother or Male Awakening or What's Wrong with America. Though he disdains teaching ("a disaster for writing"), he loves to lecture.

And Robert Bly is a passionate pontificator. "Why do I write? Why do you take a shower?" That metaphor doesn't apply, does it? "Well, I should say it this way. Why do you sing? Do you sing in the shower?" No, I sing *out* of the shower. "Why do you sing?" he persists. Because, I say, I'm a narcissist and I'm entranced by the sound of my voice. "All right," he says, laughing, "that's good enough. Also, when the body feels good, it wants to sing."

His was the first literary voice raised against the Vietnam War, according to his publisher, and I ask him to comment on his controversial image. "No," he declares. "Do *you* want to talk about it? What do you want to say about it?" Does he consider himself a catalyst of controversy? "It happens," he shrugs. "Must be a mischievous little boy in there somewhere." Well, what was he like as a child? "Ah, very straight," he replies tersely.

Does he ever harness his dreams for creativity? "Do you realize what a horrible phrase that is? They're not to be used that way," he berates me. Then has he drawn on dreams for inspiration? "Yeah, I allow them to come into a poem if they appear. But that's not the same as harnessing them," he snorts. "You know what that implies? That you've got a wild horse and you've tamed him and put the bit in his mouth. James Hilton said if you have a black snake in your dream, don't call it your mother complex—don't you realize you've just wiped out one black snake?" He laughs.

Ahem, he seems to dislike interviews. "No, no," he laughs. "I just like to tease you. So that I don't do all the work. You have to do some, too." What did he want to be as a little boy? "I didn't want to be a fireman. That's all I remember." He knew that? "I knew." But he didn't really know there was such a thing as a poet. He wrote one poem in high school, a few in college. During World War II, in the Navy, he met his first poet. "I met all kinds of people I would have never met in my hometown. As it happened, I had high mathematical aptitude, so I was put in a radar development program, and Izzy Eisenstein wrote a poem right in front of me. I couldn't believe it. I was just amazed to realize there were poets."

Rheumatic fever sprung him from the service, and he went to Harvard, where his classmates were John Ashbery, Kenneth Koch, John Hawkes, George Plimpton, and a "whole slew" of other future literary lights, and where his teacher was Archibald MacLeish. I ask him to describe himself. "Why do you want me to speculate about myself? Do you want to turn me into a narcissist? If I did it, what I'd say would come out in a poem, it wouldn't come out in conversation," he mutters.

". . . You don't understand . . . or you wouldn't keep asking these questions. You're not to harness dreams and you're not to talk lightly about certain perceptions one has of oneself. That is not to be done," he proclaims. What did he mean by saying he was "very straight" as a boy? "I'm trying to tell you I don't want to answer those questions. Don't you get it? You don't, do you? I don't want to answer those questions, because I'm interested in the world. Well, then you figure it out." What's his earliest memory? "See, this is none of your business. You don't understand the issue," he roars.

Go on, I urge him. "That if you keep asking me this you're turning me into a third person, in which I have to look back in a cold way on myself." But he does that in his poetry. "No I don't. Because there it's a poetry situation, which is very different. And there's a place for the black snake to be. You're asking me to drag out this thing and just lay it out on the table for you." The black snake? "Yeah. You're asking me to get it out! The black snake lives in bushes back there and he doesn't want to be dragged out in the daylight just because someone asks a question."

I recite the Fifth Amendment. "That's not it. You see, you really don't get the point. Because if you did, you wouldn't ask these questions. But you don't have any respect for the privacy of others. . . . Now when you ask me a question like, how do you regard yourself, this is completely Descartian, I am an insect and you are the scientist. And you ought to cut that out. That's the way it feels. You must know that. . . ."

Who is his audience? "Will you stop these questions," he barks and, in mock distress, punches me lightly on the arm. Are there any misconceptions about his work? "Who cares?" he interrupts me. Misconceptions that he'd like to correct? "Who cares?" he repeats. There are those who say that Robert Bly is belligerent, bellicose, antagonistic, and arrogant. "Why not? Of course," he murmurs disarmingly, and chuckles. "Everybody knows that."

What does he tell young folks who want to be poets? "Well, it depends on if I like the looks in their face. . . . If they have a real interest in art, I can feel it. One thing I tell them is I think you should go by yourself in some log cabin and not talk to anybody. Usually their eyes cross." What does he see in my face? "It'd take a long time. Is this part of the interview?" Yes. "I see a person with a lot of intellectual enthusiasm and generally goodwill. So I would probably give you a fairly certain answer. But also what I see in your face is what I've been getting after you for. Too much greed about the privacy, about details of other people's lives." Greed? "Yep, greed." Not zeal? "Yeah. I mean, that doesn't cancel out the other one. But you have a tendency to feed off other people instead of going inside yourself and finding your own nourishment."

He mentioned working with sound—could he elaborate? "No." Here's a good question. "What is it?" he growls. The poet as antenna of the race. "Oh, I hate that f——idea." Does he take drugs? "No. What did you say?" I repeat the question. "Never." What does he eat? "Food." Does he avoid meat? "No." He mentioned morning meditation—is he a Buddhist? "Do I look like one?" Yes. "No." He laughs. "Actually, one of my heroes was a Buddhist. We went to his house and he gave us curry, *meat* curry. So someone asked him did he eat meat? Ah no, he said, except when my students come who believe in rice, then I serve meat. That's a good Buddhist point of view.

"Last night we had filet mignon. Oh, it was gorgeous, just incredible," he exults. Usually he eats mixed grain for breakfast, "which is what my ancestors ate," and brown rice for lunch. He makes breakfast for his wife, a social worker. And when his sons, twelve and fifteen, come home, they have spaghetti, because "they won't touch anything brown." Is he a good father? "I don't know. You're always asking these nosy questions. Maybe, maybe not. You're asking me to make a judgment about myself. Either I have to praise or criticize myself. Sure that's what you asked. I'm after your a——on this.

"If you ask someone what is your favorite experience as a child, you're taking the person and dividing him into a subject and an object, compartmentalizing him, and that splits the psyche," he complains. I didn't ask him that—I asked him what he was *like*. "Well, that's the same thing. That means I'm no longer a child." Well, what was he like at five? "Then the part of me that's fifty-six has to go back and look at the part that's five? I don't want to do that at your request." Fine. "No, but that's what I'm trying to tell you. It's not right for you to do that to people. . . .

"But I do think you can figure out questions that are more whole, and they can be just as probing. One of the things I like is the questions in which a man says, in such and so and such and so you said this, and in this, you said this. Now isn't there a contradiction?" he suggests. "I think you ought to think about this—how you can develop [a different] interview. There are questions you can ask that the person can answer with his whole being. Not complicated questions, but human questions that help unify the person rather than divide them. I talk about what I'm interested in. A good one would be, 'What do you think of Descartes?' I'd have to think about others, I haven't thought much about it."

At this point we digress. I tell him a story. "That's good," he says. So I'm not a total washout. "Who said you were? One of the things I deeply believe in is a conversation rather than an interview. I mean, I'm teasing you here, but I also like to have an exchange back and forth. Because otherwise, if you ask me an intelligent question and I answer it, all it does is feed my ego. . . . There's some closedness about you. You want *me* to be open, but there's a certain reserve you have," Robert Bly counsels me. "It would be wonderful if you began this interview by saying, listen, I supported three guys and it was all stupid and have you ever done anything that dumb? And *then* we'd be talking."

AUGUST 8, 1982

BERYL BAINBRIDGE
Her Novels Nail Her Parents to the Wall

"You all right, luv?" British novelist Beryl Bainbridge quavers, suddenly slipping into thick Cockney. Rudi, her fifteen-year-old daughter, has been in the shower without a sound for what seems a very long time. The mother's apprehension is contagious: what horror lurks in the latrine?

Much later, the girl leaps out. Her head and steam-pinkened torso are swathed in fresh white towels. Her forehead is smeared with bright scarlet to suggest bullet wounds. She is holding a flouncy bride doll she has just fabricated out of toilet paper. "Hullo, Peaches, you upset Mummy. Isn't that awful?" Beryl Bainbridge says, simultaneously proud and appalled at her luridly clever child. "You have to be *normal* once you have children. But sometimes fear takes over. You realize what might be hiding behind a silence."

This scene, which transpired in the author's hotel suite during her recent stop in Philadelphia, doubtless will show up someday in a book, because that is how it is for Beryl Bainbridge. She writes novels, but "I don't write fiction," she protests. "I always use people I know. I always tell them they'll make a marvelous story. Then I note how they talk, what they say. Nobody's ever objected yet. I've never once been sued. They are pleased.

"I think life itself is so interesting you don't need to invent anything. I couldn't possibly hope to better it. Usually I base the story on newspaper headlines. Like two sisters murder their mother. Well, I never follow the case up. I just find an incident I want to write about. I don't know how it will turn out until I write it.

"Touch wood, I've never had a bad review. I've been lucky. I'm not by any means a terrific seller. What I am is kind of a small cult thing. People who read me and review me seem to like me. Oh, some critics say how odd, how sinister, how peculiar my books are. That's not obvious to me. I don't find anything in life very surprising. I find it all quite normal. That's the way my mind works."

Her mind works quite curiously, thank you. She has had a recurring dream that she was being devoured by a horse's head. She lives with her three almost grown children in an old London house where a gangster once kept his molls. She writes at night, all night, in an old piano factory reachable only by a forbidding fire escape, or at her kitchen table. She is forty-five and divorced.

"It's confusing. I've written nine books. But I don't count two of them—they weren't very good. I have done seven books in seven years. That means, not a year to write them, but they are out that year. So I write them in three or four months. Which means that I am almost a publisher's dream, to do that. My publisher [Braziller] tells me when he wants the book. I always do what I'm told, and I feel very guilty if I don't do something when I say I would. So I always do it. That's what drives me," she says, chain-smoking.

"I had a very peculiar childhood. If you are going to be a writer, the kind of childhood I had was absolutely ideal. Mum and Dad had horrible rows. I suppose I was always unhappy, thinking my mum didn't love me. I went through life feeling unwanted, unworthy. Until I was thirty-six I was constantly preoccupied with the idea of my parents, and my childhood. I never could get away from it. Once I started to write about it, I could, um, then deal with it. It seemed to work that way. Had I not written, I would have been damaged. I probably wouldn't have survived if I didn't write. It is so long ago now," she murmurs, "and my life is so different now, that I tend to forget. I don't feel that way anymore. But I used to."

The seven books are called *Young Adolf, Injury Time, A Quiet Life, Sweet William, Harriet Said . . . , The Secret Glass, The Bottle Factory Outing,* and she has adapted them for stage, TV, and film. She has desperately plundered her past: there is a romantically disappointed mother who reads novels at night in the train station. There is a ragingly melancholic father who weeps in front of the radio. There is a wholesome older brother who bowls, plays tennis, and sings in the church choir. There is a wifty, wayward sister who signs checks for her bankrupt father and wanders in the pinewoods and sneaks kisses with a German prisoner of war.

The telling has taken its toll on her. "Sometimes I feel guilty. You see, I don't know anything about literature," she admits. "Yet I go all over, to universities, to talk. The only subject I ever talk about is my mother and father, my family. This is odd, isn't it?" she wonders aloud. "I don't mind about not knowing about literature.

"It's a very odd thing," she repeats, "if you have been brought up, as I was, in that era when parents didn't talk to their children, and children didn't talk to their parents, and everything is private and secret, and all you ever talk about is your mum and dad." She shakes her head. "I couldn't have written my books if my parents were still alive. Because the books are all about them. They are about my parents, and I have absolutely nailed them to the wall.

"In the beginning I wanted to write so I could write about my childhood. I don't often write about anything else. I write to get a hold on my past, to make sense of it. I'm not particularly interested in the present. I don't think about the future. But I do like the past," she sighs. "In the beginning, I had three small children and couldn't go out. So I would scribble. I didn't intend to ever make any money from it or get published. I just liked writing. I pretended it wouldn't be published. All the things I ever felt as a child, I wrote."

What was she like? "What was I like? Wild, awkward. I don't mean clumsy. I mean difficult. And fairly exuberant." But always close to terror, real or not. She remembers dimly, as a tot, taking shelter from the sirens. "You could hear the bombers going over Liverpool. I saw the damage. There was a rumor I was going to be evacuated to America, but the boatload before the one I was supposed to go on was bombed, and all the children drowned.

"I used to talk to myself out loud. I'd ask myself who I was.

I actually asked, 'What's your name?' Then I'd reply. I don't know why. Maybe it was comforting. There was so much pain in our family. Since I was obviously so difficult and extroverted, it was my mother's idea that I should go on the stage." So she tap-danced for troops at five, did children's radio, joined a repertory theater company, and regularly appeared on a TV soap opera. Her acting career lasted ten years.

"When I say I was difficult, what I am trying to say is that I didn't seem to fit in. It was as if I was responsible for my parents' unhappiness. So I had to make them laugh, and my brother, too. I could sense the atmosphere. Because I was considered a bit of an oddity, my mother very shrewdly decided I should try theater. She pushed me. I wasn't terribly interested. Oh," she amends, "I enjoyed it well enough. I was funny. I had a good sense of timing. I probably could have developed into a happy comic person. But because of how unhappy my family was, whatever imagination I had was channeled into another dimension."

Into make-believe. Almost as soon as she could talk, she made up stories about magic carpets. She even invented a companion. "I had an imaginary dog. It was a lump of wood I found on the shore that I dragged around with me everywhere, on a piece of string. Until finally my parents got worried and bought me a real dog."

At ten she kept a secret notebook. "I started to write a daily account of my parents. I didn't want them to find out, 'cause they would be upset, I suppose. What I did was tear pages out of exercise books, then write my bit of diary, then stick it inside a big beautiful book on the life of Livingstone who went off into the jungle to meet Stanley. Such a gorgeous book, the pages were edged in gold leaf," she coos. "What sacrilege. When I think how beautiful that book was, it would be worth a fortune. But each bit of paper I added, the homemade glue I used, it became thicker and wouldn't shut. I became panic-stricken, scared my mother would read it and get angry. I don't know if anybody ever saw it or not. I burned it. I stuck it in the garbage bin and nearly set fire to our house."

At eleven she wrote a novel under the influence of Dickens, and by thirteen she had plowed through Virginia Woolf, D. H. Lawrence, Faulkner. Now, though, "I try not to read modern fiction. It's just best not to. You pick up things. I have a photographic memory, and whatever I read, I might write that way."

At twenty she married a painter named Austin Davies. "Of course it didn't last," she says. "I think I'm wary about love. It's a damn nuisance. I think it's impossible. I don't know any English woman writers with husbands. One woman novelist, thought of very highly, announced she was giving the whole thing up because she was completely happy, happy, happy. She had fallen in love, was getting married, and was having babies. That was it, she didn't want to write anymore. . . . I wouldn't want it. I am so contrary. How could I be married when I write all damn night? I'm not going to change my habits and write in the day. I like writing at night," she declares. "What's the point? A woman needs companionship, and sex, but you don't need to have somebody in the house with you all the time . . . you might as well buy a dog," she snorts.

Since she has come into her own as a novelist, "I have changed so much. Just in the last seven years. Purely because I'm happy. It isn't money, but doing something, being appreciated. Up to about seven years ago, never a day went by that I didn't ask myself, why didn't my mum love me. I'd replay that whole thing. I don't do that anymore," she exults. "Just the process of writing things down cures your neurosis, wipes it out. It's all vanished.

"When I was young, all I ever wanted to do was have lots of babies and be happy. So you have the children and get half the fantasy. What's ridiculous," Beryl Bainbridge says, "if I only knew when I was younger how possible things are. Then I wouldn't have been so, so uptight. If I had only known, the difference between happiness and unhappiness is purely confidence."

MAY 13, 1979

DICK FRANCIS
Writing at a Fast Clip

"I was known as the Queen Mother's jockey," says sixtyish best-selling thriller writer Dick Francis, who has profited considerably from changing careers, not horses, in midstream.

Looking at him—ruddy, round-cheeked, jolly, and gray—you wouldn't think that he has had horses fall on top of him, horses that just *stayed there*, badly hurt or merely winded, until someone came to haul them off; you wouldn't know that he broke an arm, broke his nose five times or his collarbone, each side, six times, or that he fractured his skull or crushed some vertebrae in his back, or even that he broke numerous ribs because you don't count those, really.

Now he sits, vaguely elegant, one leg up on a cushion in a Philadelphia hotel room. It is dusk, and he sips water as if it were wine. The occasion is the American debut of his twenty-third novel, *The Danger*, a wonderful read, which involves both horse racing and international terrorism. His day has been clearly taxing. "I signed well over two hundred books in an hour and a half, and they were queued all around the shop," he says of his visit to Encore Books.

For four of his ten years as a jockey, he rode horses owned by England's royal family. Overall, he rode in 2,305 races, won 345 of them, and placed or showed in 535 more. "For a long time, the thing people wanted to know most was about my racing life. But I think people are coming around to wanting to know how I write stories. A badly ed"—he pauses—"well, not a badly educated fellow, but someone who didn't have a top education. How do I write the stories? I don't know. My mother and father were just decently bred. And they expected me to behave like a gentleman, and I tried to behave like a gentleman. . . . I was a good boy. . . .

"And, ah," he sighs, drifting into a reverie. Yes? I prompt. "I, I, but I didn't do any sort of classical subjects in school. I left school when I was fifteen. I could write and do sums, do shorthand—which I can't do now. And I was observant, always very observant," he declares. ". . . I started reading thrillers when I was fourteen. I suppose I liked them because they were easy to read, and you know, you pick them up in railroad stations if you're going away on vacation."

Did he ever try writing anything as a child? "No." No? "Only letters. I wrote a lot of letters. Always have. I would much rather write a letter than telephone somebody," he admits. "And then when I joined the Air Force during the war, I spent three years in Africa. I used to write a lot of letters home to my family and my girlfriend and friends, and they all seemed to like receiving them. And I was able to describe things which I'd seen. And then when I started race riding after the war, I had an uncle, my mother's brother . . . I used to write a lot of letters to him and tell him how the races went, how the horses which I rode behaved themselves, and how they performed. And it all helped, I think."

With his wife, Mary, who helps him with his research, he splits his time between Oxfordshire and Fort Lauderdale. Does he live on an estate with many horses? "Ah, no, I don't. I live in an area where there are a lot of racehorses trained. My son is training racehorses, he has a stable. He lives about twenty miles from me. He's got one of mine. But I don't ride that one because it's a flat racer and I'm a bit too heavy. But I go and ride some of his bigger horses, his jumpers. I have a few days' hunting a year. I judge at horse shows a lot, I've judged all over the world."

As a jockey, was he on a constant diet? "Ah, I wasn't. I was lucky. I was—I am the ideal build for a steeplechase jockey. I'm now about 157, 160, which doesn't matter. But when one's in training, you have lunch, you see, and you have a good breakfast and a good dinner. But a lot of the jockeys do waste, waste, waste all the time. They look so ill, and how they live I don't know. But I like to eat, I like to drink."

Does he remember the first time he saw a horse? "Ah, it was

very early, I suppose. My father had a stable. And he was a professional jockey before the First World War. He didn't quite reach the highlights of the game as I did. . . . And my grandparents used to ride in . . . hunt races. And nearly all my uncles did, too. I was born to the saddle, you might say. But when I wanted to be a jockey, neither Father nor Mother was very keen for me to do this. . . . But as soon as I went into it, I made a name for myself."

What can we learn about him from his books? "Ah hah!" he says, grinning. "I don't know, I'm not as brave as I make my main characters out to be, but I think there's a lot of myself in them, I suppose. People say I, *they're* very stoic. Well, I suppose I am a stoic, in a way. A lot of my main characters suffer a lot of knocking about, or injuries, and things like that. Well, I've suffered a lot of injuries, not in the same way as I write about them, but as a racing jockey you do suffer injuries. There's many a time I've broken my collarbone and I've ridden the next day in a race. My wife would strap it down tight. I mean, it was sore, but well, wotthehell? When you get warmed up, you don't feel it."

Tell us more about his injuries? "Oh, I had a few," he mumbles, self-deprecatingly. "No, I don't think I had as bad injuries as a lot of other jockeys. But I broke a few more bones than a lot of others. My nose and collarbone seemed to suffer most." When he fractured his skull, was he out of commission very long? "They didn't know I fractured it. I didn't let on." He laughs. "I didn't ride for about three weeks, not even a month." That's not very long. "No," he agrees. "Nowadays they wouldn't let that sort of thing happen. Nowadays, jockeys, if they have a fall, if they get hurt, they have much more trouble getting back into action, because they have to have a medical examination after every quite serious fall. In those days you didn't."

Why did he quit? "Old age," he contends. "I was thirty-six, and that's old for a steeplechase jockey. Because you don't bounce when you get to your mid-thirties like you used to. I would have liked to have started when I was in my teens—I always wanted to, but the war broke out before I could really get into it. I had six years in the RAF [Royal Air Force]. And when I first went into racing, I was twenty-five or twenty-six," he recalls.

Does he still experience much pain? "I don't suffer anything from all this . . . not really, no. Oh, occasionally, I've got one finger which . . . I can't bend the muscles." Was he resting his foot because of an old injury? "Ah, it was just tired," he laughs. "I've been dashing about today."

After he retired from racing, he wrote a Sunday newspaper column on the sport for sixteen years, and since 1965 he's been writing a thriller a year. Though he can recite most of his book titles by heart, "I will admit I don't remember every character in them. But if I think hard, they'll come back to me," he says.

Which would he rather discuss—horses or books? "Horses anyday." Why? "Well, I was born to the saddle," he repeats. "Books are hard work. Writing books is hard work." Which was he better at? "I wouldn't like to say. I got to the top of the tree being a jockey. I suppose I've got there now as a writer. No," he reconsiders, "I still don't think I have got to the top. I haven't got to the top of the tree. I haven't sold the same number of books as Robert Ludlum or John Le Carré. But I might one day." How many books has he sold? "Well, a few years ago, a rough count was done, and it was over twenty million then. So I don't know. It's probably more, much more, now."

Is there anyone he envies or admires? "I admire John Le Carré. And I honestly can't say about Robert Ludlum, because I haven't read one of his books. They're too big for me to start. I don't like starting on big books," he says.

John Leonard once wrote something extremely complimentary about Dick Francis—does he remember what it was? "No." Something about to not read Dick Francis because— "Oh yes," he interrupts. How does that go? "'To say you don't like to read Dick Francis because you don't like horse racing is like you don't read'—what's his name?" he gropes. Is like not reading Dostoevsky because—"'Because you don't like God.' That's right. That was some quote, wasn't it? It was quoted on the back, my publishers quoted it on the dust covers of some of the books, too. Yes, that was something." Putting him in the same breath as Dostoevsky. "I don't" —he laughs—"I don't think I'm anywhere near that."

Appropriately modest but not falsely humble, he concedes his talents. "What they say, I've got good hands. Horses—I don't blow any trumpet—but horses seem to go a lot better for me than they do for the ordinary man in the street. There *are* lots of others, you know, people who end up to be good and successful jockeys, they've all got that gift to make horses go," he says. ". . . When I was a jockey, I used to go out with the opinion that I was going to run, win every race. I didn't, by a long way. And when I turn in a manuscript now, I'm very, very white that I'm not going to make it. But once it's got in, gone in, and I'm finished with it, I expect it to, I *hope* anyhow, it will be better than the last one. That's what I aim to do. I aim to make each succeeding novel better than the last one. Whether I manage that, I leave to other people's opinions.

"People say to me now, doesn't all this applause you're getting now and all this fanfare, doesn't it make you feel awkward? Well, I've been getting that all my life, and the coverage and fame. And it doesn't make any difference, I hope, to my head. . . . There are lots of things I still want to learn about. But it's just natural." Natural?

"I think so. Ever since I was a child, I've been in front of the cameras and winning in show rings on ponies, and winning on hunters after I was bigger. . . . And after the war I immediately went into racing, and I was always in the press and being interviewed, and since I've been writing the books it's gone on. I suppose if it didn't, if I didn't write and no one followed me around, I'd feel lost." Okay, that's a good spot to end. "Okay, I hope I've not sounded bigheaded," Dick Francis apologizes, "because I don't mean to be at all."

JULY 22, 1984

STUDS TERKEL
He Celebrates the Uncelebrated

"I steal lives." Newsreel voice grinding away, Studs Terkel talks Chicago-tough out of the side of his mouth over bacon and eggs at the Barclay. Seedy and disheveled against the white linen tablecloth, he's in the same red-checked shirt and navy jacket he's worn for the past three days.

Studs Terkel may just be this century's greatest "confidence" man. All over America they tell him the little-big secrets of their anonymous-ordinary-unique lives—soda jerks and retail clerks, census takers and candlemakers. And Studs Terkel commits his "larceny" with a Uher-4000, the same make tape recorder Richard Nixon used. Then, from these interviews, he makes book, or books, like *Working, Hard Times, Division Street: America.*

For three days I have followed him around Philadelphia. To his Penn lecture on the tape recorder as human communications tool. To a book-signing party at the Pennypack Park home of a Beaver College prof. To an interview so obscenely early he tries to sleep instead. But, finally fortified by three cups of coffee, Studs Terkel holds forth, and there is no holding him back.

"What I take is far more than I give," he barks. "Lives are invaluable, beyond price. There was a fireman who shamed me once. He said, 'After I spent all afternoon telling you my life, you won't even have dinner with me?' I had already unplugged my tape recorder. Jesus, I said, I'm supposed to see some hotel clerk across town. 'You're running off like that?' he accused me. How could I be so insensitive," Terkel berates himself. "A thief-in-the-night feeling. The fireman stunned me into facing up to it.

"Sure I pay people to talk to me. You gotta. I work like a Chinese doctor. Fifty dollars to a maid, $1 to a millionaire. Clement Stone, that big insurance guy who bankrolled Nixon, he gave me two cigars in exchange for the dollar. What was he doin' with those Cuban cigars? 'Take a look, Studs,' he says, 'that's before Castro took over. I've got warehouses of them.' He's incredible," Terkel says with amazement.

"There's an everyday poetry to people's experiences that always surprises and delights me. A waitress says she moves past tables 'like a ballerina or a gypsy holding out a tambourine and they throw out a coin.' A gas meter man says his fantasies are of women, his reality dogs. A steelworker wishes his name would be inscribed on a skyscraper he helped build like some incredible proletarian sculpture 'cause he feels *hey* that's his! A black woman says, 'There's a feeling tone. You ain't got it, baby, you're dead.'"

Studs Terkel celebrates the uncelebrated. "It's like unchartered territory talking to anonymous people. They're eager to reveal their lives, provided you give a damn that what they have to say matters. Years ago," he explains, spreading his scrambled eggs across a piece of toast, "it was strange for anyone besides actors to speak into a microphone, but today most people can forget the mike and the interview can become conversation, not inquisition."

Though he deals with human self-definition, Studs Terkel tends to hide himself behind the anecdote that deflects personal probing. "Sure I get embarrassed by personal questions," he admits. "I don't discuss my family, 'cause this is my work. Let me tell you a story. Remember Diana Barrymore, the actress? She had a rough life, guys and booze, was known for her escapades, and finally committed suicide. Well, I interviewed her once on my radio show in Chicago and she asked me, 'Haven't you forgotten something? You haven't asked me about my personal life,' meaning all those romances. I said it was none of my concern. We know you through your work, your art. But she had become so accustomed to being constantly humiliated that she nearly started crying because it was literally the first time she was treated with respect, as a person," he whispers reverently.

"Me? The year the *Titanic* sunk, I rose up. I was born in 1912. My father was a tailor until he got sick, and my mother ran a rooming house. If I were to choose the word that has governed my life, I'd say 'improvisatory' rather than helter-skelter or ad lib. I like to wheel freely, to improvise. I guess that's why I got to like jazz as a kid. My middle brother always went to dance at a ballroom nearby where jazz bands played, and I'd tag along. I guess I was twelve and he was seventeen. He kept trying to chase me home because he wanted to make out with the girls. But all I wanted to do was listen to the music. When I got older I was even a jazz deejay and wrote a book called *Giants of Jazz*. But that's later." He backtracks.

"Hell, I went to school to be a lawyer and all these things came about, through an 'accretion of accidents,' the way Duke Ellington might rehearse something and it went wrong and that going wrong became something good. Well, that's how it was with my life. I went to law school dreaming of Clarence Darrow and I woke up to see ["Chicago Seven" Judge] Julius Hoffman. I wasn't made for law. After two attempts I finally passed the bar exam because I'm good at faking." Faking? "I'm kind of an actor. I did act for a while.

"Chicago was the home of soap operas. They kept casting me as a gangster. They'd say, 'Gimme Bogart, gimme Cagney' and I'd croak 'Against the wall, youse guys' and they'd say 'That's it.' I didn't do all those voices. Nah. They're all the same. I couldn't do any of them. But they thought I was great just the same." He grins wickedly.

"I liked it, but I had horrible tenure—like a radical college professor who was always getting fired. If I wasn't arrested or sent up for life, I usually came to a sudden violent end. Each time I got 'killed' I got another job. Once I even had to wear a tuxedo though it was radio, 'cause we had a studio audience. So I rented one, walked in very self-conscious, and a guy says

I looked like a bookie goin' to his sister's wedding, and I said isn't that crazy, that's the role I was playing," he recalls.

"It's a goofy kinda thing. I was blacklisted in the fifties, but I wasn't really damaged. All these curious crazy things that have happened to me—the radio show I've been doing twenty-two years, TV, the books. But, for a while, the American Legion was after me," he says ruefully. "Why? Who knows?" At this point, Studs Terkel rises and makes a prearranged getaway to the airport in a taxi, past smokestacks and stalled freight trains and mountains of junked cars. I tag along.

Does he ever see himself as a sophisticated extension of a machine? "That's a good question. No, the machine doesn't dominate me, bad though I am." Bad? I wonder. "I'm lousy technically," he confesses without embarrassment. "I goof up. Sometimes I press the wrong buttons. And then it doesn't work. But the people I'm talking to notice, and tell me. It makes them feel needed.

"There's nothing wrong with using a tape recorder," he protests. "I like the idea of it being an instrument of revelation"—his eyes dance—"rather than blackmail or repression or surveillance. When a person I'm talking to asks me to play some of the tape back and I do, then they murmur with amazement, 'I never realized I felt that way before.' Well, that's quite an astonishing moment," he observes, "when the person didn't know something till he heard it. We're *both* transformed."

"Why do I do this? I love the *vox humana*," he rhapsodizes. "The humor, the whimsy, the craziness, the nobility. It's exciting. Do I see myself as a voyeur? Am I manipulative? I'm curious, I'm curious," he repeats. "I want to know what's going on. I want to be there. I want to know what people are thinking. I am," he breathes, "an emotional yo-yo. I become the type of person I'm talking to. My voice changes. I'm a chameleon. Am I performing at my end of the tape recorder? Yeah, subconsciously.

"You know," he says, returning to the man who fascinates him with the same queer attraction a cobra holds for a mongoose, "Richard Nixon is actually an extension of Descartes' philosophy, *Cogito, ergo sum*—'I think, therefore I am.' For Nixon, it was 'I tape, therefore I am.'"

But wait, I say. That's Studs Terkel, too. Hasn't he built *his* reputation on tape? "Oh, that's funny. I tape, therefore I am. Play that back for me, won't you?"

APRIL 27, 1975